THE GUN DIGEST BOOK OF SINGLE ACTION REVOLVERS

By Jack Lewis

DBI BOOKS, INC., NORTHFIELD, ILLINOIS

About Our Cover: Your eyes aren't playing tricks on you! The Ruger Super Blackhawk .44 magnum on our covers is, indeed, in stainless steel. Ruger has been an industry leader in the use of rust resistant stainless steel for some time now; and, with that in mind, a stainless Super Blackhawk is only natural. It will, no doubt, prove to be a winner with wheelgunners who want the most durable, rugged single action magnum ever made. Holster courtesy of Red River Frontier Outfitters. **Photo by John Hanusin**.

PUBLISHER
Sheldon Factor

PRODUCTION DIRECTOR
Sonya Kaiser

ART DIRECTOR
Dana Silzle

PHOTO SERVICES
Kristen Tonti

PRODUCTION
Betty Burris

COPY EDITOR
Dorine Imbach

CONTRIBUTING EDITORS
Mark Thiffault
Dean Grennell
Roger Combs
Jack Mitchell
George Virgines
Massad Ayoob

Produced By:

Charger Productions

CONTENTS

INTRODUCTION

The single-action sixgun has been maligned in recent years as inadequate for self-defense, lacking rapid reloading capability for law enforcement work and has been given the status of a relic in many instances. Be that what it may, the single-action still maintains a mystique all its own and is a prime target for enthusiastic gun collectors, fanciers and historians.

With Colt's announcement that the Single Action Army model would be discontinued there were those who did everything short of cry in their bore. This particular handgun has become something of a classic. For those brought up on the tales of Wild Bill Hickok, Jesse James and then watched the movie cowboys from William S. Hart to Hopalong Cassidy, there remains the logic that the gun that tamed the West must still be a potent force no matter what is said about it.

I think this is true. Just as Bill Ruger has reworked his revolvers to make them more safe, I feel certain we once again will see a revised edition of the Colt SAA in short order. The internal workings may be different in an effort to call off the lawyers and the judges who tend to blame firearms rather than carelessness by the shooter as the offender in injury cases, but I suspect the exterior will be much the same as the 1873 issue.

And to replace the Colt during this suspected temporary absence, we are certain to see a host of copies — foreign and domestic — based upon the long-expired patents. Some will be good, others will be not so good; all will be based upon the feeling that there is a market for nostalgia and if Colt does not want to fulfill that need, others will.

We are well into the Space Age and perhaps *Star Wars* is not so far away as we might like to think. But whatever the technology, I suspect that close combat in such a terrestrial setting may well be fought with single-action space guns.

This tome, incidentally, could not have been completed without the help of a lot of people, including Patt Bogush of Colt; Jim Triggs of Ruger; Dick Dietz of Remington; George Virgenes, a true authority and author of *Saga Of The Colt Six-Shooter;* Roger Combs; Dean A. Grennell; Massad Ayoob; Jack Mitchell; and Tommy L. Bish. All offered freely of their knowledge and expertise.

Jack Lewis,
Capistrano Beach, California

Chapter 1

A LOOK AT TRADITION

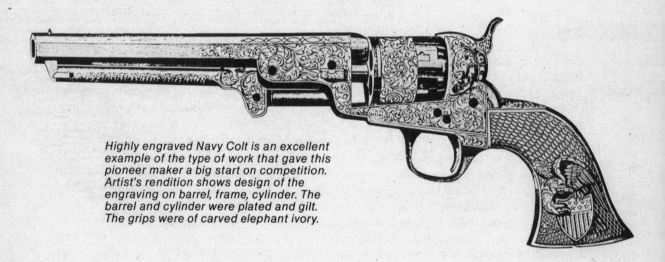

Highly engraved Navy Colt is an excellent example of the type of work that gave this pioneer maker a big start on competition. Artist's rendition shows design of the engraving on barrel, frame, cylinder. The barrel and cylinder were plated and gilt. The grips were of carved elephant ivory.

THERE ARE those writers of history who have called Samuel Colt the father of the single-action and the inventor of the revolver. Neither is precisely true. To qualify this claim further and say Sam Colt was the father of the single-action revolver does not make the statement entirely true, either.

First, let us take a look at definitions: The term single-action, in relation to a handgun, indicates that the hammer must be drawn back to the cocked position by thumb or finger pressure, then the trigger must be pulled, activating the mechanism to cause the hammer to fall upon the firing pin and thus fire the cartridge.

Generally speaking, double-action means that the handgun can be fired by pulling the trigger, causing the hammer to go through a full cycle, arcing to the rear and releasing automatically so that the hammer can fall forward and make contact with the firing pin.

First off, virtually all of the early handguns, whether flintlock or percussion, required single-action firing. Since these fired only one round, then had to be reloaded, chanc-

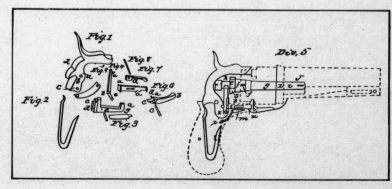

Patent application for Samuel Colt's first design was accompanied by these drawings. Issued in February 1836, this particular model never was placed in actual production.

Sam Colt Came Up With A Gun Design That Is Second Only To The Wheel For Mechanical Longevity!

es are no one gave much thought to the possibilities of a double-action design.

As for the revolver, more than a decade before Sam Colt came up with his basic design for a revolver a number of European gunmakers were building what has come to be called the "pepper box." This mechanism did not feature a cylinder as such. Instead it had several barrels set in a circle to rotate around a primary axis. In the earliest versions the barrels were not turned mechanically. After a round was fired it was necessary to install a new percussion cap on the single nipple, then to rotate the circular device so the next barrel could be aligned and fired. Crude though it was, the pepper box was somewhat faster than firing a single-shot, having to reload each time before the next shot could be taken.

So much for definitions.

There still is little doubt that Sam Colt revolutionized the design of handguns and, other than the wheel, few inventions have remained as close to the original concept as has the single-action revolver from Colt's initial patent drawings. There have been improvements, certainly, but the theory continues to flourish in firearms factories around the world. It may well be that other inventors came up with innovations that could have been equally as important, but there was one thing that Samuel Colt had that perhaps the others did not. He recognized the value of showmanship. Today it might be called promotion or public relations, but Colt drew upon his early show-business background to aid in development of much of the interest eventually shown his brainchild.

Only 18 years old at the time, Sam Colt attempted to apply for a patent on his first revolver in 1832. According

Forerunner of revolver designed by Colt was the pepper box, which had several barrels. It usually had to be turned by hand, with a new percussion cap installed each time.

There has been little change in design of Colt's Single Action Army model from time of its introduction to the modern-day fast-draw practitioner use.

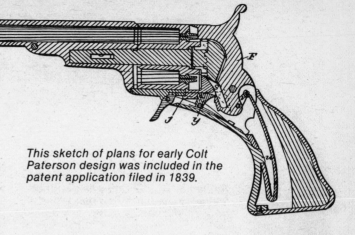

This sketch of plans for early Colt Paterson design was included in the patent application filed in 1839.

to legend he had carved the original model from wood while serving as a member of the crew aboard a sailing ship. Colt was put off by Henry Ellsworth of the infant U.S. Patent Office, who insisted the erstwhile inventor needed a more perfect model than the one submitted.

That's where Sam Colt's knowledge of show biz entered. A substance called nitrous oxide had recently been discovered — becoming popularly known as laughing gas — and Colt toured the eastern states from New Orleans to as far north as Canada demonstrating the properties of this gas before audiences that could afford to pay for a ducat at the door. Funds derived from this enterprise, lowly though it may seem, were used to further develop his design. Several working models were made for him by Maryland gunsmiths he had contacted during his travels.

Perhaps disappointed at his earlier reception at the U.S. Patent Office Sam Colt went to England, where he filed his first handgun patent in December 1835. According to old records Colt also felt that Europe might be a lucrative field for sale of his invention, but when he learned that France and the United States were on the verge of war he returned immediately to this country. He arrived in Washington, D.C., in February 1836, where he was granted his first patent for a firearm. The fact that it already had been regis-

tered on British soil may have made it easier. The patent number, incidentally, was registered in August 1839.

His first handgun came to be called the Paterson Colt, since it was manufactured in Paterson, New Jersey. As described in the patent documents the invention featured centrally placed nipples or tubes at the rear of the cylinder; each nipple isolated by partitions to prevent simultaneous discharge; rotation of the cylinder by cocking the hammer; the cylinder was locked in proper adjustment at the moment of discharge and unlocked by lifting the hammer when cocking. Colt also claimed invention of the percussion nipple, but later filed a disclaimer admitting that others might have used the system previously.

The original Colt factory was located on Passaic River at Paterson, New Jersey, so water power could be utilized to power the machinery required to manufacture.

The famed Walker Colt was designed for cavalry and mounted police use. It weighed something over four pounds.

The Walker Colt was protected in this holster, which was issued with the revolver. It was hardly the thing to haul around on a gunbelt. Instead, it attached to the saddle.

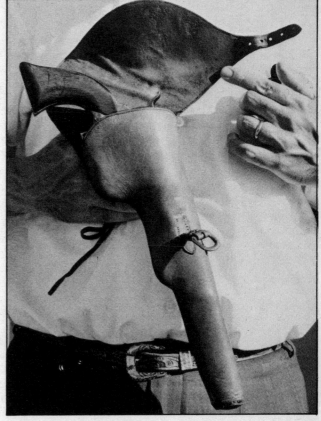

Texas Ranger and cavalry soldier, Capt. Samuel H. Walker worked closely with Samuel Colt to perfect the design of the so-called Whitneyville-Walker Dragoon for army use.

The original Paterson Colt sold for as little as $16 or as high as $100, depending on ornamentation. The original factory was located on the Passaic River to take advantage of the water power available. Samuel Colt's brother, Christopher, used the upper story as a silk mill, later selling that portion of the business.

Colt's new firm was named the Patent Arms Mfg. Co. Falling back on his old show-business experience, Sam Colt called on President Andrew Jackson — who occupied the White House from 1829 to 1837 — presenting him with a well decorated specimen: the first Presentation Colt.

Perhaps as a result of this contact Samuel Colt was allowed to submit arms for the Army Ordnance trials. Rather than a handgun, however, this first test weapon was a revolving musket. The tests were negative, although a number of rifles were used by the Army during the Seminole Indian War in Florida. Since the price of these rifles was in the neighborhood of $150 each — a monumental cost in those days — there were few takers.

However, in 1839 Samuel Colt did receive an order for Colt handguns from the Navy of the Republic of Texas. In the same era the poorly manned Texas Rangers were issued a number of the Texas Navy Colts. Jack Hays, a famed Ranger of the time, led fifteen of his men against a Comanche war party and killed forty-two of the marauders. He credited the Colt for this battle success.

Colt continued to improve his patents and also to add accesories to make loading easier. The early Patersons soon were available with powder flasks, bullet moulds, cappers and loading tools. At the suggestion of J.R. Poinsett, Secretary of War, a permanently attached loading lever was installed. This improvement came about in 1840.

That same year Colt was able to arrange another test of his carbine with the War Department, while the United States Navy expressed willingness to try out both the carbine and his pistols. At best the resulting reports were conservative.

The Paterson, of course, featured a five-round cylinder — the Colt had yet to become the famed sixgun — and Colt felt his future perhaps was on the frontier rather than with the armed services. As a result he sold a number of pistols and carbines in Texas at his own manufacturing cost. Thus came about the model known among collectors as the Texas Paterson. This was a .36 caliber style featuring a large grip.

However, a financial depression had come upon the land. The comparative high price of Colt arms combined with the lack of available money brought internal strife in the company; a number of lawsuits further drained the firm's funds.

When the Patent Arms M'f. Co. eventually filed bankruptcy at least one of the employees was paid off in parts. He later assembled the guns and sold them. During the period of the firm's existence, however, more than fifty variations and sizes of the Paterson-made Colt revolver were made.

Although Samuel Colt had his patents returned to him in the bankruptcy actions, a number of copies of his Paterson pistol already were being made in Germany and Belgium. The tools and equipment at the Paterson plant had been sold at a sheriff's sale for $6209, which meant Sam Colt suddenly was an inventor and gunmaker without a plant!

Colt Texas Paterson, forerunner of the Whitneyville-made Walker, has seven-inch barrel that proved itself on the frontier against Indians and outlaws. Above it is later Dragoon that was designed for use by the U.S. Cavalry.

Captain Samuel Walker was slain by a Mexican soldier with a lance while he was awaiting delivery of the first of the Colts he designed. His death took place during the Battle for Vera Cruz, which was recorded in art by Remington.

In the five years after the failure of the Paterson-based firm Sam Colt worked on other ideas, perfecting a marine telegraph cable and producing the first underwater explosive mine. Meantime, the Republic of Texas had been admitted to the Union in 1845 and the Mexican War had begun.

Enter Captain Samuel H. Walker and the Dragoon era.

Born in Maryland in 1817, Walker had fought in the Seminole Wars in Florida, then had gone West to sign up with the Texas Rangers commanded by the legendary Jack Hays. Ultimately General Zachary Taylor asked the governor of Texas for 5000 volunteers made up of two mounted regiments, plus two regiments of infantry. As a result the Texas Rangers were taken into the United States Army in April 1846. It was in that integration that Walker was awarded the rank of captain. Recognizing their successes with the Colt Paterson revolver against Indians and badmen, these former rangers urged that mounted troops be armed with that type of sidearm.

After what must have been a good deal of thought General Taylor sent Captain Walker to Washington, D.C., on a dual mission. The Mexican War was not popular with northern businessmen, who considered it the cause of higher taxes; also, others felt that the admission of Texas to the Union had increased the strength of slavery. Walker, however, was well connected politically, through his brother. In addition, the captain was considered a hero in the East and had made himself something of an expert on Colt firearms. His mission, as outlined by Zach Taylor, was to attempt to recruit a company of volunteers for service in the Mexican War and also to work with Colt in developing a handgun that would provide sufficient firepower to make up for the general's scattered, undermanned forces.

As a result of meetings with W.L. Marcy, the Secretary of War, Captain Walker was granted authority to negotiate a contract with Sam Colt to produce a thousand revolvers. Walker, as history shows, had some definite ideas as to the design of the proposed handgun.

After the meeting with Walker, Sam Colt was in a quan-

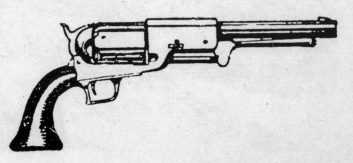

The Whitneyville plant where Samuel Colt was able to contract for his government order was located in what now is the city of Hamden, Connecticut. The factory belonged to Eli Whitney, wo insisted the contract be assigned over to him.

dary. He and the officer had agreed on the design of what was to become known as the Walker Colt or the Walker Dragoon, but Colt now was a man with a contract and no manufacturing facilities. He also had little if any financing for such a project.

Colt approached Eli Whitney, the son of the man who invented the cotton gin. The latter, a tough Yankee businessman, was totally aware of Colt's circumstance. As a result the inventor was forced to sign over the government contract to Whitney. However, under the terms of the agreement Colt was guaranteed a profit and would retain ownership of all of the equipment that would be acquired in order to fulfill the contract.

The first thing Colt did was journey to Paterson, New Jersey, to round up as many of his old employees as possible. With the men furnished by Whitney he had a fifty-

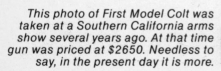

This photo of First Model Colt was taken at a Southern California arms show several years ago. At that time gun was priced at $2650. Needless to say, in the present day it is more.

Colt-made firearms — as well as numerous copies — were in use on both sides during the Civil War. This painting of General Sheridan's charge in Virginia in 1864 documents handgun use. It now is in Library of Congress collection.

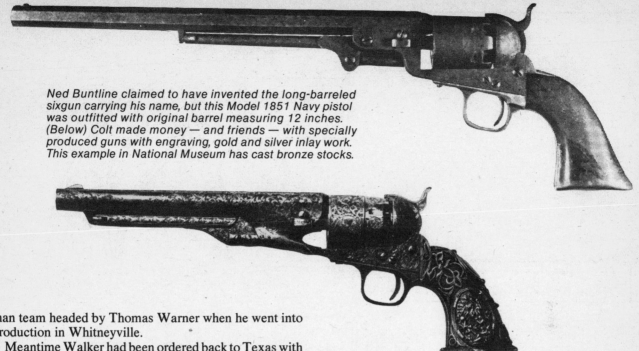

Ned Buntline claimed to have invented the long-barreled sixgun carrying his name, but this Model 1851 Navy pistol was outfitted with original barrel measuring 12 inches. (Below) Colt made money — and friends — with specially produced guns with engraving, gold and silver inlay work. This example in National Museum has cast bronze stocks.

man team headed by Thomas Warner when he went into production in Whitneyville.

Meantime Walker had been ordered back to Texas with his newly recruited company of volunteers. As a show of his appreciation Samuel Colt made two special Whitneyville-Walker Colts, as they were called. These dragoons were forwarded to the soldier in Mexico, but it is doubtful whether Walker ever actually saw them. Captain Samuel H. Walker was killed by a Mexican soldier armed with a lance during a charge at Vera Cruz on October 9, 1847. The matched Walker Colts apparently still were among replacement supplies being held at his company headquarters at the time of his death.

Chamber capacity of the Walker Dragoon was increased to six rounds over the five-round cylinder of the earlier Paterson, and a number of internal improvements were made in the basic design to make the revolver stronger and less subject to malfunction.

The original group of Colt Walker handguns was contracted to the War Department at $28 per gun. Sam Colt offered another one thousand guns of the same design for that price, but also offered the government the alternative of purchasing five thousand guns at only $5 each. The War Department settled on the lesser order at the higher price — a practice that seems to have descended to modern-day military buying — and Colt moved his operation from Whitneyville to his old home at Hartford.

Following the move Captain William A. Thornton of Army Ordnance took an active part in reducing the length of the barrel and the cylinder of the Walker design, thus developing the first standard Dragoon that was to be turned out en masse for the nation's military.

While fulfilling the military contract, in 1848, Colt again turned out pocket pistols. His first from the Hartford facility was in .31 caliber. Although it had no attached loading lever, the rest of the gun resembled the Dragoon in design and often was referred to as "the little Dragoon."

With the end of the Mexican War in 1848, it was thought the demand for handguns might drop, but the West was being opened against the Indians and gold had been discovered in California. This opened a whole new market

Samuel Colt may well have been the father of cooperative advertising. In mid-1850s he furnished illustrations to hardware stores and others to advertise his own guns.

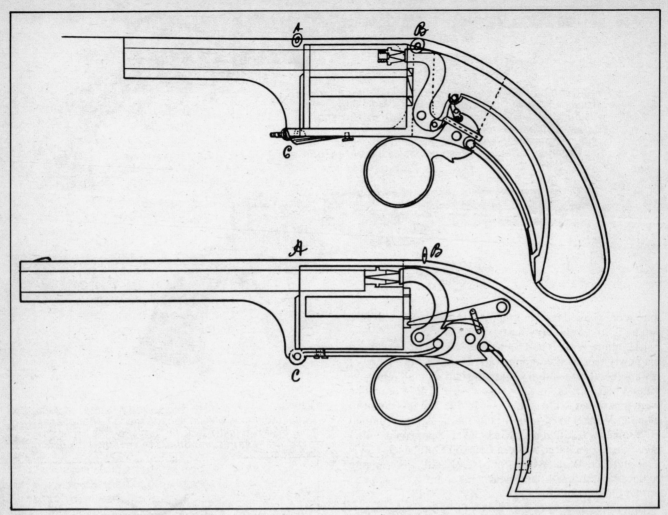

From the Colt archives, this sketch is for proposed six-shot pistol with a round trigger ring, as well as a flat main spring. It's proof that the inventor was always seeking new ideas, but this one never got into production.

for Colt. As the handgun had been noted by the Mexicans during the war, it also found favor in the country south of the border and Sam Colt began to sell guns there.

Meantime President James Polk had become a bit miffed with the gunmaker, since the President wanted to pay a small royalty of $4 per gun and make the Colt patents in government armories. Colt declined this offer on the grounds that he could make them better and to more exacting standards in his own plant. In view of this approach Colt took precautions to renew his patents in October 1848.

In the years that followed Colt was awarded more military contracts and went abroad himself to explore the foreign markets, which he found lucrative. Along the frontier his sixguns were becoming the standard for lawmen, outlaws, cavalrymen, settlers — and even Western artists. George Catlin, an early artist who concentrated on frontier and Indian scenes, carried a Colt Dragoon and later was to do advertising art for the Colt firm. Another who was to do such commercial art for the company's ads was Frederic Remington.

Ever seeking to improve design and reliability Colt and

his staff continued to file new patents and to incorporate a number of these in design variations. The Army was suggesting that its soldiers needed a lighter pistol than the four-pound-plus Dragoon style, but Sam Colt had opened a plant in London and was furnishing Dragoons to the British Army for use in the Crimean War during which England, Turkey, France and Sardinia fought Russia. During this two-year war starting in 1854, Colt found his facilities jammed and even endeavored to have some handguns made in Belgium under contract.

Colt had completed a new factory in Hartford in 1855 and even went so far as to manufacture gunmaking equipment, which was sold in England and in Russia. He took time out from adding to his wealth and successes to wed one Elizabeth Hart Jarvis in 1856 at the age of 42. After a honeymoon trip to Europe Sam Colt returned to his factory, aware that his patents were about to expire.

Despite his best legal efforts Sam Colt was unable to protect the patents and they suddenly were public domain. It was only a matter of months before handguns based on his patents began to flow from the plants of Massachusetts Arms Company, Remington, the Manhattan Arms Com-

This civilian version of the Model 1860 Army revolver has no provision for a shoulder stock. Obviously made to sell for less, back strap was of iron, not brass. (Below) Although at first glance, this appears to be a Navy Colt, it is a six-shot .36 caliber copy that was made in same era by Metropolitan Arms Co. of New York.

pany, and Colt's old partner, Whitney.

Colt, however, did have the advantage of being first and the publicity and acceptance his designs had received over the years helped to maintain the business without serious problems during this era. In addition, the fact that he had modernized his plant helped him to produce Colt revolvers at a more competitive cost than some of those who sought to cash in on his imagination.

An added plus for the business lay in the fact that there were rumblings of discontent below the Mason-Dixon Line and hundreds — perhaps thousands — of his firearms were being taken south and secretly stored. More thousands were in private hands, of course, and found use during the Civil War. Of those stockpiled early in the South, many in the hands of collectors today bear the official markings of the Confederate States of America.

Heading the Army's plea to reduce the weight of his Dragoon, Colt and his design staff came up with the version that is popularly known as the Model of 1860. This handgun was designed as a holster gun and weighed two pounds nine ounces, as opposed to the weight of the Dragoon at a couple of ounces over four pounds. The new 1860 model immediately underwent government tests and was reported as being both efficient and strong.

The so-called Army Holster Pistol — or Model of 1860 — scaled down the bulk of the Dragoon and, while it was made in .44 with a choice of 7½- or 8-inch barrels, there were a surprising number of variations, including a so-called Civilian model. The round cylinder, roll engraved

With incorporation of a shoulder stock, Samuel Colt called this his new stocked carbine. Stock was quickly detached and could be switched to another revolver that was loaded, increasing the amount of available fire power, ads said.

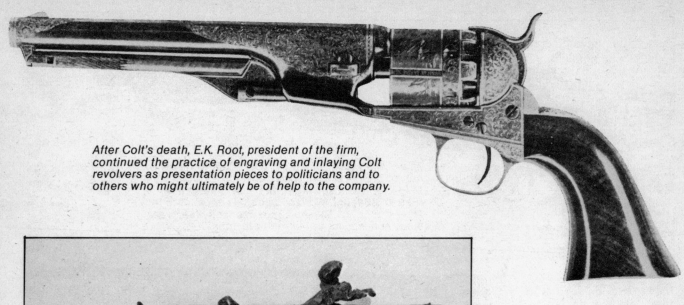

After Colt's death, E.K. Root, president of the firm, continued the practice of engraving and inlaying Colt revolvers as presentation pieces to politicians and to others who might ultimately be of help to the company.

This badly melted Colt, now in a private collection, was found in the ruins of the factory after the fire that completely destroyed it.

Although large by today's standard, Model 1849 Pocket Model was popular even through the Civil War as a hide-out gun. Few examples found today are as well preserved.

with a ship scene similar to that used on earlier Navy pistols, was bored for six rounds. (No effort will be made here to discuss the various configurations of interest primarily to collectors. Countless volumes already have been written on the subject and are available.)

Not content to put all of his guns in one military basket, Sam Colt had designed a belt pistol for the Navy as early as 1851. It was called the Model of 1851, but became known ultimately as the Navy Colt in popular usage. It was manufactured in .36 caliber with an octagon barrel measuring 7½ inches, although special orders produced longer and shorter barrel lengths. The roll engraving on the cylinder featured an engagement between the Texas Navy and ships of Mexico. An improved version was the Model of 1861.

Detachable shoulder stocks, incidentally, were available for the Navy Colts, as well as for Third Model Dragoons and the Model 1860 Army revolver. There is no record of such stocks ever being used successfully in a combat engagement and it is doubtful whether they were a major success. Most frontier types tended to carry a pistol and a rifle, although often in the same caliber so ammunition was interchangeable.

The 1860 Army Colt in .44 caliber was a mainstay of Union troops during the Civil War and thousands were issued. Today, most of those that remain are in collections.

The Oriental-looking cupola that tops the Colt plant in Hartford has been present since this factory was built in 1864. The landmark has become something of a trademark in its own right, being featured in some Colt advertising.

Later, Army Ordnance technicians converted some to cartridge-firing guns.

Samuel Colt did not live to see the end of the Civil War. He died in 1862. In February 1864 the Hartford Colt plant literally burned to the ground. However, Colt's widow and Elisha K. Root, who had succeeded Sam Colt as the president of Colt Patent Fire Arms Manufacturing Company, decided to begin rebuilding immediately.

The fire, of course, was a blow to the firm's production and finances, since only part of the damage was covered by insurance. In more modern times the blaze has been considered damaging to Colt collectors, since all of the records of manufacture prior to the date of the fire were destroyed.

While the Colt revolver became well known throughout the world among military leaders, one cannot ignore its importance along the frontier. While another company has stated it was its rifle that "won the West," that particular

The part played in the winning of the American West by the Colt revolver and other maker's single-actions has been well defined by Frederic Remington and a host of other artists. Remington later painted advertising art for Colt.

This short-barreled version of the 1862 Police Model has no loading lever. A loading tool carried separately was used. It is thought only a few were manufactured.

Colt began using engravings early on his firearms. This particular pattern was seen on the Model of 1855 side-hammer revolvers. These were five-shot guns, which may have made up in decoration what is lacked in efficiency.

model did not come along until 1894 — after the West had been pretty well tamed. If credit must go to any particular firearm for the winning of the West, the Colt certainly cannot be ignored.

When John Butterfield began his stagecoach line, starting at St. Louis and passing through El Paso, Yuma and Los Angeles, to terminate in San Francisco, he armed his employees — more than 750 of them — with Colt firearms. The distance from St. Louis to San Francisco was some 2760 miles with the trip taking up to twenty-five days, depending upon Indians and weather. Fare was $100 for the entire route, with mail being sent along at ten cents per half-ounce. The Butterfield line, however, went bankrupt during the Civil War.

Wells, Fargo & Co., founded in 1851 in San Francisco,

became a major purchaser of Colt pistols and a special model of the Model 1849 Pocket Pistol was designed specifically for the firm's use. It became known as the Wells, Fargo model.

It is not surprising that such firms tended to supply arms for their employees, as they became frequent targets of highwaymen. For example, Wells, Fargo suffered 347 stagecoach holdups and eight train robberies between 1860 and 1884, losing $917,726. In fact, following his capture and ultimate release from prison, the firm found it better to pension the infamous Black Bart — nee Charles E. Boler — at $125 monthly than to worry about his activities! It was not until the introduction of the express money order that things slowed down in the stagecoach robbing business. While Wells, Fargo continues today as a well

Always the showman, Sam Colt tended to incorporate an air of adventure in his engraved scenes used on the cylinders of his revolvers. He may well have been right, as competitors rarely matched his continuing sales.

Sam Colt was slow to accept any suggestions relative to a bored-through cylinder, but eventually a number of guns were converted to cartridge use by means of a unit designed for percussions by Thuer.

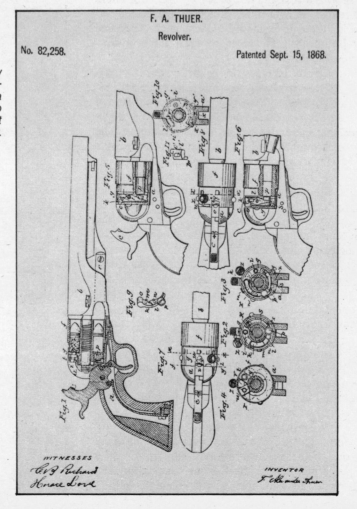

F. A. THUER.

Revolver.

No. 82,258.   Patented Sept. 15, 1868.

Conversion to black powder cartridge for percussion Colts was designed by C.B. Richards and used by Colt firm for some guns purchased for cavalry.

known banking chain in the West, its express enterprises were merged with the now defunct Railway Express Agency in 1918.

The fact that it required nearly a month to get a letter across the nation by stagecoach in the Fifties and Sixties led to formation of the Pony Express. Although hundreds of volumes have been written about the daring of these riders and they have been the subject of countless motion pictures, the Pony Express was short lived. It was established in 1860 at an expenditure of some $100,000. There were 190 relay stations and some eighty experienced riders, including a young William F. Cody, later to become known as Buffalo Bill. However, by 1861 the Pony Express had become history.

Most of the Pony Express riders carried two Colt revolvers as well as a carbine. According to historians the revolver issued by Russel, Majors & Waddell, founders of the Pony Express, was the Navy Colt. However, the riders soon found that the added weight was a hindrance. The first piece of armament to be turned in was the carbine because of weight and its bunglesome nature on a fast-running horse. Many of the riders also gave up one of the Navy Colts, although the smart ones learned to retain the second cylinder fully loaded for use in a brush with road agents or Indians. When the first six rounds were fired, the fresh loaded cylinder could quickly be slipped into the frame of the Navy Colt for double the normal fire power.

Completion of the telegraph line to the West Coast marked the end of the Pony Express. At the same time, the Union Pacific Company had been organized to build a transcontinental railroad and was being subsidized by the government. Every effort was being made to complete the line during the Civil War, as Lincoln and his military leaders felt it would be a vital force in ending the hostilities. However, the war ended first. The rails did not meet until 1869 when Chinese workmen laying track from the West for the Central Pacific linked up with the Irish immigrant laborers of the Union Pacific.

The Indian Wars in the West went on for another twenty years. It was not until 1889, with the last big uprising of the Sioux Nation, that the frontier became safe from hostile tribesmen. During this era the Colt percussion models, then the cartridge guns, did their share to tame the West.

The Civil War no doubt brought about the introduction of the metallic cartridge and spelled the ultimate doom of the percussion firearm.

Two New England gunmakers, Rollin White of Hartford and Smith & Wesson of Springfield, had been working on such an invention to replace the paper cartridges that had been developed for faster loading. The paper-encased units had been used primarily in single-shot rifles during the war, but they were easily damaged and exposure to moisture made them useless.

Rollin White submitted two patents for metallic cartridges in the late 1850s, while Smith & Wesson introduced a rimfire ammo design in April 1860. At the same

Colt no doubt was in the midst of designing the Single Action Army Model of 1873, when Richards had patent for cartridge conversion issued in 1871, thus only a few Colt percussion guns were converted by the factory.

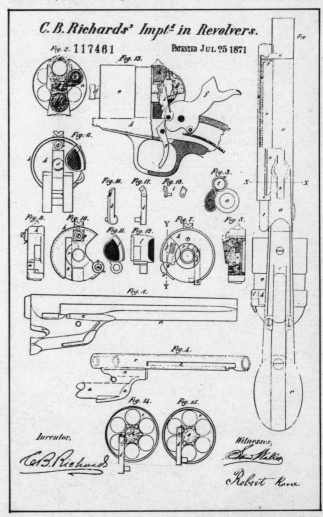

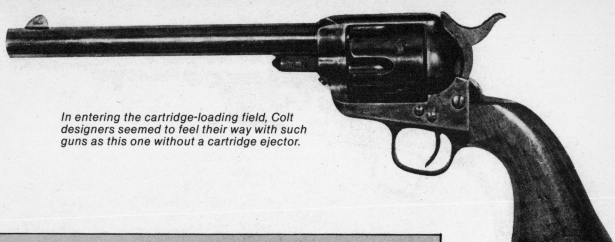

In entering the cartridge-loading field, Colt designers seemed to feel their way with such guns as this one without a cartridge ejector.

Noted Western artist Frank E. Schoonover painted this frontier lawman for use in a Colt promotion in the 1920s. Note that the Colt SAA has been displayed prominently.

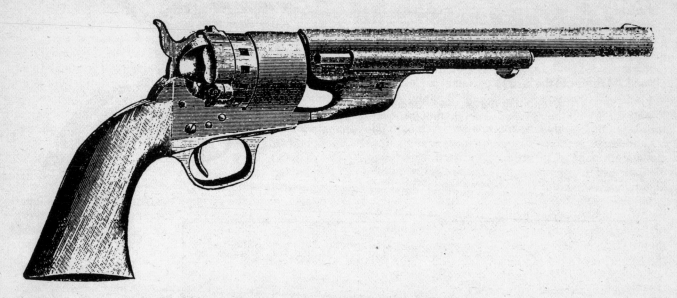

This illustration was used in an 1872 advertisement that offered Colt's metallic cartridge Army six-shot revolving pistol. Actually, it was a percussion conversion that sold at that time on retail basis for only $16.

time variations called pin-fire and cup-primer cartridges were being developed in Europe.

By the end of the Civil War rimfire cartridges were being made in this country in .22, .32, .38, .41 and .44 calibers, with even larger cartridges for rifles such as the Spencer. Meantime a number of small manufacturers were experimenting with firearms conversions that would make it possible to use cartridge ammunition with reworked percussion models.

Perhaps the most successful of these early conversions was the Thuer system, which was patented in September 1868. This conversion unit was designed for .31, .36 and .41 caliber guns, including a larger size for Army and Navy revolvers, one smaller for police and pocket models.

The cylinders were bored through and finished at the rear, with a new ratchet installed. This work was done only on nonfluted cylinders and the converted gun ended up with six chambers regardless of the original model. The cartridge designed by Thuer was tapered for front loading in the cylinder. There also was a conversion ring in proper size. In the face of the ring was machined a deep annular groove, leaving room for a rebounding firing pin. The groove was designed to contain the ejecting mechanism.

The cartridge designed by Thuer used a standard conical bullet cast with a Colt bullet mould. Along with black powder the round was loaded with a tapered brass cartridge case and a thin primer, a lubricating wad being positioned between the powder and the bullet.

The result was a center-fire cartridge, perhaps the first produced in the United States. However, it found no great success. The War Department did some testing with the unit, but found it lacking. The idea was marketed by Colt in

The Colt Bisley model was made primarily for the British market. This target model was blued, with uncheckered walnut grips. Note that this one has no case ejector.

its London catalog in 1869, then dropped.

Perhaps Colt's lack of continuing interest in the Thuer cartridge is reflected in the fact that the Hartford manufacturer had been experimenting with its own cartridge design for some time. Colt owned patents for metallic-cartridge firearms prior to 1868 and introduced such a model in both .38 and .44 rimfire to the War Department in 1869. Meantime both Winchester and the Union Metallic Cartridge Company, the latter founded in 1867, were introducing metallic cartridges for rifles.

Colt's first cartridge-firing revolver was a .44 rimfire model that loaded a 200-grain bullet ahead of 23 grains of black powder. This gun apparently was a factory rework of the Model 1860 Army. The firing pin, designed specifically to convert the 1860 to rimfire, is held by two rivets. It was installed after metal had been cut away on the left side of the hammer. The operation also involved some grinding on the hammer face and neck of the original percussion model.

While this stop-gap creation served as the forerunner of the famed Single Action Army model, it was not especially successful. As nearly as can be determined, fewer than 7000 guns were made in the Colt factory.

During this period there were all sorts of conversions on all types of Colt handguns, all designed to give the individual model cartridge-firing capability. The Colt factory did a number of these conversions, while individual gunsmiths did more. There is not sufficient space in this volume to cover the entire range, but let it be noted that there were factory-installed conversions of both the Model 1851 and Model 1861 Navy Colts, most ordered by the Navy's Bureau of Ordnance; there were conversions of 1862 Navy and Police models to both .38 rimfire and .38 center-fire; other models also were converted on a special-order basis.

The War Department and the Navy had come to favor a center-fire or, as it was termed then, a "central fire" cartridge over the rimfire. Winchester's Model 1873 rifle came to influence the Colt designs, too. The riflemaker was chambering its model and supplying ammunition in .44-40, .38-40 and .32-20 calibers. A match-up seemed obvious.

Development of cartridge ammunition brought about the introduction of the Single Action Frontier revolver, which became known also as the Single Action Army model, the Peacemaker and, with minor variations in design, by several other names. Also known as the Model 1873, because of its date of introduction, the basic design

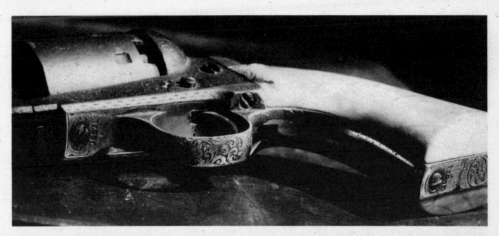

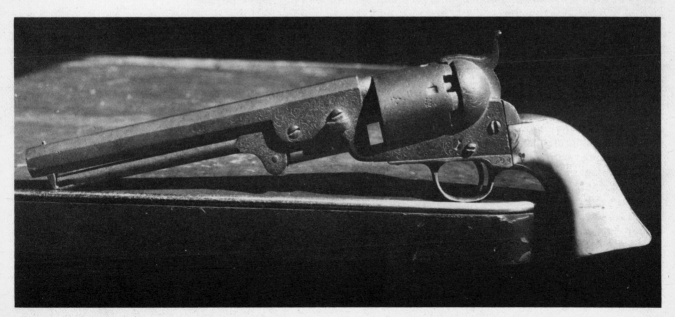

This ivory-stocked percussion model, much of its engraving still visible, was discovered in Latin America about 1960.

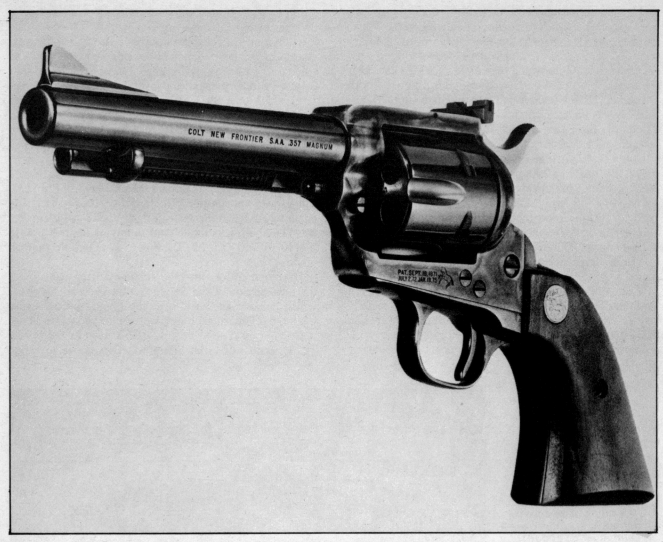

In the early 1960s Colt marketing personnel came to realize that others were reaping fortunes off obsolete patents once owned by the company. They began making a new single-action, including new flat-top Frontier model.

has been produced on a more or less continuing basis until 1982, when Colt announced it was being dropped — in its present form — from the line, once and for all.

The Single Action Frontier is the most copied firearm in history. In the past, when Colt discontinued its manufacture for a period, a host of copies suddenly appeared on the market. Many of them were relatively cheap, inferior copies coming from Europe; while others, such as Sturm, Ruger & Co., improved upon the basic internal mechanism while retaining much of the original Colt design to produce a superior single-action revolver. More will be said on this in subsequent chapters.

In its introductory phases in 1873 the model — listed by the manufacturer under the formal name of Colt's Single Action Army and Frontier Revolver — was made in standard and target styles. The standard Frontier was available initially in .45 Colt, .44-40, .38-40, .32-20 and .41 Colt. The Frontier Target model was chambered for .38 Colt, .45 Colt, .22 rimfire, .41 Colt and .450 Eley, the latter for the English market.

The later variation called the Bisley model also was made in standard and target configurations. The standard Bisley was chambered for .32-20, .38-40, .41 Colt, .44-40 and .45 Colt, while the target version was chambered for .32-20, .38-40, .38 Colt, .45 Colt and .455 Eley.

According to Colt historians, some 312,000 Frontier-design Colt single-actions were produced between the introduction in 1873 and discontinuation in 1941, when the plant's facilities were turned over to arms production for World War II. Of this number some 45,000 were of the Bisley design, while 2000 or so were in .44 rimfire. The latter caliber was made between 1875 and 1880, when it had become obvious that the big-caliber rimfire cartridge was a thing of the past. Between 1873 and 1891 some 37,000 revolvers were ordered by Army Ordnance. These were in .45 caliber and featured 7½-inch barrels, becoming designated as the Single Action Army model.

Another variation introduced during this period was the short-barrel Storekeeper model, which was built without the ejector rod standard on other Frontier stylings. This

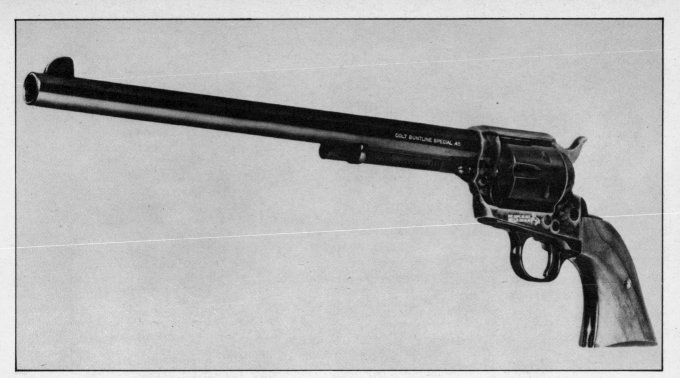

The popularity of the Wyatt Earp television series in which Hugh O'Brien carried a long-barreled Buntline Colt brought about the reintroduction of that model by Colt. They also made it in a Frontier Scout .22 rimfire version.

Although many do not consider it particularly practical, the chrome-plated Colt SAA introduced in the 1960s had a broad following, as it or cheaper copies were carried by a host of the video cowboys then making the scene.

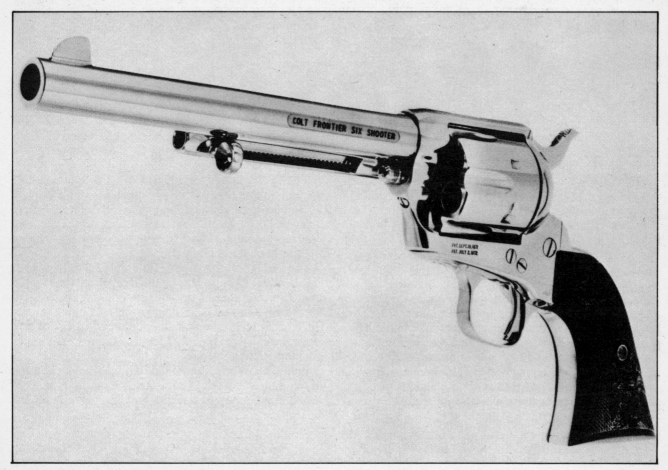

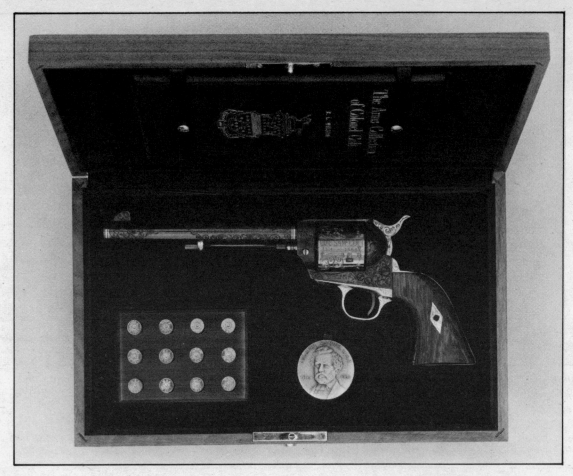

When Colt marked its 150th anniversary, they issued a series of commemorative .45 Single Action Armies.

version was available in 3-, 3½- and 4-inch barrel lengths.

Another variation was the long-barrel Buntline Special. This version, often with a barrel as long as twenty inches, could be ordered with a shoulder stock. The name came from the fact that Ned Buntline, the hack writer who brought fame to Buffalo Bill, is supposed to have originated the idea of the long barrel and ordered a number of such guns to present to well known lawmen such as Wyatt Earp and Bill Hickok. It is possible that Buntline did present such guns, but he certainly did not originate the long barrel, as it has been found as originally installed on such models as the 1851 Navy.

As the popularity of the so-called Peacemaker grew around the world new calibers were added. In rimfire the gun appeared in .22 short, long and long rifle; .22 WRF and .32 rimfire. Ultimate center-fire chamberings not listed earlier included .38 Eley, .44 German, .44 Russian, .450 Eley and .476 Eley, as well as a host of others. Standard barrel lengths were listed as 4¾, 5½ and 7½ inches, although longer lengths were available on special order.

To list the various changes and improvements over the years would require another volume. We suggest that the interested reader check one of the many detailed references available. An excellent source is *Colt Firearms (from 1836)* by James Serven.

The Bisley variation was meant primarily for the British market. At that time in England there was comparatively little interest in the American frontier, so Colt marketing personnel came up with the name Bisley, as the shooting range of the same name had been the gathering place of British shooters for many decades.

The Bisley differed slightly from the Frontier model in that the frame had a flat rear surface where it abuts the stocks and grip strap. This helps provide additional length for the Bisley grips. The Bisley Colt was introduced in England in 1894 and was discontinued in 1912. Some examples carry the legend *Model 1894,* but most are simply marked *Bisley Model.*

Following World War II Colt officials apparently felt demand for the Single Action Army model was dead. It was not until they saw others building fortunes on the

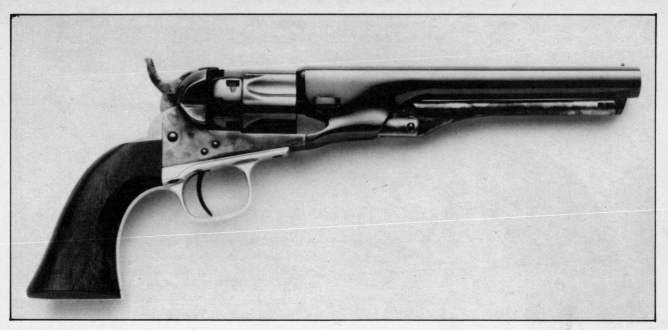

With the advent of this decade's boom in black powder shooting, Colt resurrected such old-timers as the 1862 Police revolver. While others had copied old patents of the company, maker insisted it was a continuation.

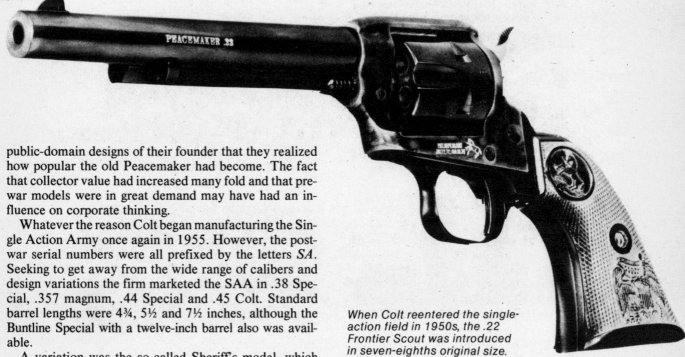

When Colt reentered the single-action field in 1950s, the .22 Frontier Scout was introduced in seven-eighths original size.

public-domain designs of their founder that they realized how popular the old Peacemaker had become. The fact that collector value had increased many fold and that pre-war models were in great demand may have had an influence on corporate thinking.

Whatever the reason Colt began manufacturing the Single Action Army once again in 1955. However, the postwar serial numbers were all prefixed by the letters *SA*. Seeking to get away from the wide range of calibers and design variations the firm marketed the SAA in .38 Special, .357 magnum, .44 Special and .45 Colt. Standard barrel lengths were 4¾, 5½ and 7½ inches, although the Buntline Special with a twelve-inch barrel also was available.

A variation was the so-called Sheriff's model, which was built under special contract for Centennial Arms of Chicago. This particular model, made in 1961, was in .45 Colt, with a three-inch barrel and no ejector rod. It bore a stirring resemblance to the old Storekeeper model of the last century.

The last single-action in the Colt line was the Frontier

Colt Storekeeper's Model was made during last century as a short-barrel self-defense gun. A number of makers have copied design for current-day sales.

Scout introduced in 1957. While it had the basic design of the Single Action Army revolver, it was scaled down to seven-eighths size and was made only in the .22 rimfire range from shorts through magnums. Barrel length was 4¾ inches only, except for the so-called Buntline Scout, which was introduced in 1959 with a 9½-inch barrel.

In 1974 history began repeating itself. With the growing interest in black powder shooting Colt dug out the designs for its old Third Model Dragoon and the 1851 Navy, start-

Special run of chrome-plated Buntline Frontier Scouts were marketed with a plaque commemorating the late hack writer.

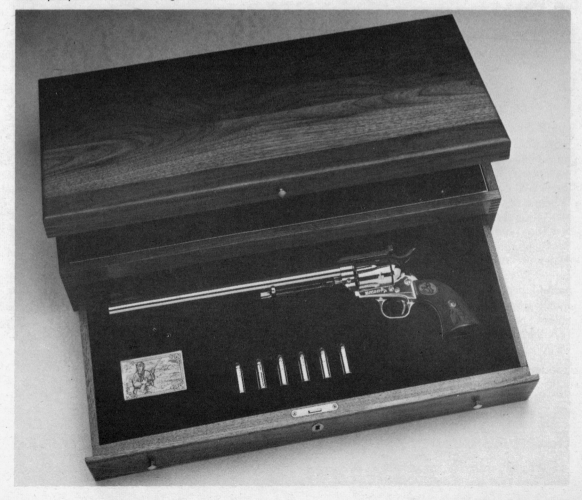

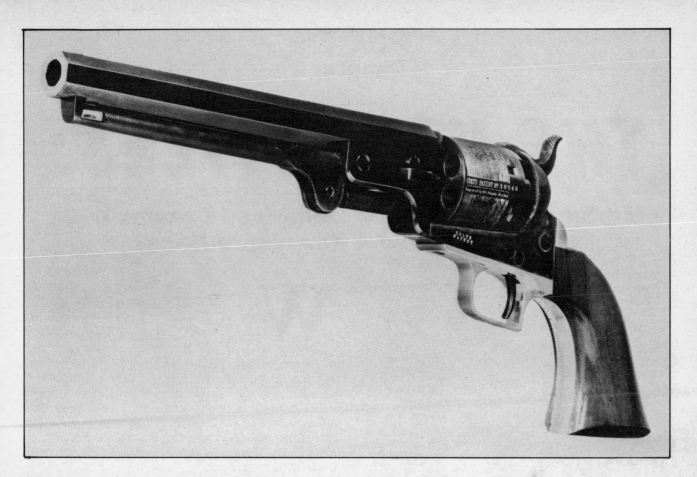

The continued line of Colt percussion revolvers was discontinued in 1982. They followed design of originals with exactness. (Left) Colt .22 Buntline Scout handled all lengths of that cartridge through the .22 magnum.

ing to manufacture them once again for this segment of the shooting public.

While others had been making replicas of these models for decades — most of them manufactured in Italy and imported — Colt insisted that their version was not a replica; instead, it was simply a continuation of models that had been dropped a century or so ago. In addition Colt offered a complete line of accessories, which were exacting in the same detail as the antique originals. These guns were discontinued once again in 1982.

In 1981 the Colt Firearms Division of Colt Industries announced that the Single Action Army and the Colt Frontier Scout would be discontinued. The latter popped up a year later in a slightly different internal design, but Colt officials insist that when current contracts were met — most of the final guns being made from parts available — the Single Action Army as we have known it for nearly 110 years will cease to exist.

As a fitting departure the final 3100 guns are being made up during 1982 as a John Wayne — American Legend issue with ivory grips and gold-inlaid engraving bearing the late actor's likeness. There is little doubt that John Wayne was an American legend, as was the Colt Single Action Army. Perhaps it is only fitting that both be laid to rest in the same decade.

Chapter 2

THE VERSATILES:

Mr. Smith & Mr. Wesson Combined Dreams With Brains To Build A Respected Name

Daniel F. Wesson was one of the fathers of cartridge handguns, since his experimentations with ammunition led to the introduction of the cartridge revolver.

WHILE the major credit for development of the percussion revolver goes to Samuel Colt, the contributions of Daniel B. Wesson and Horace Smith can hardly be ignored. They pioneered much of the practical development of the cartridge handgun, although numerous others had been approaching the same problem both in this country and abroad.

For example, a number of similar developments featured a bullet that had a powder charge impregnated in the rear of the projectile itself, thus making a cartridge case unnecessary. However, this approach never was particularly successful.

Rollin White, a designer of the period, had approached Colt with a design featuring a chamber that was bored completely through the length of the cylinder, but it had been rejected by Colt as too dangerous and unreliable.

Edwin Wesson was the inventor of a revolver that featured a hand-turned cylinder. It, too, had shown little evidence of success, but when he died he left to Daniel B. Wesson and other heirs a patent application for a revolver that featured a mechanically turned cylinder. Horace Smith had dabbled in the firearms business earlier, but had exhausted most of his capital by the time he joined Daniel Wesson in a partnership. They formed the Massachusetts Arms Co. to manufacture a revolver with a hinged frame. This design, born of Edwin Wesson's patent, allowed the barrel to tip up so the cylinder could be removed easily. Colt, however, filed a lawsuit charging patent infringement and the courts seemingly agreed. The infant firm was ordered out of the revolver business.

Smith and Wesson, aware that Sam Colt's patents would run out in a few years, joined with B. Tyler Henry, designer of the famed Henry repeating rifle, in a project to produce a rifle. The principle was used also in a pistol of the time. Both arms featured a tubular magazine and utilized a hollow-based bullet propelled by fulminate of mercury inserted in the cavity. These arms were made in .31, .36 and .44 calibers.

Meantime Daniel Wesson continued to experiment and eventually developed a cased cartridge that featured an internal primer. This eventually was patented, at which time they sold their repeating rifle and pistol patents with the fixed ammunition design, to Oliver Winchester. The latter formed the Volcanic Arms Co., forerunner of Winchester, with Henry.

The cash derived from the sale gave Smith and Wesson the funding needed to pursue their own aims.

Incidentally, a verbal agreement between the partners and Winchester stated that Smith and Wesson would not involve themselves in rifle production and Oliver Winchester would not investigate the handgun market. Winchester did ultimately make a few single-action revolvers, then dropped the project. It has been only in recent years that S&W has introduced rifles into its line; these invariably have been imported from overseas for distribution through the S&W sales force.

While waiting for Colt's patents to expire, as they did in 1857, Daniel B. Wesson continued his cartridge experiments, coming up with a practical rimfire cartridge design. This particular cartridge utilized fulminate of mercury in the rim as a detonating device. This, in turn, ignited the black powder load behind the bullet crimped in the case.

Although they now had a cartridge, Smith & Wesson didn't have a pistol in which to fire it. They contacted Rollin White who had patented his revolver in which the cylinder was bored completely through. This was the design that had been offered to Colt and rejected as too dangerous and too costly to make. Smith & Wesson bought White's patents, although the contract allowed Rollin White to use the designs in his own manufacturing. The inventor did manufacture a few pistols, but he made a great

Horace Smith already had lost a good deal of money in attempting to develop firearms when he joined Wesson. He left the firm, but his name continued.

The Volcanic repeating pistol was the first handgun Smith and Wesson produced. It was sold to Winchester and the funds used to start in revolver competition.

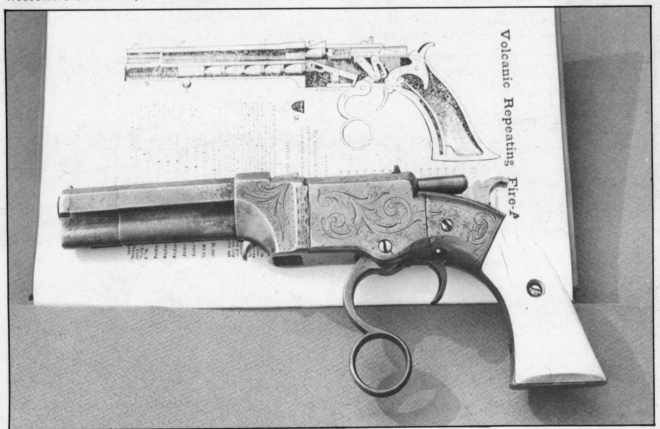

Smith & Wesson's Model 1 put them in competition with Samuel Colt, who claimed patent infringement and was able to halt their efforts to market any type of revolver until Colt's patents had run out.

deal more money in later years with his manufacture of the White sewing machine, which he designed.

Meantime, others were taking a long, hard look at the new-fangled cartridges and were attempting to design handguns to handle them. Remington, making a percussion revolver at the time, didn't rush to change their design, which allowed S&W a chance to get the lead. In 1857, the partners offered their first cartridge-loading revolvers — and the ammunition to fit them. The guns were in .22 caliber and fired the equivalent of today's .22 short, then loaded with black powder. Manufacture of this particular model continued until 1869.

In 1861, S&W had brought out what they called their Model 1½. This was the same basic design as their first revolver, but was chambered for the .32 rimfire cartridge.

The partners had experimented with larger calibers, but with cartridge cases made of copper at that time, they had experienced difficulties. Cases of this particular metal would not withstand the pressures caused by heavier powder charges of larger calibers.

There was no government contract for Smith & Wesson pistols during the Civil War, but they became popular with Union officers, who carried them as the equivalent of today's "hideout gun." Before the model was discontinued in 1874, more than 76,000 of them had been made and sold. This particular .32 rimfire fired a 90-grain bullet ahead of 13 grains of black powder.

It wasn't until 1870 that S&W was able to come out with a revolver to handle a larger cartridge, although several smaller makers had attempted to market pistols in .38

The S&W Model 2 Army revolver of 1855 may have the name, but it did not prove of interest to the War Department.

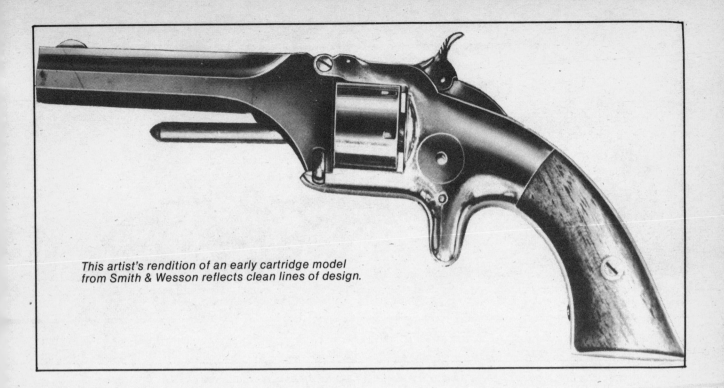

This artist's rendition of an early cartridge model from Smith & Wesson reflects clean lines of design.

caliber. The newest cartridge was .44 caliber and the handgun for firing it was called the Smith & Wesson .44 American. The cartridge, a center-fire, featured a 218-grain bullet propelled by 25 grains of black powder. The bullet traveled along at an estimated 650 feet per second (fps), although there was no way of chronographing it in that era.

The .44 American was tested by the War Department, but it was the Colt Model 1873 Peacemaker or Single Action Army Model that was adopted. However, history shows that at least one regiment of cavalry was equipped with the S&W revolver. In spite of the legendary role credited to the Colt revolver in taming the frontier West, no one can deny that the S&W .44 American had its share of enthusiasts and the model featuring an eight-inch ribbed barrel was shipped to the West by the thousands.

The center-fire cartridges manufactured by S&W at that time were based largely upon the Berdan cartridge developed in Europe for military use.

Although the firm carries his name to this day, Horace Smith left the firm in 1870. Shortly thereafter, the com-

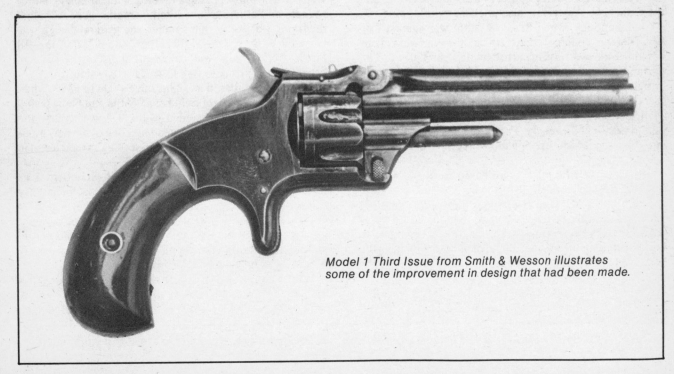

Model 1 Third Issue from Smith & Wesson illustrates some of the improvement in design that had been made.

A revolver that was destined to become a classic was the 3d Model American, which was used by one regiment of cavalry on the frontier. It also was favored by many pioneers because of its dependability of design.

pany introduced the .44 Russian model, receiving an order for some 200,000 of these monstrous revolvers. Virtually all, as the name implies, were exported to Russia for use by the Czar's army. This particular model had a shortened barrel measuring 6½ inches, plus other minor cosmetic changes. The cartridge, developed by a Russian arms designer, has a muzzle velocity of about 750 fps. It featured a 246-grain bullet ahead of 23 grains of black powder. The Russian model reputedly was more accurate than the earlier .44 American, also packing more power.

Oddly enough, when Russia went to war against Turkey, the latter country ordered still another variation chambered for the .44 rimfire cartridge made in Turkey. This particular round seems to have been a virtual steal from the design of the earlier .44 Henry cartridge. Some 5000 of these revolvers were shipped to the Ottoman Empire.

Incidentally, all of the .44 caliber center-fire revolvers of that era — and even the Turkish rimfire — were designated as the Model 3. All are variations of the same basic design.

Elmer Keith, who made a prolonged study of the early Smith & Wesson models, feels the hinge was the weakest feature on this Model 3 revolver, although the Smith & Wesson tended to be more accurate than the Colt Peacemaker. Rough treatment, such as stapling barbed wire to fence posts with the butt, tended to damage the hinge of the S&W .44 American. Not so with one-piece frame of the more rugged Colt single-action.

Daniel B. Wesson had done some additional work on his cartridge and had reduced it in size to .36 caliber. He called

this the .38 Smith & Wesson; it carried 14 grains of black powder behind a bullet of approximately 150 grains.

The first .38 S&W revolver had a fluted cylinder to hold five rounds. It had a 3¼-inch barrel and relatively crude sights. There were several improvements in the design over the years, with some 108,000 made from the time of its introduction in 1876 to the end of the second model's production in 1891. This model, too, saw its share of service on the frontier, being a favorite with gamblers, storekeepers and others who wanted a smaller gun. Although the frame was somewhat smaller, the general design was the same as that of the .44 Russian Model 3, thus the .38 Single Action, as it was called officially at the factory, became popularly known as the Baby Russian.

The Model 3 reared its sights once again in 1871, when Major George W. Schofield heard of the gun being tested by the Army. Then assigned to the Tenth Cavalry, the major asked that the factory send him one of the new models, stating that he was interested in serving as their agent in Kansas and Colorado.

The major's brother, General John M. Schofield, was president of the Army's Small Arms Board. Apparently someone felt the younger brother had some degree of influence, for he was sent a revolver with five hundred rounds of ammunition. A factory representative also wrote to Schofield, stating they could supply him with as many Model 3s as he wished at $15 per gun!

Within a year, Schofield had sold sixty-eight of the guns for Smith & Wesson, but he didn't feel the gun, as designed, filled all of the needs of the cavalryman. He began to improve upon the gun's design with new patents issued in his own name. The first new development was a barrel latch registered with the U.S. Patent Office in June 1871. The Schofield latch was built on the frame rather than the barrel. This was an advantage to the man on horseback; to open the revolver for reloading, one simply pulled the latch toward the hammer with the thumb.

Seemingly smitten with his initial success, Schofield set about virtually redesigning the whole gun for cavalry use. He submitted his plans to Smith & Wesson asking that they build several guns to his redesign. The company deferred, saying they were too involved in meeting the contract with the Russian government. Officials did agree to furnish all necessary parts, if the Army officer would have someone else do the finish work.

Schofield was issued a second patent in April 1873, after several Model 3s had been completed utilizing his ideas. One feature of the redesigned gun was an extractor system that replaced the rack and gear used on all Smith & Wesson models to that time.

Schofield, now a colonel, attempted to sell his design to the Army, but the Colt Model 1873 Army already had been adopted. Nonetheless, following Schofield's visit, the Ordnance Board agreed to test the Schofield design. It was found to be equal to any other tested and in September 1874, S&W signed a contract to complete 3000 Schofield-design Model 3s for the Army. Cost, under terms of the contract, was $13.50 per gun.

There was one drawback: the Army wanted the Schofield to be chambered for the .45 Long Colt cartridge so ammo would be interchangeable with the Colt 1873 Army. Daniel B. Wesson, however, contended that the Colt cartridge would not work properly with the Schofield's extractor system. He submitted the design for a shorter cartridge that would function in the Model 3.

At the time the 3000 contract guns were delivered to the Springfield Armory in July 1875, Colonel Schofield was on the frontier as an Indian fighter. He no doubt was pleased that the Army had contracted almost immediately for a second lot of 3000 guns.

The Schofield Model 3 delivered to the U.S. Army differed greatly from the standard model. In .45 caliber, the barrel latch was situated on the frame rather than the barrel in keeping with Schofield's patent and the rack and gear extractor had been replaced by the extractor cam of the soldier's design. The cylinder retainer also had been redesigned so the cylinder could be removed by rotating the front cylinder retaining spring half a turn. The top of the barrel also had been grooved to aid in sighting.

Perhaps it was a long time between Indian campaigns on the frontier and Colonel Schofield had the time to reconsider his work, but the first order of revolvers no sooner had been delivered than the officer began to suggest modifications for the second order to be delivered to the Army. Thus, the second batch of contract revolvers boasted a barrel latch that had been somewhat rounded; the top was

The Smith & Wesson plant in Springfield became a local monument, showing the favor with which S&W products were received by buyers. In background is mansion of Daniel Wesson, who continued the business in lifetime.

knurled for a positive grip when unlatching the revolver for reloading on the back of a horse.

The second 3000 guns were delivered in October 1876; a third order of 1000 guns was delivered to Springfield Armory in April 1877. All guns delivered to the army were blued. However, in each order there was an overrun of several hundred guns. These were offered on the civilian market, either blued or nickel-plated and minus the Army markings. Price was $17.50, with Colonel Schofield receiving fifty cents per gun as his royalty.

There were glowing reports on the Schofield-design Smith & Wesson by those who tested it, but they were not the ones using the revolver in the Indian wars. The Schofield S&W and the Colt Peacemaker were being issued to cavalrymen in the same unit despite the difference in ammunition. While the S&W obviously could be reloaded more rapidly on the back of a running horse, mix-ups in ammunition occurred on the battlefields of the West. The Colt SAA fired a longer cartridge that could not be used in the S&W Schofield. At the other extreme, the Smith & Wesson ammunition could be used in the Colt-made gun. It was not long before the Army ordered the Schofields dropped from inventory.

The Schofield revolvers were sold as government surplus in 1880. Some were purchased for use by National Guard units, but the majority went to such surplus dealers as Francis Bannerman, who resold the guns to civilians on the frontier. Many were stripped of the blue finish and nickel plated, while the barrels were cut to five inches in length. Wells, Fargo & Co. purchased a number of the five-inch models for issue to their express agents/stagecoach drivers in the West.

In all, fewer than 9000 Schofield-design guns were produced by Smith & Wesson and sales by the company ended in 1878. At the other extreme, Bannerman and other surplus dealers made minor fortunes in selling the remnants to civilians.

Daniel B. Wesson came to realize there were improvements that could be made to the Model 3 to make it more acceptable in the civilian marketplace. The grip shape of the Russian model was altered, while a different mainspring tension unit was devised; a shorter extractor system also was incorporated, done by J.H. Bullard of the S&W staff.

The reworked design was called the New Model No. 3 or the .44 Single Action, production beginning in 1878. It became the longest lived of the firm's single-action revolvers and was produced in six separate designs before being dropped once and for all in 1912. The six variations have been segregated by today's arms collectors as the .44 Single Action, the Turkish model, the Revolving Rifle, followed by Frontier Target and Winchester models.

The .44 Single Action came off the production line in 1878 pretty much as Bullard had designed it, featuring a 6½-inch barrel, .44 S&W Russian chambering and grips of black or red hard rubber or walnut. Available with either blued or nickel finish, the gun later was issued in barrel lengths ranging from 3½ to eight inches. The U.S. Government ordered 280 of the guns which were turned over to the State of Maryland, but the greatest interest was in Japan. That government purchased nearly one third of the 35,796 guns made for issue as the official sidearm of the Japanese navy.

In time, the New Model No. 3 was manufactured in a variety of calibers including .32 S&W, .32-44 S&W, .320 S&W, .38 S&W, .38-44 S&W, .41 S&W, .44 Henry Rimfire, .44 S&W American, .44 S&W Russian, .45 S&W Schofield, .450, .45 Webley, .455 Mark I and .455 Mark II. Production was halted in 1898, but Smith & Wesson continued to catalog the model until 1912.

The New Model 3 Turkish version was produced specifically for the Turkish Government. The contract, signed in 1879, called for delivery of 5000 units in .44 Henry rimfire chambering They were to be blued, have 6½-inch barrels

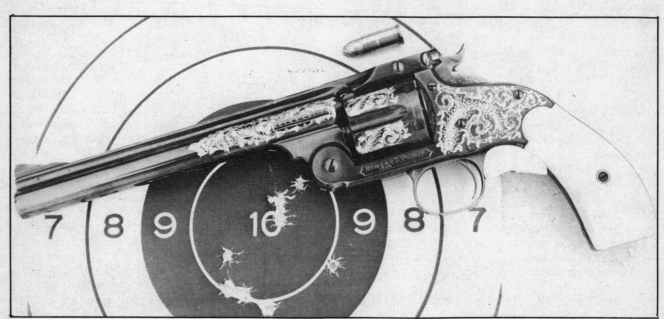

This Smith & Wesson .44 Russian 1st Model has been engraved but not yet reblued. Gun owner Bob Furst fired the target group during tests conducted by him in 1957. Ten shots stayed in the black.

The 3rd Model Russian revolver was made in several configurations. Note the shape of the trigger guard and the fact that this example boasts a ring on butt for lanyard. One version fired Russian-made rimfire.

and walnut grips. In all, 5461 guns were delivered in the first order with a second order for 278 delivered in July 1883. The overrun of 183 Turkish revolvers were sold on the commercial market, according to existing records.

The next variation of the Model 3 was listed as the Smith & Wesson .320 Revolving Rifle. Introduced in 1879, it bore some general resemblance to the Colt percussion revolving rifle made earlier in that century. It was less than a success, since only 977 of the rifles were sold between its introduction and 1890, when it was dropped from the catalog.

The revolving rifle had the same frame as the pistol except for a feature that allowed for changes in the point of trigger engagement, thus governing the weight of the trigger pull. The rifle had a red hard rubber forearm and grips, while the stock was of walnut with a black hard rubber butt plate. Barrel lengths were 16, 18 or 20 inches. Of the more than nine hundred made in the decade-plus, seventy-six had a nickel finish; the rest were blued. The rifle, priced at $23 when dropped from the S&W line, is a much sought collector item today. Made in smaller supply, the nickel-plated versions bring premium prices.

The next version was the New Model No. 3 Frontier, introduced in 1885. Chambered for the .44-40 Colt cartridge, one of the selling points was the claim that it made an excellent companion piece for the Winchester lever-action carbine that fired the same cartridge. The only change in design was the lengthening of the top strap and cylinder to handle the longer cartridge.

The Frontier version found little favor with buyers. Although available in either blued or nickel finish and a choice of 4, 5, or 6½-inch barrels, only 2072 guns were made. Ten years later the factory still had more than half the inventory. The answer was to convert them to .44 Winchester caliber and sell them to Japan. Thus about forty percent of the inventory found its way to the Far East.

The New Model No. 3 Target version was made originally in .44 S&W caliber and numerous records were broken with it before Ira Paine, a professional shooter, convinced Wesson that the target revolver should be produced in a smaller caliber. The result was introduced in 1887 as the .38-44 and the .32-44, indicating the caliber of the cartridge being fired on a .44 frame. The target version had a windage-adjustable rear sight and a bead front sight designed by Paine. The rebounding hammer was eliminated from this particular model, allowing for a smoother action. Some 4333 of these smaller calibers were made before being dropped from the line in 1910.

The last of the Model 3 variations was the .38 Winchester, introduced in 1900 and dropped from the catalog in 1907. Should you run across one of these models today, you could send your children to college on the proceeds. With only seventy-four guns sold during the period it was carried, this is the rarest gun ever made by Smith & Wesson.

The total number of guns made and marketed from the Model 3 design between its introduction in 1870 and 1912 was financially rewarding. Records show that 250,820 guns of this design left the factory during those forty-two years.

Mention already has been made of the smaller single-action pocket pistols patterned after the Model 3. A new

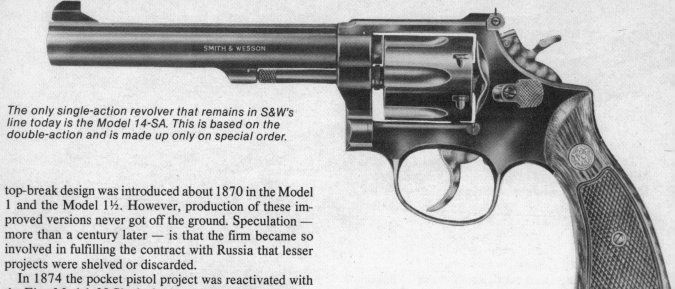

The only single-action revolver that remains in S&W's line today is the Model 14-SA. This is based on the double-action and is made up only on special order.

top-break design was introduced about 1870 in the Model 1 and the Model 1½. However, production of these improved versions never got off the ground. Speculation — more than a century later — is that the firm became so involved in fulfilling the contract with Russia that lesser projects were shelved or discarded.

In 1874 the pocket pistol project was reactivated with the First Model .38 Single Action — mentioned earlier as the Baby Russian. Initially, the gun was designed as a rimfire, but D.B. Wesson decided upon a new center-fire of .38 as more acceptable. The first of the new guns coming off the line in late 1875 were chambered the new center-fire .38 Smith & Wesson cartridge, which became a standard around the world. The gun was available in numerous variations of barrel length and grip materials, but the nickel-finished version quickly proved more popular than the more practical blued finish.

The gun was redesigned in 1877 and production continued for another year and a half. During that time, more than 25,500 guns were made and sold.

The .38 Single Action was redesigned by D.B. Wesson and J.H. Bullard as the Second Model. They shortened the length of the extractor housing to save costs. Bullard also circumvented the extractor system patented by Colonel Schofield. Between 1877 and 1891, when production on this single-action ended, the Massachusetts facility marketed 108,225 of these guns. At one point — 1887, the peak year — the Second Model was offered with barrel lengths of 3¼, 4, 5, 6, 8 and 10 inches.

The Ladysmith was designed personally by Daniel Wesson as a self-defense handgun for ladies. However, when he learned that it was being sold primarily to the prostitutes of the era, he dropped it from S&W line.

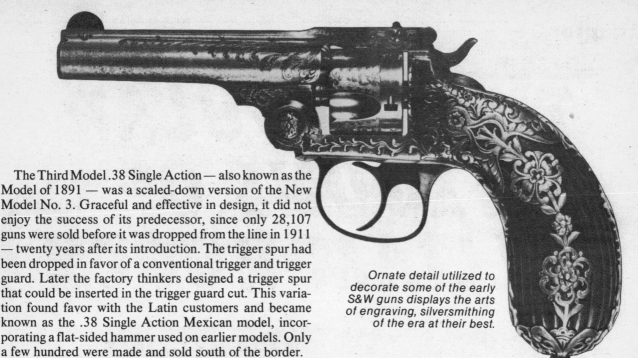

The Third Model .38 Single Action— also known as the Model of 1891 — was a scaled-down version of the New Model No. 3. Graceful and effective in design, it did not enjoy the success of its predecessor, since only 28,107 guns were sold before it was dropped from the line in 1911 — twenty years after its introduction. The trigger spur had been dropped in favor of a conventional trigger and trigger guard. Later the factory thinkers designed a trigger spur that could be inserted in the trigger guard cut. This variation found favor with the Latin customers and became known as the .38 Single Action Mexican model, incorporating a flat-sided hammer used on earlier models. Only a few hundred were made and sold south of the border.

Ornate detail utilized to decorate some of the early S&W guns displays the arts of engraving, silversmithing of the era at their best.

Perhaps supporting the contention that nothing really is new in firearms design, once the .38 Single Action was on track, D.B. Wesson offered some serious thought to introducing a .32 caliber pocket pistol. He turned to the Model 1½, which had been redesigned as a top-break, but never had been put into production.

The .32 Single Action was patterned after the Second Issue Model 1½, maintaining the popular bird's head grip. Again Wesson opted for a reloadable .32 center-fire, using a crimp like that of the .38 cartridge designed for the .38 Single Action. The resulting .32 Smith & Wesson, originally loaded with black powder, still is manufactured with smokeless powder.

production of double-actions as early as 1872, designing a gun for the Russian market. That marked the beginning of the end of an era.

Today, Smith & Wesson still markets one single-action revolver which is listed as the K-38 SA M-14. A six-shot version in .38 Special only, it has a six-inch barrel and service-type checkered walnut grips. It is the same as the manufacturer's double-action Model 14, except for the single-action feature and is available only on special order.

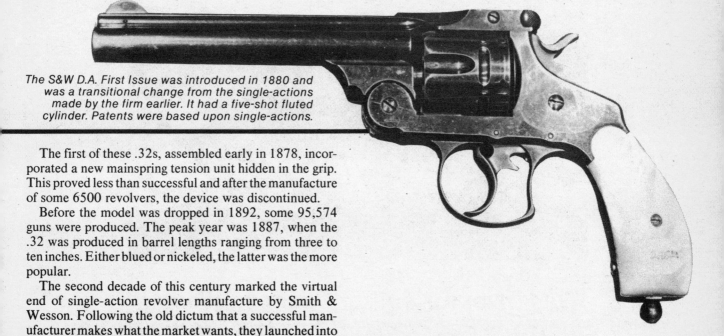

The S&W D.A. First Issue was introduced in 1880 and was a transitional change from the single-actions made by the firm earlier. It had a five-shot fluted cylinder. Patents were based upon single-actions.

The first of these .32s, assembled early in 1878, incorporated a new mainspring tension unit hidden in the grip. This proved less than successful and after the manufacture of some 6500 revolvers, the device was discontinued.

Before the model was dropped in 1892, some 95,574 guns were produced. The peak year was 1887, when the .32 was produced in barrel lengths ranging from three to ten inches. Either blued or nickeled, the latter was the more popular.

The second decade of this century marked the virtual end of single-action revolver manufacture by Smith & Wesson. Following the old dictum that a successful manufacturer makes what the market wants, they launched into

Chapter 3

THE SINGULAR SIXGUNS OF WILLIAM RUGER

This Inventor's First Success Was An Auto, But He Is Recognized For His Single-Actions

I N SOUTHPORT, Connecticut, stands a small frame building that has become something of a shrine among gun buffs. It is the structure where the first handguns of Sturm, Ruger & Company were made. Perhaps not so oddly, the antiquated frame building also holds a special spot in the heart of William Ruger, currently the chairman of the board of the company.

While the name of the company continues, anyone who has anything to do with sporting arms, thinks of a firearm made by this company simply as a Ruger. This perhaps is partially due to the fact that Alexander Sturm, co-founder of the firm, died in the infancy of the company. But it also reflects the genius and guidance of Bill Ruger that has made this firm, in little more than three decades, the equal of any in the world when it comes to the manufacture of quality firearms.

The company had what can be described only as a modest beginning, shortly after Bill Ruger and Alex Sturm discovered in the late Forties that they had much in common. They both were gun collectors and felt that better guns than some then being marketed should and could be made . At that time Bill Ruger was in his thirties, while Sturm was a few years younger.

History shows that William Batterman Ruger was born in Brooklyn, New York, in June 1916. He attended public schools there, then was sent to Salisbury Preparatory School in Conneticut before enrolling at the University of North Carolina in Chapel Hill.

The Ruger family originally came from Germany in 1848. Bill Ruger's grandfather made his living as a portrait painter, while his father was a lawyer. The elder Ruger enjoyed hunting and often took his young son duck hunting on what then was a remote Long Island Sound. Many of young Bill Ruger's formative summers were spent on his grandfather's farm on Long Island, where he usually had close at hand the .22 Remington with which he had been gifted on his twelfth birthday.

Ruger did not graduate from the Chapel Hill campus, since he wanted to get into the arms business. While still a student at UNC, he converted a Model 99 Savage from lever-action to a gas-operated autoloader. That was in 1939. Instead, Ruger — recently married — returned to his wife's hometown of Greensborough, North Carolina, where he concentrated on designing a machine gun. The design was sold to the Auto Ordinance Corporation in Connecticut and Bill Ruger was awarded an employment contract along with the sale. He spent the years of World War II in that firm's machine gun development shop.

These were valuable days for young Ruger, as he not only learned more about gun design but had an opportunity to become acquainted with the problems of transfering a design from paper to a functioning firearm. He learned about manufacturing costs, knowledge that would stand him in good stead later.

At the end of WWII, Ruger opened a small plant in Southport, Conneticut, where he began to manufacture a line of carpenter's tools. He soon found that his manufacturing costs were too high to allow him to compete with lesser lines and the business folded.

That was when he began to work out the Ruger automatic pistol design. It was about that time that he met Alex Sturm, a brilliant young man who expressed an interest in investing in the Ruger design.

In January 1949, Sturm, Ruger & Company, Incorporated, was founded with the two as partners. Initial production began in the red barn where Ruger had built his

The old red barn, where Ruger made carpenter's tools in the days before he joined with Alex Sturm to build what has become a firearms empire, is still nostalgic site.

Alex Sturm, a sensitive young poet, offered financing to form the company and wrote the first advertisement, sales brochure. He also devised firm's crest.

carpenter's tools. The first gun was the Ruger Standard Automatic .22 that gained almost immediate acceptance. A variation still is in the line, but it has been with single-action revolvers that Bill Ruger has gained much of his fame.

In those first days, Sturm, Ruger & Company had twelve employees, some of whom still are with the firm. While Bill Ruger concentrated on design and production problems, Alex Sturm wrote the firm's early ads and designed the now famous Ruger insignia that has become the firm's trademark. Sturm, incidentally, was both an accomplished artist and writer, having been graduated from the Yale University School of Art. He drew upon his interest and expertise in heraldry in designing the corporate trademark, designing it as a falcon with wings spread. As for his own thoughts concerning design of the image, Bill Ruger

says, "Alex respected the past. Our bird may be rather Teutonic. I'm not sure what he had in his mind, except that he thought human progress came to a halt abruptly in the Twelfth Century."

Over the years, Ruger has been described in many ways. His longtime friend John Amber called him "an American gun genius" in the *Gun Digest*. Others have described him as "a modern Teddy Roosevelt," "a modern Victorian" and as "a Renaissance Man." He may be all of these, but the tall graying inventor obviously had a spot in his heart for his partner. When the Sturm-designed falcon first appeared on the .22 auto, it was emblazoned in red. At the time of Alex Sturm's death in 1951, Ruger ordered that it should be black as a sign of his grief at the death of his friend and partner. It wasn't until 1972 that a silver eagle trademark appeared on Ruger single-actions.

The first single-action to make its appearance from Ruger was the .22 caliber Single Six. (Right) The Bearcat .22 with a 4-inch barrel also was an early Sturm, Ruger production item.

As soon as it was obvious that the Ruger auto had found a market, Bill Ruger began design of a single-action revolver. As a youngster, he had been an admirer of the Colt Single Action Army and had become a student of frontier history. Colt, of course, had discontinued the SAA at the beginning of World War II and had not seen fit, at that point, to reissue it. Meantime, television had become a new national pastime and hordes of film cowboys were cluttering the screens, most of them carrying single-action revolvers. Thus, a new interest was created in the old model among the young, while collectors had begun to hoard the old pre-WWII Colt versions. Ruger was convinced that there was a market for a new single-action.

But Bill Ruger did not rush his work. He designed his first single-action, a .22 lookalike of the Colt SAA, carefully taking more than three years in design and tooling. When it appeared, it was called the Single Six and varied internally to a great degree from the model that had inspired it.

All springs were of steel piano wire, while an alloy steel firing pin was mounted in the frame. The barrel measured 5½ inches on the initial models and the gun weighed thirty-five ounces. To hold down the weight, the grip frames were of aluminum alloy. The frame is of chrome moly steel and resembles the Colt Flat Top SA. Case-hardened frames were advertised, but never were put into serious production. The only known examples are in Ruger's own collection.

The first guns into the marketplace featured hard rubber grips with sharp diamond checkering; the black eagle emblem was inset in both grip panels. The grip frame was enlarged slightly in 1962 and at that time walnut grips became standard.

The loading gate was a flat plate with a notch to open it for loading. Later, Ruger changed the flat plate to a round gate. In later years the maker also offered the Single Six in longer barrel lengths and with engraving. In 1959, for example, the gun was offered in .22 Winchester rimfire magnum with a 6½-inch barrel. Stag and even genuine ivory grips were offered as options at one point, although these were phased out in 1962.

Engraving on the Single Sixes was done by Charles H.

These two Ruger flat-top models are rare, as they have 10-inch barrels. At top is the .357 magnum version and beneath is the .44 magnum, which found instant sales.

Jerrod, who contracted at $30 a gun to handle this phase of the work. On these special guns all steel parts have a high luster blue finish, the grip frames are polished rather than anodized and virtually every part of the gun — including the screws, but excluding the hammer — has some degree of engraving. The total number of engraved guns produced between October 1954 and May 1958 was approximately 250.

But Bill Ruger was not happy with simply producing a selling single-action .22. He began thinking in terms of variations. For example, the Single Six soon was being marketed — initially in 1961 — as a convertible. The frame was built to handle a .22 magnum cylinder, while an extra .22 long rifle cylinder was included. This continued until the Ruger New Model single-action was introduced in 1973.

In 1958 Bill Ruger introduced the Bearcat, which was chambered to handle .22 shorts, longs and long rifles. The barrels on the initial run were four inches in length; the entire handgun weighed only seventeen ounces, with its frame of aluminum alloy. The Bearcat also featured an alloy trigger guard anodized in a brass color. Lock work was of heat-treated steel and, as with the Single Six, the springs were of steel piano wire. Overall length was 8⅞ inches; the grips were of plastic-impregnated wood and the gun was polished and anodized with a blue finish, except for the trigger guard.

There were numerous improvments and changes of a minor nature in the Bearcat in the years that followed and in 1972 Ruger announced the Super Bearcat. Basically the same design as the Bearcat, the frame was of steel, bringing the weight to 22½ ounces. Later that year a steel trigger guard was incorporated to replace the alloy type.

In 1964 Ruger came up with the Super Single Six Convertible, which again included dual cylinders to handle the .22 magnum and .22 RF cartridges. The major improvement was better sights, the rear being adjustable for windage and elevation. Barrel lengths were 5½ and 6½ inches, although a few were made with 9½-inch barrels. Walnut grips also were incorporated into this design.

When Ruger introduced his New Model single-action, the changes were incorporated in the Super Single Six.

Left: Bill Ruger has been interested in firearms design from boyhood and was a gun collector while still in his teens. He learned much about design from specimens.

Lawman and outdoor writer Charles "Skeeter" Skelton was one of the early proponents of the Ruger .44 magnum line. He also was one who advocated the .41 caliber for use by law enforcers across nation.

Gun writers, ballistics enthusiasts took great delight in wringing out the new Ruger Blackhawk to determine whether the manufacturer's claims actually were met.

Most of the changes in the entire single-action line came about as a result of safety standards then being proposed by the federal government. The New Model Single Six — like all other New Model Ruger single-actions — has a safety bar between the firing pin and hammer. This does not rise until the hammer is reaching its rearmost position. An improved grip frame features lugs to engage a spring, thus returning the trigger and lowering the transfer bar to the safe position.

The New Model Super Single Six was introduced with barrels in 4⅝, 5½, 6½ and 9½-inch lengths. In 1974 a stainless steel version was introduced in all of these barrel lengths. The 9½-inch stainless model was dropped in 1975, the 4⅝-inch variation in 1976.

In 1975 Ruger also issued a Super Six that was not convertible. It came only with the .22 RF cylinder. These were available both in blued finish and stainless steel.

Long before this, however, Bill Ruger had entertained the idea of center-fire calibers. His first design was introduced in 1955 as the familiar .357 Blackhawk single-action.

Known as the Flat Top model because of the design of the frame, the first Blackhawks were introduced with a 4⅝-inch barrel. The chrome-moly steel frame was heavier than that of the Single Six, but followed the Ruger innovation of using coil springs of steel music wire throughout. With overall length of 10⅛ inches, the gun weighed thirty-nine ounces. The Blackhawk, built for accuracy featured a Patridge-type blade on a matted ramp. The rear Micro sight was adjustable for windage and elevation with click screws. Standard grips were of hard rubber with sharp checkering and a black gloss finish; stag, ivory or walnut were available as an extra-cost option.

In 1957 engraved Flat Top Blackhawks were adver-

Ruger Super Blackhawk is compared to a pair of Colt single-actions to show the design similarities of two.

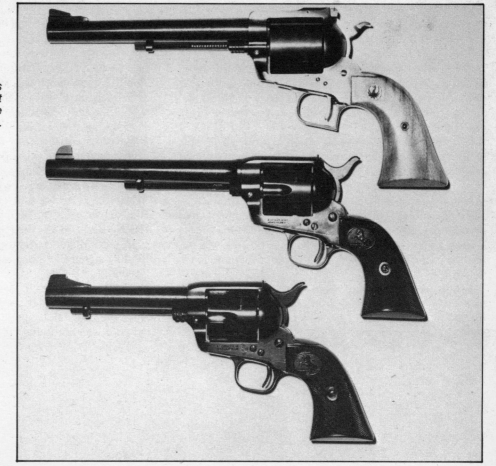

The power of the Ruger .44 magnum is made obvious in this test wherein a gallon carton of milk is hit by bullet.

tised, but only a few were made. Today, they bring premium prices among collectors.

The .357 Blackhawk went through numerous cosmetic changes over the years and in 1962 the frame was redesigned to provide protective ribs on each side of the rear sight. At one point the line included a ten-inch barrel and during 1972 the Blackhawk was offered with a brass grip frame.

With the introduction of Ruger New Models in 1973, the Blackhawk also underwent the internal change aimed at increased safety. It became known, of course, as the New Model Blackhawk, and in 1974 a stainless steel version in 4⅝ and 6½-inch barrel lengths was introduced.

By this time, American handgunners seemingly had become macho-oriented; bigger was better. Much of this interest can be credited to Elmer Keith, who once was described as a man "who feels a .458 is not overgunning for field mice."

Whatever one's feelings about Keith's philosophies, he had been involved in getting Smith & Wesson to introduce the .44 magnum Model 29, which became an almost instant success for the makers.

But Bill Ruger also had been looking at the .44 magnum potential, and a year after the introduction of the .357 magnum Blackhawk, he introduced the .44 magnum Blackhawk with a heavy flat-top target frame of chrome-moly steel. The handgun measured 12½ inches overall, featured a 6½-inch barrel, yet weighed only forty ounces; an ounce more than the .357 Blackhawk with its 4⅝-inch barrel.

Materials used for the .44 Blackhawk were virtually the same as those in the .357 version. With the first three hundred manufactured, hard rubber grips were standard, but uncheckered walnut then was substituted and remained the standard until the gun ws dropped from the line in 1962 to be replaced by the Super Blackhawk. About 30,000 .44 Blackhawks were made. Of these, 1000 had 7½-inch barrels, while 1500 left the factory with ten-inch barrels.

In 1959 Ruger introduced the Super Blackhawk, again in .44 magnum, although some were chambered for .44 Special.

The first Ruger single-action to boast protective ribs on the frame, it was introduced originally in a 7½-inch barrel length; unlike other single-actions made by Ruger, the cylinder was not fluted. This big handful measured 13⅜ inches overall, with a weight of forty-eight ounces.

In the beginning the Super Blackhawk — made on either a long or short frame — was shipped in a mahogany box. Later the handgun was relegated to a cardboard box. At its introduction the .44 Super Blackhawk was equipped with a Micro adjustable rear sight; in 1968 a target sight of factory design and manufacture was substituted. The early guns were polished and blued, but in 1961 the model was given a high-luster finish.

Variations in barrel length also were introduced. In 1963 a number of Super Blackhawks were made with ten-inch barrels and in 1966 about six hundred guns with 6½-inch barrels were marketed. A 1967 option was a Brass Dragoon-type frame.

In 1973 the Super Blackhawk became the New Model with incorporation of the transfer bar and redesign of other internal parts. In 1979 Sturm, Ruger marketed the model with a 10½-inch barrel.

If there ever was an unsuccessful gun to come out of the Ruger works it had to be the single-shot single-action Hawkeye. This was built specifically for the Winchester .256 cartridge, which had been introduced originally in a Smith & Wesson revolver, but which suffered functioning difficulties. In the S&W gun we tested in 1962, the cartridge cases tended to back up in the chambers upon firing, effectively locking up the gun. It became a job for a gun-smith to remove the fired cases. The S&W chambering was quickly discontinued.

It is possible that Ruger was aware of this difficulty, for he made this gun for the .256 as a single-shot on a modified Blackhawk frame. The gun was introduced with a barrel of 8½ inches and target sights. As nearly as we have been able to determine, no more than 3000 of these guns were made, which makes it a highly marketable item on today's collector market. An oddity of collecting is the fact that the least successful guns often become those most sought.

In the mid-Sixties there was a flurry of interest among law enforcement agencies for the .41 magnum cartridge and several manufacturers introduced models for this round, feeling it served as a sort of middle ground in those police departments that banned the .44 magnum as too dangerous to the general populus for normal street use.

Bill Ruger, however, had introduced a .41 magnum Blackhawk as early as 1956 in 4⅝ and 6½-inch barrel lengths. With the exception of the substitution of an aluminum ejector rod housing and redesign of the ejector rod in the mid-Sixties, the design of the gun remained constant until the New Model became the standard in 1963.

Other variations in caliber with minor changes in design over the years have been introduced to meet what Ruger considered a specific market. For example, the Blackhawk appeared in 1971 in .45 Colt, featuring 4⅝ and 7½-inch

The Sturm, Ruger plant in Southport, Connecticut, is a far cry of the beginnings of the firm in the old red barn.

The New Model Ruger Single Six .22 features target sights, with other modifications to make it more safe. (Below) The New Model Single Six is still in production, but discontinued stainless model with 9½-inch barrel is rare.

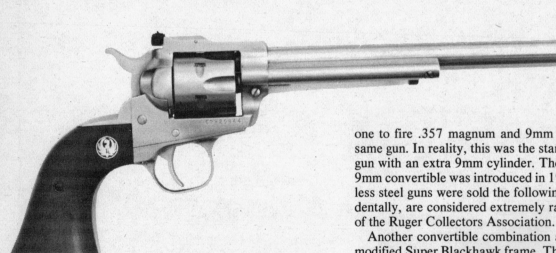

barrels. This was virtually the same gun as the Super Blackhawk, except that the .45 featured a fluted cylinder. In 1972 it was offered with a Dragoon-style brass grip frame. And as with all of the Ruger models, its innards were redesigned for an introduction in 1973 as the New Model.

Ruger had offered a convertible Blackhawk that allowed one to fire .357 magnum and 9mm cartridges from the same gun. In reality, this was the standard .357 magnum gun with an extra 9mm cylinder. The New Model .357/9mm convertible was introduced in 1973 and a few stainless steel guns were sold the following year. These, incidentally, are considered extremely rare among members of the Ruger Collectors Association.

Another convertible combination also was made on a modified Super Blackhawk frame. This was the .45 Colt/.45 ACP offering, which was introduced at the same time as the .45 Blackhawk. Again, it was the same gun with an additional cylinder to handle the .45 ACP. It was made in 4⅝ and 7½-inch barrel lengths, undergoing the same internal modifications in 1973 to become the New Model.

Meantime, Bill Ruger had become intrigued with the growing interest in black powder shooting. His answer was the .44 Ruger Old Army percussion revolver, which bears a vague resemblance to the Civil War-era Remington

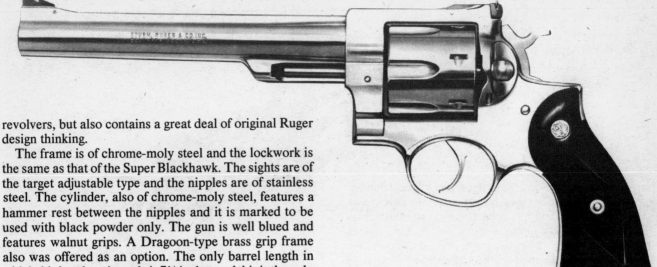

revolvers, but also contains a great deal of original Ruger design thinking.

The frame is of chrome-moly steel and the lockwork is the same as that of the Super Blackhawk. The sights are of the target adjustable type and the nipples are of stainless steel. The cylinder, also of chrome-moly steel, features a hammer rest between the nipples and it is marked to be used with black powder only. The gun is well blued and features walnut grips. A Dragoon-type brass grip frame also was offered as an option. The only barrel length in which this handgun is made is 7½ inches and this is the only gun in the Ruger line that did not undergo the internal designs of 1973 leading to the New Model designation. A stainless steel version was introduced in 1975.

With literally thousands of war surplus M-1 carbines in the country — not to mention others that had been made from the more or less public domain designs — Bill Ruger felt that a companion handgun chambered for the .30 Car-

The Redhawk was the first double-action .44 magnum to be introduced into the Ruger line, although the Security Six line designed for law enforcement was an earlier double-action.

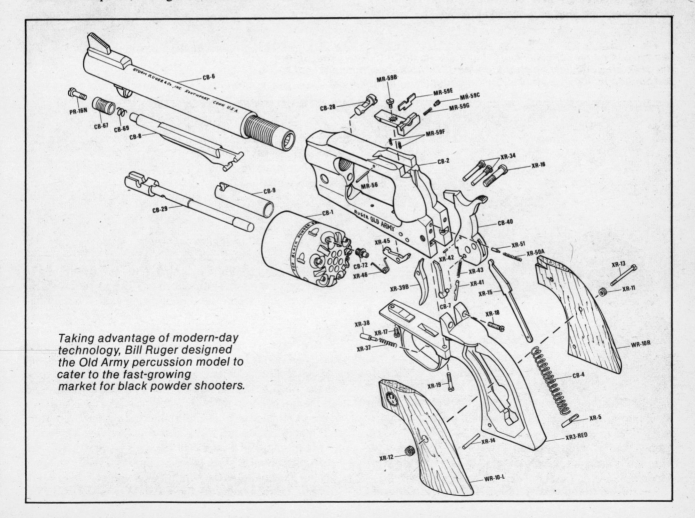

Taking advantage of modern-day technology, Bill Ruger designed the Old Army percussion model to cater to the fast-growing market for black powder shooters.

The Ruger Old Army black powder shooter has refinements such as target sights that the old frontiersmen never dreamed of, it has features modern buffs appreciate.

bine cartridge might do well in the marketplace. It would appear he was correct, since this version of the Blackhawk still is in the line and has been since its introduction in 1967. The gun was introduced with a 7½-inch barrel, featuring the Super Blackhawk frame and a fluted cylinder. It continued through the New Model redesign phase and weighs forty-four ounces. In 1972 a brass grip frame was available as an option.

Along the way, Ruger has been involved in numerous special orders and commemorative editions. In 1975 Ruger built the so-called Mag-na-port Mark V Edition consisting of some 250 guns. These were built with five-inch barrels for the most part and all were Mag-na-ported with the Mag-na-port logo engraved on the top strap. Hammers and triggers were jeweled and nickel-plated.

When it came time for expansion, Ruger moved north to New Hampshire. His gunworks and casting operation are at Newport, a community that is surrounded by the hills and forests that Ruger has always loved.

Above: The New Model Blackhawk was introduced with a 7½-inch barrel and was chambered for .30 Carbine and .45. (Left) The 4⅝-inch version was available in .357 magnum, .41 magnum and old standby, .45 caliber.

In 1976 a series known as the Tomahawk Custom was made up in a lot of two hundred guns. These guns featured 4⅝-inch barrels that had been Mag-na-ported. A tomahawk was engraved on the hammer, while the top strap was engraved with the same tomahawk and the Mag-na-port logo.

The Mag-na-port Classic was manufactured in 1978 with a 7½-inch Mag-na-ported barrel, with the term Mag-na-port Classic engraved on the top strap and gold filled. The serial numbers also are gold filled and the grip screws are gold plated as well.

In 1979 Ruger issued the Safari Mag-na-port Super Blackhawk .44 magnum, which featured the same barrel venting. Changes from the standard were numerous from a cosmetic point, including an Omega Maverick rear sight, gold-plated hammer, trigger, center pin, center pin release, ejector rod and grip screw. A .44 magnum cartridge was

inlaid in the antiqued walnut grips and the cylinder was engraved with a Cape buffalo.

In 1980 Ruger brought out the Safari II in elephant, rhino, leopard and lion editions. On these the specific animal was engraved on the cylinder and the same figure was featured on scrimshawed ivory set in the grip.

It should be noted, incidentally, that with the Mag-na-port editions, all of the actions are sealed to lock the hammer and trigger, thus preventing the cylinder from being turned.

Ruger took a lead from Colt and others, when he chose to enter the commemorative business on a limited basis. The difference between his operation and others lay in the fact that his commemoratives were pre-sold prior to production. These will be discussed at greater length in another chapter.

Although a double-action, note should be made of the

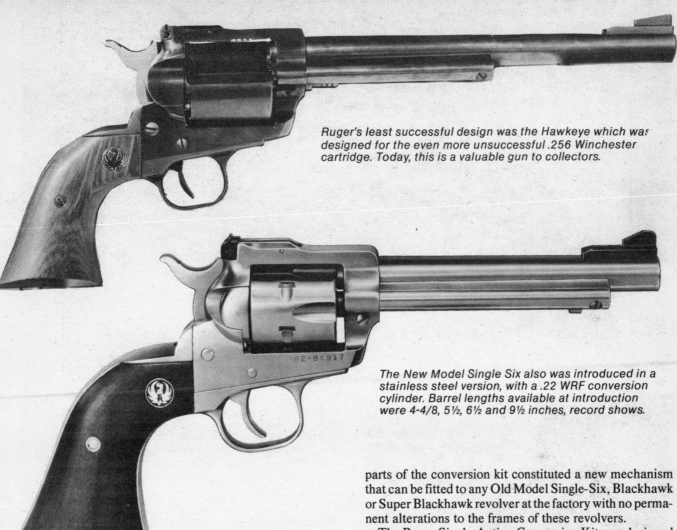

Ruger's least successful design was the Hawkeye which was designed for the even more unsuccessful .256 Winchester cartridge. Today, this is a valuable gun to collectors.

The New Model Single Six also was introduced in a stainless steel version, with a .22 WRF conversion cylinder. Barrel lengths available at introduction were 4-4/8, 5½, 6½ and 9½ inches, record shows.

Ruger Redhawk model, which was introduced in 1979. This particular version had the lines of the Super Blackhawk, but has been made only in stainless steel. As a direct but less expensive competitor to the Smith & Wesson Model 29 double-action .44 magnum, Bill Ruger was not wrong when he felt that gun enthusiasts would be standing in line to obtain one!

There was a time in this country, if an individual shot himself accidentally, he was willing to accept the blame for his own stupidity. More recently, with more and more attorneys coming out of law schools and fewer and fewer finding high-paying positions, a new dimension has entered the area of responsibility.

Bill Ruger redesigned his entire series of single-action revolvers in 1973, adding safety factors, as outlined earlier, but several lawsuits persisted, all of them based upon alleged accidents with the pre-1973 or Old Model Rugers.

So, early in 1982, Sturm, Ruger & Company introduced a new invention for the owners of Old Model Ruger single-action Single-Six, Blackhawk, and Super Blackhawk revolvers — the Ruger Single-Action conversion kit. The parts of the conversion kit constituted a new mechanism that can be fitted to any Old Model Single-Six, Blackhawk or Super Blackhawk revolver at the factory with no permanent alterations to the frames of these revolvers.

The Ruger Single-Action Conversion Kit was designed to provide the owners of Old Model Ruger single-action revolvers with the advantages of a modern transfer-bar mechanism by the replacement of a few key parts in the revolver. The seven new parts that comprise the Ruger conversion kit are the hammer, pawl, transfer-bar, trigger, cylinder latch, cylinder latch spring and cylinder base pin.

A close examination of these parts will reveal some of the truly unique characteristics of this invention," Ruger stated at the time the kit was introduced. "The use of thin spring steel to fabricate the rugged new transfer-bar has made it possible for this part to lie in a shallow recess in the side of the hammer, and the use of hardened alloy steels and spring steels in all of the new parts has resulted in a mechanism which functions perfectly and has tremendous endurance and reliability.

The transfer-bar-type mechanism of the conversion kit prevents the kind of accidental discharge that can occur if the hammer receives a heavy blow while resting over a loaded chamber. With the trigger fully forward, the hammer rests directly on the frame and cannot contact the firing pin. The kit's transfer-bar is positioned between the hammer and the firing pin to transmit the hammer blow to the firing pin only when the trigger is pulled and held all the way to the rear.

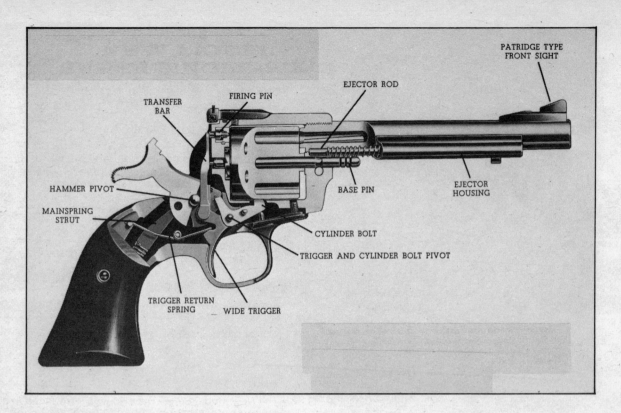

TRANSFER BAR · FIRING PIN · EJECTOR ROD · PATRIDGE TYPE FRONT SIGHT · HAMMER PIVOT · MAINSPRING STRUT · BASE PIN · EJECTOR HOUSING · CYLINDER BOLT · TRIGGER AND CYLINDER BOLT PIVOT · TRIGGER RETURN SPRING · WIDE TRIGGER

Ruger's New Model Super Single Six incorporated many improvements that are reflected in cut-away drawing. (Left) In 1982, he introduced a conversion kit to be installed in Old Model Ruger single-action revolvers that would make these more safe, retain their value.

"This invention provides the owner of an Old Model Ruger single-action with most of the advantages and convenience of the Ruger New Model single-action revolvers, although the conversion kit does not provide the loading gate/hammer interlock feature of the Ruger New Model revolvers," we were told.

In 1973, when Sturm, Ruger & Company discontinued the Old Model Single-Six, Blackhawk and Super Blackhawk and introduced the New Model single-actions, many shooters were critical. The old model revolvers represented a classic, time-tested design widely accepted by shooters everywhere, while the New Model had different handling characteristics. Despite the criticism, Ruger felt he had invented a mechanism that represented a new state of the art in the manufacture of modern single-action revolvers.

In the years since 1973 the discontinued Old Model Ruger single-actions rapidly achieved collector status and their values increased substantially.

"With the New Model revolvers gaining acceptance, all would have been well, but in recent years it has become apparent that some people have been suffering injuries with the old model single-actions, because of a disregard for the basic rules of firearms safety. Also, people were not taking the trouble to learn the mechanical characteristics of the particular firearms they were using. The company attempted to determine the causes of as many of these accidents as possible, and the results were surprising."

Ruger and company came to the conclusion that most of these accidents had occurred because the shooter had allowed the hammer to rest in its full forward position, with the firing pin contacting the primer of a large cartridge in the chamber aligned with the barrel. This was in spite of specific instructions to the contrary that were packed and shipped with all old model Ruger single-actions since production began in 1953.

Given the fact that a cartridge primer detonates by percussion (a sharp blow), and that the basic single-action design dates back well over a century, and that it is possible to place the firing pin in contact with the primer of a live cartridge in many firearms, common sense should tell the shooter not to let the firing pin rest directly on a primer, even if he had *not* read the instructions packed with the old

William B. Ruger is justly proud of the fact his efforts on behalf of shooters led contemporaries to elect him as American Handgunner of the Year in 1975. The permanent bronze trophy was presented him as a part of award.

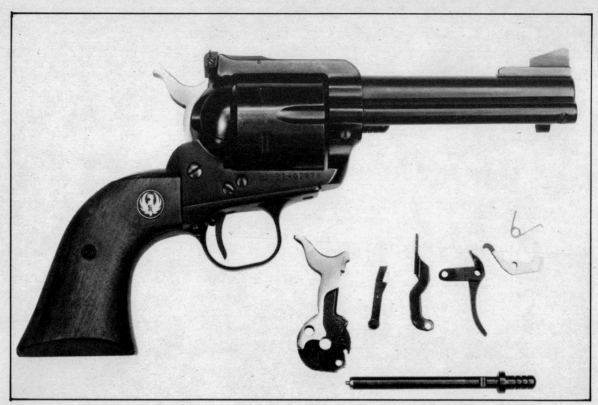

Pictured beneath this Old Model Ruger single-action are the parts of the conversion kit that may be installed to increase safety. The old parts may be retained by collectors to insure the handgun is of collector quality.

model revolvers. Nevertheless, some shooters still experienced tragic accidents by ignoring these well known principles.

As a result of the firearms accidents that had become apparent, and single-action revolver accidents in particular, Ruger began to publish an unprecedented campaign of safety messages dealing with the handling characteristics of the old model single-action revolvers, and the widely known and recommended practice of loading only five cartridges and resting the hammer on the empty chamber.

While it is true that the Ruger New Model single-action revolver, with its patented transfer-bar type mechanism, can help to prevent accidental discharges from the conditions previously described, the Ruger New Model revolver is entirely different from the old model revolver, and the mechanism parts of the Ruger New Model and old model revolvers are not interchangeable.

While virtually all single-action revolvers have been safe to use when handled properly, Sturm, Ruger & Company developed the single-action conversion kit to be fitted to any old model Ruger single-action. These parts are designed to protect the shooter from an accidental discharge resulting from a severe blow to the hammer if he has forgotten to load only five cartridges and to keep the hammer down on an empty chamber.

The company has been offering to fit any old model Ruger Single-Six, Blackhawk, or Super Blackhawk revolver with this new mechanism at no charge. The new mechanism can be fitted without alteration to the revolver and without changing its outward appearance in any way.

Installation of the conversion kit parts will not affect the collector value of old model Rugers and the original parts can be re-installed by the owner for collector purposes at any time.

Although the Ruger Single-Action Conversion Kit is furnished at no charge, it must be fitted at the factory. Customers should write to the company at the following address for details: Sturm, Ruger & Company, Inc., Lacey Place, Dept. OM, Southport, CT 06490.

Do not ship your old model Ruger revolver until you are contacted by Sturm, Ruger & Company with shipping instructions.

The new Ruger Single-Action Conversion Kit can help to protect careless shooters from the consequences of their actions, but all firearms are dangerous, and the best safety device is a careful shooter. Never rely on *any* mechanical safety device to prevent accidents. Follow the standard safety practice of loading only five cartridges in any older single-action revolver, and always carry the revolver with the hammer resting on an empty chamber.

There is no such thing as a foolproof gun!

At this writing, as Sturm, Ruger & Company is well into its fourth decade, Bill Ruger remains chairman of the board and continues to oversee much of the development work at both the plant in Connecticut and a newer facility in New Hampshire. However, another generation has come upon the scene. William Ruger, Jr., the eldest son, now is president of the firm, while Tom Ruger is sales manager. Other family members, including son-in-law Steve Vogel, also are closely allied with various facets of management.

Chapter 4

THE GOOD GUYS

The Sixgun Helped Win The West, While Some Of Its Proponents Wore Gray Hats Rather Than White!

THE SIXGUN, through fact, fiction — and sometimes fact made legend by fiction — has become an American mystique in its own right. This quality has been nurtured in the last century by both the historians and the hack writers who have glamourized our Western frontier and the part played by the Colt Single Action Army, the Smith & Wesson American and the Remington 1875 Army, as well as other revolvers of lesser repute.

In the writings of the last century and well into the 1900s, individuals tended to be painted as either black or white, authors often underestimating the intelligence of their readers or perhaps not being intelligent enough themselves to realize that there are shades of good and bad.

In putting together this chapter on the so-called Good Guys and the sixguns they used in allegedly taming the West, it becomes obvious that the Good Guys and the Bad Guys often were interchangeable. Which category they eventually ended up as representing often depended upon circumstances, twists of fate and — in some cases — press agentry.

Buffalo Bill Cody, for example, has been pictured as a great frontiersman who won the West from the back of a white charger. Until only recent years the fact went ignored that, while Cody did ride the Pony Express and shoot a batch of buffalo, he became a showman who may have believed his own press agents and the writings of Ned Buntline, one of the hack writers of the period, who tended to use real names and totally fictitious stories. Also ignored for the most part lies the fact that Bill Cody was a lousy businessman, whose Wild West Show ultimately went at a sheriff's sale and that this man on the white charger ultimately developed a serious drinking problem.

If one goes back to the Thirties and reviews Wild Bill Hickok through the eyes of the movie writers with Gary Cooper in the title role and Cecil B. DeMille directing, we reach the conclusion that Hickok never did anything but good deeds throughout his life. The truth more likely is that he was a profesional gun-for-hire who made a point of doing most of his killing while standing behind a badge. The same has been said of Wyatt Earp, the legendary marshal who cleaned up Tombstone and a lot of other towns along the way. He was the subject of legends, but some members of the Earp family later came to admit that he also controlled or had a piece of a lot of the gambling and vice in those frontier communities where he was hired to keep the law.

Judge Roy Bean is another case in point. As the self-proclaimed Law West of the Pecos, he was pictured as dispensing justice with a common sense approach to the law. Actually, he tended to use the law to his own advantage. The one thing that can be said is that there was law, even if it was of Roy Bean's own making.

At the other extreme, there are many who tend to glamourize such names as Jesse James, Billy the Kid, Sam Bass and a host of others. They have been made legends and those legends no doubt will continue to exist long after the truth dies of disuse. They no doubt had their good points as well as their bad, but the fact remains that they killed and hurt a lot of people along the way, while showing occasional flashes of a Robin Hood syndrome. But has anyone ever considered what the opinion might be today had Jesse James been a country constable or even a town marshal? His name probably would never had made the history books.

So, in writing about the Good Guys who helped make the sixgun famous — or infamous — on the side of good, we have attempted to show that these individuals were as much victims of their own circumstance as were the Bad Guys.

The fully engraved Colt .45 Single Action allegedly presented to Judge Roy Bean now is in the new Frontier Historical Museum in Temecula, CA. (Inset) Judge Roy Bean was the self-styled Law West of the Pecos in Texas.

JUDGE ROY BEAN

The Law West Of The Pecos Conducted Court With His Sixgun Close At Hand

ONE OF the oldest characters ever to pack a single-action .45 Colt in his varied arsenal was one Roy Bean, better-known in history as "Judge Roy Bean, the Law West of the Pecos."

Today, the highly engraved handgun which aided him in maintaining his curious brand of law is enshrined in Temecula, California, as part of the Bianchi Museum, which is devoted to maintaining the memorabilia of the Western frontier.

Judge Roy Bean was one of a raft of nearly illiterate Old West jurists who distilled law, liquor and larceny into a legendary blend that — like the watered whiskey he poured at his combination saloon/courthouse — many find hard to swallow today, a century after his death.

Roy Bean was born in Mason County, Kentucky, probably in 1825 — it's hard to say, since he changed his history to suit his mood. His introduction to firearms is unknown, but he was familiar with their use by the time he ventilated a bandido as a young man in Chihuahua. He high-tailed it for San Diego, where he found trouble again: He served a month in jail for killing a man in a horseback duel. This was his introduction to the legal system he later would prostitute.

Roy Bean's story almost ended following his release from the hoosegow. He wandered up to Los Angeles and got involved with a senorita. Her Mexican boyfriend objected, there was a scuffle, and Bean blasted him. The boyfriend's compadres then hauled Bean outside and strung him up, leaving him for dead. Bean claims he was later cut down by the senorita and thereafter took to wearing neckerchiefs to hide the rope burn scars.

He dropped out of history until the Civil War erupted, when he turned up in Old Mesilla, New Mexico. He sided with the Confederates, but never got close to the battlefield. Rather, he organized the Free Rovers, a guerilla band known locally as the "Forty Thieves." Clearly, he was interested in furthering his own fortunes along with those of the South.

He was to move east as far as San Antonio, where he began running the blockade from Mexico with supplies for the Confederacy. How successful he was is unclear, since old records indicate he spent lots of time in courtrooms, defending allegations of fiscal misconduct. This courtroom time was well-spent, since Bean was to learn more of the law than most of his peers.

Now in his thirties, Bean took his only wife during this time, a child named Virginia Chavez. She bore him two sons and two daughters before leaving him.

He again dropped out of history's gaze for about twenty years, until about age 56. The Southern Pacific railroad was pushing through west Texas, with towns emerging from the barren landscape like wildflowers after a desert storm; and they were to wither just as fast.

But when they were flowering, there was money to be made. Roy Bean opened a saloon in the tent town of Vinegaroon. He somehow got himself elected a justice of the peace in 1882 — he could read haltingly and barely write — then followed the road gangs to Langtry, twenty miles west of the Pecos River. It was here that Bean was to create legend.

The bull-voiced, whiskey-soaked Bean opened a combination saloon, gambling hall and courtroom called "The Jersey Lilly Saloon," named after the English actress Lily

Roy Bean's courthouse and saloon, where justice and libations were dispensed freely, was located in Langtry, Texas.

Langtry, for whom he carried a torch. (Lily was misspelled by a sign painter arrested as drunk and disorderly who was working off his fine...chances are that Bean never knew the difference.) Bean was later to claim that he named the town after the actress, but it more likely was named after one of the town's prominent citizens of the same name.

Such as he was, Roy Bean was the closest thing to a judge within two hundred miles, so the Texas Rangers began bringing in their prisoners for trial. With an 1879 copy of the Revised Statutes of Texas as his guide, Bean began dispensing justice — along with whiskey to attorneys during recesses he called for that specific purpose. Cases were heard by the portly, white-bearded Bean between hands of poker on the other side of his "courtroom." He would open the proceeding by bellowing, "Hear Ye! Hear Ye! This honorable court's now in session and if any galoot wants a snort before we start, let him step up and name his poison!"

Bean's brand of justice was tempered by realities of life. Like the time an Irish railroad worker was hauled into court for killing a Chinese laborer and two hundred of his Irish mates showed up to see justice was done. He had been a good customer at the bar, too, so Bean leafed through his lawbook and solemnly declared: "There ain't a damn line here nowhere's that makes it illegal to kill a Chinaman. The defendant is discharged!"

When another good customer was charged with opening a prodigious hole through the middle of a Mexican worker, Judge Roy Bean declared that "it served the deceased right for getting in front of a gun."

The fines levied by the judge varied with the circumstances and inevitably ended up in his pocket. When questioned by another judge about disposition of the fines, Bean declared: "My court is self-sustaining."

"The Law West of the Pecos" showed genuine ingenuity when it came to getting money. Like the time a worker died because of a three-hundred-foot fall. Judge Bean, acting as coroner, pronounced the man dead at the scene. But he wasn't thrilled at the $5 fee he was to receive for arranging burial, so he ordered the corpse searched. There was $40 and a revolver on the deceased, and Bean promptly announced: "I find this corpse guilty of carrying a concealed weapon, and the fine is $40."

The judge also presided over weddings and divorces; the former earning him $2, the latter $5. He would always end his marriage ceremony with the solemn pronouncement: "May God have mercy on your soul."

Bean was compliant when divorces were sought. When informed by a federal magistrate that his granting of divorces was beyond his power as a justice of the peace, Bean retorted: "Well, I married 'em, so I figure I've got the right to rectify my errors!"

For twenty years, Bean ruled over Langtry and there's no record of his ever using the ornate, engraved Colt .45 shown in the photo (and being worn by the judge in the courthouse picture). At first, Bean was elected — the election was conducted in his saloon. But in 1896 his hated rival, Jesus P. Torres, won the office: A count of the ballots showed 100 more people than actually lived in the town had voted for Bean!

Bean was undeterred, however, and continued trying cases on his side of town. He was known to be harsh to offenders who didn't patronize his saloon, and even ordered non-offenders to buy the house a round. He shortchanged sightseers to his court, figuring that was his payment for their visit. Perhaps it was; they even got to see his pet bear, kept chained to his bedpost for many years!

The judge did his share of hanging, too. Upon pronouncing sentence on a cattle rustler brought before him, a newspaper reports Bean said:

"You have been tried by twelve good men and, true, not of your peers, but as high above you as heaven is of hell, and they have said you are guilty.

"Time will pass and the seasons will come and go. Spring with its wavin' green grass and heaps of sweet-smellin' flowers on every hill and in every dale. Then sultry summer, with her shimmerin' heat waves on the baked horizon. And fall, with her yellow harvest moon and the hills glowin' brown and golden under a sinkin' sun. And finally winter, with its bitin', whinin' wind, and all the land will be mantled with snow.

"But you won't be here to see any of 'em; not by a damn sight, because it's the order of this court that you be took to the nearest tree and hanged by the neck till you're dead, dead, dead, you olive-colored son of a billy goat!"

Before the grizzled judge died of old age and bad liquor in 1903, he did once see the actress whom he once described as: "By gobs, by ziggity, what a purty critter!" During her tour in 1888, Lily Langtry came to San Antonio. Judge Roy Bean bought a front-row seat for her performance.

While details of their association are scanty, it appears Lily Langtry knew of Bean some years earlier, when she sent him the engraved pistol shown in the accompanying photo. According to an affidavit of authenticity sworn by L. Robinson Perry at the time of sale of this gun to the Bianchi Museum, the gun is a Colt Single-Action Frontier Revolver with barrel shortened to 4¾ inches, serial number 8054, nickel-silver finish, completely scroll-engraved. "Judge Roy Bean, Law West of the Pecos," along with numerous early Texas cattle brands including X.I.T. Brand, the King Ranch Brand, Snake River brand, Little & Little brand, and the Rocking Chair brand. The gun has one-piece ivory grips.

Perry recounts the revolver's history: "This six-shooter was acquired from the State Treasury Office in Austin, Texas, in 1919, by Captain E.B. Averill, late of Phoenix, Arizona. Texas state authorities confiscated this gun, along with other real and personal property of the late Judge Roy Bean, for non-payment of fines collected in his official capacity as judge.

"This gun was examined by Cole Agee, the noted gun engraver, at Fort Worth, Texas, in 1947," the deposition continues. "He identified the engraving as the work of a Mexican engraver by the name of Sergio Moreno of San Antonio, Texas, about 1885. This revolver was identified as belonging to Judge Bean by his daughter, Zulema Bean Voss, of New Orleans, Louisiana, in 1947. She stated that the gun was sent to her father by the British stage actress, Lily Langtry..."

Lily Langtry visited the town and the Jersey Lilly Saloon after Bean's death in 1903. The townspeople presented her with the judge's bear, which promptly ran away.

The eccentric jurist died at about 80 years of age, thus ending a colorful — and checkered — period of handgun history.

There is some doubt as to whether Judge Roy Bean and Lily Langtry, the actress, ever actually met, but numerous legends were born of his admiration of the lady.

Wyatt Earp .45 Colt originally owned by old-time Tombstoner Fred Dodge that's now in Frontier Museum Historical Center. With this gun Earp reputedly killed notorious cattle rustler, Curly Bill Brocius.

COLT SINGLE ACTION #69562 USED BY WYATT EARP Collection of Capt. Fred W. Dodge Chief Special Officer Wells Fargo & Co. Express

WYATT EARP

A Controversial Figure Who Left His Mark On The History Of The Old West

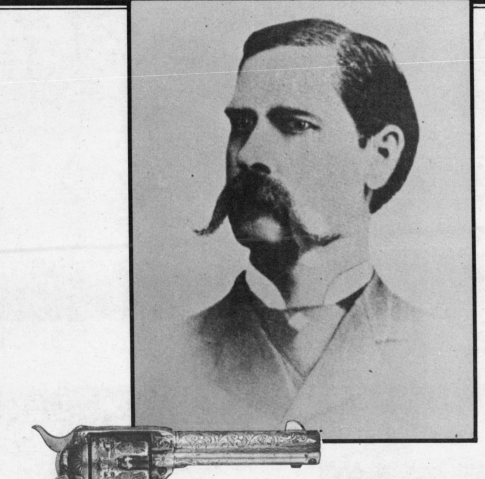

Wyatt Earp at age 38 was known to work both sides of the law, but is remembered most for fun at OK Corral.

Easy handling was just one benefit of 4¾-inch barreled Colt Peacemaker .45.

WYATT BERRY STAPP EARP was another of the Western figures who inspired intense feelings either of admiration or dislike. Had he not been wearing a star, many feel his actions would have been deemed unlawful.

Wyatt was born to Nicholas Porter and Virginia Ann Cooksey Earp on March 19, 1848, at Monmouth, Illinois. He learned farming on the family homestead near Pella, Iowa, and listed his occupation during the 1870 census as farmer. He had married Irilla H. Sutherland and set up housekeeping near Lamar, Missouri, where his family had moved in 1869. His first term as a lawman was served in Lamar, where he defeated half-brother Newton J. Earp for the post of constable. But when his wife died less than a year later he resigned and moved to the cowtowns...and infamy.

During this footloose time Wyatt and some pals "procured" two fine horses owned by one William Keys of Fort Gibson. Despite an elaborate escape plan, Earp and friends were arrested, charged with horse stealing, released on $500 bail, then vamoosed to Kansas beyond Arkansas' jurisdiction. (One of the group who did come to trial was subsequently released.)

From 1871 to 1874 Wyatt Earp kept a low profile, earning his living as a gambler in towns like Hays City, Ellsworth, Wichita, and Dodge City. Wichita alone shipped nearly a quarter-million head of cattle and that meant lots of cowboys and cash at the railheads. At six feet two

PAT. SEPT. 19. 1871.
" JULY. 2. — 72.
" JAN. 19. — 75.

Assorted views of Capt. Dodge's Wyatt Earp .45 that's now part of the Frontier Museum Historical Center in Temecula. As a collector gun, this is top value since good history has been established, certifying ownership.

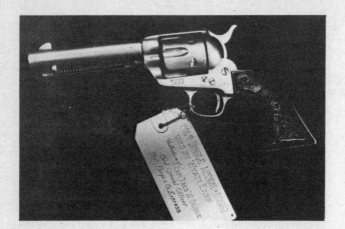

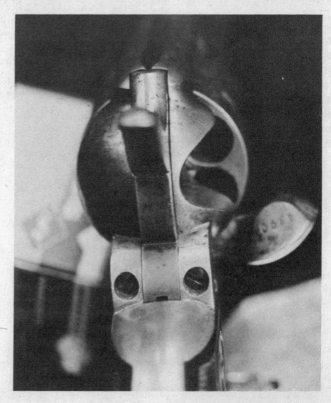

battle when appointed a city policeman by Wichita Marshal Michael Meagher. For $60 a month — and, it was learned later, a portion of the fines he skimmed during collection — the blue-eyed, ash-blond Wyatt Earp kept peace and harmony in the hoary cowtown.

In April 1876 Earp's boss, Marshal Meagher, was facing tough competition for reelection. Some say he put Wyatt up to it, but whatever the reason, Wyatt severely beat former marshal Billy Smith and limited his campaign potential. Earp was arrested and charged with disturbing the peace. He was fined $30 plus $2 court costs, and his boss was reelected by an almost two-to-one margin. The action resulted in Wyatt's dismissal from the Wichita police force, and the police commission recommended he and brother Morgan be arrested for vagrancy. Before officers came looking for them the pair had moved to Dodge City where Wyatt was hired upon Bill Tilghman's recommendation by 307-pound Marshal Larry Deger. His salary in Dodge was $75 per month plus $2 for every court conviction and Wyatt supplemented this with gambling.

John Bianchi holds just one of the many single-action historical handguns that form fascinating part of his Frontier Museum Historical Center. Gun is priceless.

inches, Earp was a lean and mean 185-pounder who swaggered through the red-light districts and gaming halls that lured swindlers and cowboys alike. Popular cowboy sport was to "hurrah" a town — ride at the gallop, yipping and yahooing, firing guns into the air. In Dodge City, the railroad tracks cutting Front Street separated respectability from riot. The assemblage of whorehouses, dance halls and saloons was dubbed by citizens as "across the Dead Line." So tough was the territory that even business owners paid protection money — to the police!

In his stay at Wichita Wyatt was joined by brother, James, who worked as a barkeep and part-time hack driver, and Jim's wife, Bessie, who ran a whorehouse which included among the stable of talent one "Big Nose Kate" Elder who later was to become the steady girlfriend of Wyatt Earp's best friend, Doc Holliday. The slogan of the town was "Everything Goes in Wichita" and cowboys, railroad workers, and drifters sought to live up to that claim. In 1874 alone authorities collected $5600 in fines.

There's disparity over the town troublemakers; some writers claim cowhands loosed from their herds with full pockets caused most of the problems, although George Hinkle, bartender at a Dodge City saloon, pointed a finger at drifters and railroad men "who caused more trouble than the cowboys." Whoever, Wyatt Earp was ready to do

Wyatt Earp formed a fast friendship with John Henry Holliday, a tubercular dentist with hot temper and quick trigger who was participant in OK Corral episode.

Virgil, eldest of Earp trio of lawman-brothers, was persuaded by Wyatt to head for Tombstone and destiny from his job as U.S. Marshal of Yavapi County. After OK Corral shootout, he was bushwhacked at night in Tombstone. His left arm was shot up, ending gun career.

In the nine years between 1875 and 1884, Dodge City shipped just short of 350,000 head of cattle — a record for any Kansas cowtown. There were plenty of cowboys and the railroad men required to move their charges to keep authorities like Wyatt Earp toiling. Of the thirty-three revelers occupying real estate in Boot Hill, only one may have been dispatched by Earp before his resignation in 1877. Of his performance, buddy Bat Masterson remembered thirty years later in a story for *Human Life Magazine:* "Wyatt on a great many occasions, at the risk of his life, rendered valuable service in upholding the...law... While he invariably went armed, he seldom had occasion to do any shooting in Dodge City..." And were Wyatt Earp the blood-thirsty outlaw with a badge many writers would have us believe, he surely would have gunned down giant Red Sweeney who used his six-foot six-inch, 245-pound bulk to maul Wyatt during a barroom brawl over a dance hall girl.

Others, like barkeep George Hinkle, disagreed. In Dale T. Schoenberger's *The Gunfighters,* Hinkle is quoted as describing Wyatt as "a big blow" whose veracity could always be doubted and "a fighting pimp." Another non-admirer, cowboy Pink Simms, in a letter said that Wyatt

was an intelligent, efficient police officer who didn't like to work alone, and invariably surrounded himself with a group of killers.

Earp left for the Dakota Territory but returned to Dodge City after less than a month. He was arrested and fined one dollar for slapping a dance hall girl named Frankie Bell, with whom he'd collided and who had cursed him. (Frankie was jailed and fined $20 plus costs.) Wyatt left Dodge again and followed the gambling circuit throughout Texas and in 1877 met Doc Holliday, the tubercular dentist who was to lend a hand — shotgun would be a better word — in a fray at Tombstone's OK Corral.

Earp returned to Dodge City in early 1878 and with him was a mistress named Mattie Blaylock. Wyatt was appointed assistant city marshal at $75 per month and $2 arrest fee, which he strengthened with a percentage of the gaming take from the Long Branch and Alhambra saloons and protection money paid by businesses "across the Dead Line." Life went on, punctuated with a very occasional gunshot, and in the fourteen months he remained on the police payroll before moving on in September 1879, Wyatt arrested thirty-two of the seventy-eight persons arrested and charged in Dodge City.

The Old West at its worst: Two dead cavalrymen decorate mud-spattered boardwalk of rough-hewn timber following a night of revelry "across the Dead Line." Paid-off cattlemen or soldiers on payday whooped and died.

Earp moved on to Mobeetie, Texas, and was run out of town for trying a "gold brick" hoax, drifted with mistress Mattie to New Mexico and on to Tombstone and the zenith of his career. He stopped by Prescott to collect brother Virgil, deputy U.S. marshal for Yavapi County, and soon was joined by brothers Morgan and Jim from Dodge City, and Baxter from California. Wyatt profited through mining interests and filled in slow times riding stagecoaches as a shotgun messenger for Wells, Fargo & Company. He ws hired as deputy to Tombstone's Charles Shibell in October of 1880 and in his tenure arrested and pistol-whipped the notorious cattle rustler Curly Bill Brocius, whose real name was William Graham, and claims to have later killed him.

Now in the Frontier Museum Historical Center in Temecula, California, is one of Earp's many pistols, a Colt Single-Action .45 with serial number 69562 that came from the collection of old-time Tombstoner, Captain Fred Dodge. It was with this gun that Earp reputedly shot Curly Bill Brocius.

Was it in retalliation for Curly Bill's theft of a Colt Frontier revolver, gold and silver engraved with 7½-inch barrel in caliber .44-40 with serial number 42850? The pistol was presented to Wyatt from a group of Chinese in Tombstone and Curly Bill took it along with a rifle from Earp's Wells, Fargo office with the help of another outlaw named Johnny Ringo. The pistol, now in the aforementioned collection, was confiscated by one-time sheriff of Tombstone, John Slaughter, when he arrested Ringo.

Virgil Earp was later appointed to a lawman slot in Tombstone, and Wyatt was dismissed by Shibell and replaced with John Behan. Earp and Behan then sought the post as sheriff of Cochise County and Behan got the job. To really make things hot between them Earp won the heart and whatever of Behan's mistress, Josephine Sarah Marcus; Wyatt was also to keep living with Mattie.

Besides a gambling stake in Tombstone's Oriental Saloon, Wyatt made money with his brothers hiring out as possemen and one of these posse actions led to his famous Fremont Street shootout. Six U.S. Government mules were stolen and pursued to the ranch of Tom and Frank McLaury at Charleston, some six miles from Tombstone. The posse found the mules in the corral, but the McLaury brothers would not come out to face the pursuers. They struck a deal in which the mules would be returned if the Earps left, but the McLaury's reneged on their half of the bargain and got on the bad side of the Earp boys. Dislike deepened when friends of the McLaurys were sought for a stage robbery many felt was the work of Doc Holliday or the Earps proper. Then Billy Clanton, a McLaury comrade, was found astride a horse lately owned by Wyatt. Two other McLaury chums, logger Pete Spence and Cochise County Deputy Sheriff Frank Stilwell, were arrested by the Earps for robbing the Bisbee stage.

The bad blood boiled on October 25, then spilled into dusty Fremont Street on the 26th. Morgan Earp and Doc Holliday taunted Ike Clanton, a McLaury friend who was

Frank McLaury, reputedly the best shooter of the Clanton-McLaury bunch, was first to be shot when gunfire began on Fremont Street in Tombstone.

Bad blood between Tom McLaury and Earp clan came to boil when Wyatt slapped and pistol-whipped him after they collided outside the Tombstone courthouse.

temporarily unarmed. Angered, Ike later got a pistol, told Wyatt he'd happily fight in the morning, then settled into an all-night poker game after which he and Virgil Earp exchanged none-too-pleasantries. Virgil pistol-whipped Ike and with Morgan's help hauled him to police court for a $25 fine for carrying a gun within city limits. Morgan and Ike quarreled further inside the court, and Tom McLaury jostled Wyatt Earp outside the court, for which Wyatt slapped and pistol-whipped him. Wyatt and Frank McLaury had words later in the day, and about 2:30 it was time for a showdown.

Sheriff John Behan, no friend of the Earps, tried to negotiate a last-minute settlement to avoid bloodshed, but the heavily armed Earps, Holliday in tow with sawed-off shotgun under his coat, would not be mollified. They approached Frank and Tom McLaury, standing with Ike and Billy Clanton, and another friend named Bill Claiborne who fled when the fight was imminent. Shots rang out — who fired first and whether or not some of the McLaury

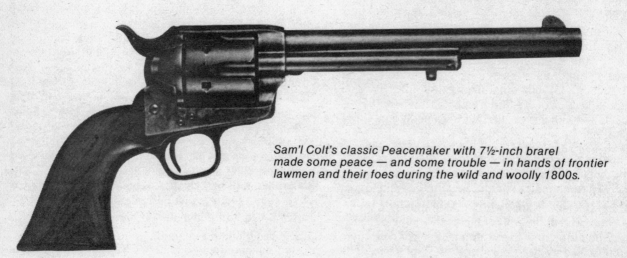

Sam'l Colt's classic Peacemaker with 7½-inch brarel made some peace — and some trouble — in hands of frontier lawmen and their foes during the wild and woolly 1800s.

Ike Clanton spent night before OK Corral playing poked with Earps and in morning argued with Virgil, who arrested him with Morgan's help. Bad situation.

Stilwell's legs and body which led to murder warrants being issued against them. Eluding the posse, Earps' band sought Pete Spence, but instead found Indian Charlie Cruz and quickly dispatched him. They never got Spence and with a posse hot after them, the Earps and Holliday skedaddled for Las Vegas, New Mexico, then on to Colorado.

For the next few years Wyatt wandered through the West as a gambler or dealer. He accompanied the expedition to Dodge City to help friend Luke Short regain his kingdom in 1883, and tried mining through Idaho 'for which he was twice convicted of claim jumping. He wandered to San Diego, San Francisco, Fort Worth and Denver, and made another ripple in the public consciousness when he refereed a prize fight in San Francisco in '96. He awarded the heavyweight championship to Tom Sharkey over Robert Fitzsimmons because of an alleged foul, although Fitzsimmons was clearly winning the bout and the resulting uproar pleased him no end for the notoriety he had regained.

Wyatt then tried racing horses, operating a saloon in Alaska, and several alleged bunco plots before dying in Los Angeles on January 13, 1929, of a cancerous prostate and chronic cystitis. He was another who had seen the passing of the Wild West and glimpsed what the future held for the quiet country we know today.

Morgan Earp was young firebrand who continued to exacerbate disintegrating relations between his brothers and McLaury-Clanton camp. He was killed by Frank Stillwell and friends while playing pool.

band were unarmed is debated still — and when the smoke cleared both McLaurys and Billy Clanton were dead and Morgan and Virgil Earp were wounded. Holliday, Wyatt Earp and Ike Clanton were unhurt.

Because testimony after the shooting indicated some of the McLaury group were unarmed and because the Earp bunch pressed the fight, murder warrants were issued by Sheriff Behan for the Earp group. All were acquitted after trial.

In late December Virgil Earp was ambushed and his left arm permanently crippled. In March 1882 Morgan was assassinated playing pool and Wyatt took a bullet through the hat. Morgan's assailants were Frank Stilwell, Pete Spence and a Mexican-Indian named Indian Charlie Cruz, among others. They fled town, but Stilwell was caught by Wyatt and Baxter Earl and Holliday in a Tucson railyard while they were accompanying Morgan's body to the family home in Colton, California. Six slugs were fired through

BAT MASTERSON

This Dapper Lawman Was Dedicated To Cleaning Up Frontier Towns — With A Little Vengeance Thrown In!

Many people picture actor Gene Barry when you say Bat Masterson, because Barry starred in the popular television series. This is the gent about whom the Bat Masterson series was created, and Bat is subdued in dress on this occasion. He must have made a sight in his crimson sash, sombrero, yellow neckerchief and silver-plated, pearl-gripped single-action pistols.

WILLIAM BARCLAY "BAT" MASTERSON is more familiar than many lawmen and gunslingers because of a television series popular during the Sixties. He was dapper in his black suit crowned with ebony bowler, he was smooth in his easy-going manner, and he was formidable when aroused.

Bat, born in 1853, was the second of five sons of a homesteader on the Kansas prairie. An elder brother, Ed, and third-born, Jim, later were involved as was Bat in law enforcement in the wild and wooly cowtown known as Dodge City.

Before Bat and two of his brothers deserted the farm for the badge, there was some legend-building to do. In 1872 this trio sought fortune as buffalo hunters on the plains of southern Kansas, and while Bat followed the thundering bison herds south to the Texas Panhandle, brothers Ed and Jim returned to the farm.

Bat was involved with thirty-five other hunters in a five-day standoff against five hundred Indians attacking a two-building burg called Adobe Wells, Texas, and later hired on as an Army scout for Colonel Nelson Miles who was tasked with quelling the rampaging Kiowa, Comanche, Cheyenne, and Southern Apache tribes. Safe to say he learned how to shoot quickly and accurately during these years, training that was to keep him alive in his first gunfight in Sweetwater, Texas, in 1876.

Details are sketchy, but historians surmise that Masterson's coal-colored hair and slate-blue eyes won him the affection of one Molly Brennan, who had been previously enamoured with an Army sergeant named Melvin King. When King confronted the new twosome in a Sweetwater watering hole, legend has it that Molly threw herself in front of the sergeant's drawn pistol. She was killed instantly, but the slowed bullet only wounded Bat's pelvis; while he'd limp for a spell, he would otherwise have been crippled. As he fell, Masterson unholstered his pistol and fired a round at King, who was cocking the hammer of his single-action revolver for another blast. King was hit and died the following day.

After he recovered, Bat Masterson moved on to Dodge City, where his brothers had preceded him; Ed was the assistant marshal, and Jim had bought into a saloon/dance hall. The 23-year-old Bat made quite a picture: Sombrero with rattlesnake hatband, scarlet silk neckerchief and Mexican sash, ivory-handled, silver-plated sixguns in silver-studded holsters, gold-mounted spurs on his boots. One cheeky observer suggested that his attire might give Bat an edge in a gunfight — by blinding his opponent!

Larry Deger was a whole mountain of marshal and the 307-pound lawman grappled with Bat Masterson when the young man complained about how Deger was escorting a drunk to jail — with Deger's foot. Bat then found himself in the slammer, but he got even. Dodge City was a hoary cowtown (below) that could offer a cowhand all the trouble he wanted.

Bat (standing, second from right) joined with Luke Short's "invasion force" to recover holdings out of which Short felt he'd been swindled. Standing left to right: W.H. Harris, Luke Short, Masterson, and W.F. Petillon. Seated, left to right: Charles E. Bassett, Wyatt Earp, M.F. McLane, and Neal Brown. Short was restored.

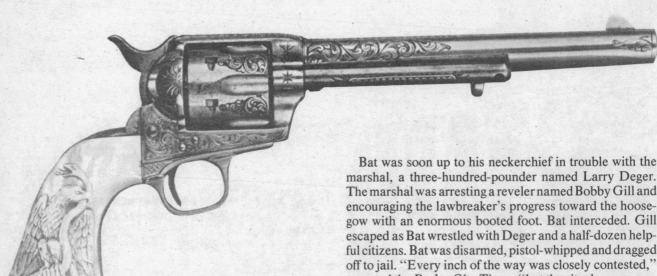

While this carved mother-of-pearl grip sports the Mexican emblem, its ornate finish is typical of what was available — and favored by flashy, dapper Bat. It was silver-plated, too, and expensive!

Bat was soon up to his neckerchief in trouble with the marshal, a three-hundred-pounder named Larry Deger. The marshal was arresting a reveler named Bobby Gill and encouraging the lawbreaker's progress toward the hoosegow with an enormous booted foot. Bat interceded. Gill escaped as Bat wrestled with Deger and a half-dozen helpful citizens. Bat was disarmed, pistol-whipped and dragged off to jail. "Every inch of the way was closely contested," reported the *Dodge City Times*, "but the city dungeon was reached at last, and in he went. If he had got hold of his gun before going in, there would have been a general killing."

Bat was subsequently fined $25 and released, then began plotting with resident politicians to gain revenge by the ouster of Deger. Masterson ran against the big lawman for

Another photograph of the handsome former buffalo hunter turned lawman. When he finished a term or was turned out by voters, he worked as a gambler.

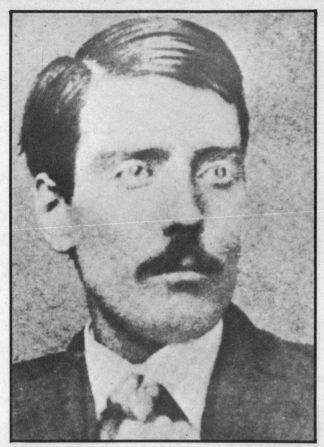

Ed Masterson was a popular lawman in Dodge City who preferred talk to gunplay, a mistake never made by brother Bat. When Ed died trying to disarm rowdy cowboys, the whole town closed to mourn his passing.

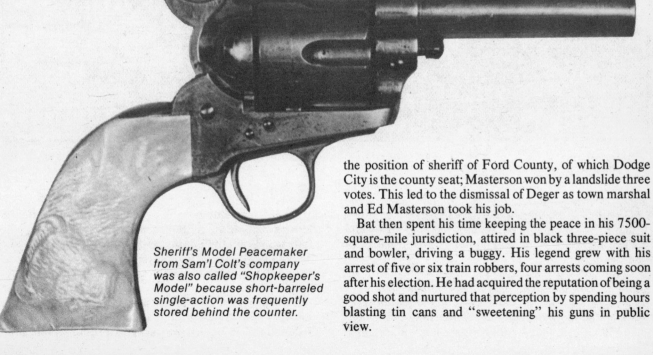

Sheriff's Model Peacemaker from Sam'l Colt's company was also called "Shopkeeper's Model" because short-barreled single-action was frequently stored behind the counter.

the position of sheriff of Ford County, of which Dodge City is the county seat; Masterson won by a landslide three votes. This led to the dismissal of Deger as town marshal and Ed Masterson took his job.

Bat then spent his time keeping the peace in his 7500-square-mile jurisdiction, attired in black three-piece suit and bowler, driving a buggy. His legend grew with his arrest of five or six train robbers, four arrests coming soon after his election. He had acquired the reputation of being a good shot and nurtured that perception by spending hours blasting tin cans and "sweetening" his guns in public view.

The third Masterson involved with law enforcement was brother Jim. After Bat had left Dodge City for other haunts, he would come a'running if Jim gave a yelp. One-thousand-mile jaunt is recounted in text.

"We used to file the notch of the hammer till the trigger would pull sweet, which is another way of saying that the blamed gun would pretty near go off if you looked at it," he later recalled.

Masterson also told of the requisites for longevity in the gunfighter's trade — the ability to shoot straight and fast — thusly: "To accustom his hands to the pistols of those days, the man who coveted a reputation started in early and practiced with them just as a card sharp practices with his cards, as a shell game man drills his fingers to manipulate the elusive pea, or the juggler must practice to acquire proficiency. When he could draw, cock and fire all in one smooth lightning-quick movement, he could then detach his mind from that movement and concentrate on accuracy."

Bat Masterson's willingness to use his firearms to settle disputes contrasted to brother Ed's reticence. That Ed was killed during an incident with a couple of cowboys suggests

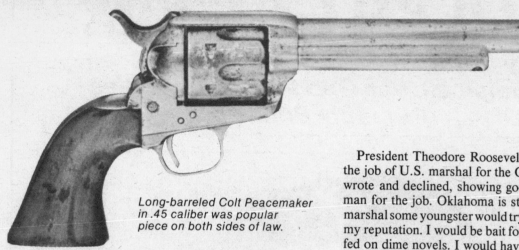

Long-barreled Colt Peacemaker in .45 caliber was popular piece on both sides of law.

might-over-mouth was a preferred course. Jim Masterson was then elected to his brother's former post.

Bat was voted out of office in 1881, but returned to the calming cowtown when brother Jim summoned. In one incident, he trained in from New Mexico to settle a dispute between Jim, a saloonkeeper and a bartender. Upon dismounting from the iron horse, he spied the troublemakers and sang out: "I have come over a thousand miles to settle this. I know you are heeled; now fight!" Bat sought cover behind an embankment and in the short gun battle, sent a slug through the bartender's lung. Bat paid a $10 fine and departed the same night.

Masterson drifted throughout the boomtowns of the West, working as a lawman or gambler. But age was slowing his draw and Masterson sagely sought employment without firearms as tools. He married an actress and bought a saloon/theater in Denver, but went bust over bad bets on fights he had promoted. He left Denver for New York City in 1905 and finished up oddly as a sportswriter.

President Theodore Roosevelt offered Bat Masterson the job of U.S. marshal for the Oklahoma Territory. Bat wrote and declined, showing good sense: "I am not the man for the job. Oklahoma is still woolly, and if I were marshal some youngster would try to put me out because of my reputation. I would be bait for grown-up kids who had fed on dime novels. I would have to kill or be killed. No sense to that. I have taken my guns off, and I don't ever want to put them on again."

As for the guns Masterson used during his lawkeeping career, these are subject to doubt. Some say he gave them away, when he took off for New York to become a sportswriter. However, there are a number of Bat Masterson sixguns in private collections around the country. All are authentic, if you look at it in that light, since they came from Masterson.

As indicated elsewhere in this tome, Masterson may have had a touch of the con man in his character, but it is a known fact that when memorabilia collectors would visit him and say they were willing to pay for a "genuine Masterson Colt," the sports reporter would put them off long enough to get to the nearest hock shop, where he could buy a Colt SAA, cut a few notches in the grips, then rub in enough dirt to make it look old and worn. According to the memories of some who were his fellow newsmen of the day, Masterson would charge from $50 up for a battered sixgun that had cost him no more than $5 in the neighborhood loan emporium.

So much for authenticity.

This Colt single-action revolver once belonged to Bat — allegedly. It has nickel finish, 4¾-inch barrel and gutta percha stocks. It allegedly was purchased on July 30, 1885. But sadly for arms collectors, Bat was wont to "fudge" on ownership.

WILD BILL HICKOK

History Is Vague As To Whether This Lean Frontiersman Was Good Or Bad; He Was Probably Both!

Long hair, fur-trimmed buckskin, enormous Bowie frog sticker in belt and ivory-handled single-action revolvers, grips forward — Wild Bill Hickok.

HISTORIANS SEEM split over James "Wild Bill" Butler Hickok: They either like him and ignore, excuse, or explain away his often questionable behavior, or they dislike him and downplay the positive contributions attributed to him. Both sides agree his exploits were blown out of proportion by "journalists" — which may have been Wild Bill's fault.

James Butler Hickok was born in Homer (now Troy Grove), Illinois, on May 27, 1837. The fourth son born to William and Polly Hickok, he learned farming before heading West in the 1850s. He landed in Leavenworth

Opposite page: J.B. Hickok as a young buffalo hunter. Protruding upper lip earned him nickname "Duck Bill" from David McCanles, Hickok's victim.

where he held odd farming jobs and joined General James H. Lane's Free State Army, served as constable of Monticello, drove teams for stage lines and the Pony Express. He was working as a stock tender at the Rock Creek Station, Nebraska, site of a macabre incident that irrevocably altered his life's course on July 12, 1861.

Rock Creek Station had been sold on terms by a bullying farmer named David McCanles to a stage line headquartered in Brownsville. The station was operated by Horace Wellman and his common-law wife. Besides Hickok, the only other employee was stable hand J.W. "Dock" Brink.

The stage line was in financial trouble. Unarmed, McCanles came for payment accompanied by two unarmed farmer chums, James Woods and W.N. Glenn. Also present was his 12-year-old son, Monroe. McCanles asked for Horace Wellman, who refused to come outside. But James Butler Hickok stepped to the door in a move that surprised McCanles, according to pioneer settler and banker George W. Hansen, who wrote of the Rock Creek Station episode in a 1927 issue of *Nebraska History Magazine.* He had no quarrel with Hickok, whom McCanles had dubbed "Duck Bill" because of Hickok's protruding upper lip when not cloaked by facial hair. McCanles asked and was provided with a tin cup of water, probably buying time. After drinking he walked to another door while Hickok stepped behind a calico curtain separating the rooms. McCanles entered Wellman's room prepared to settle with him and Hickok, who had interjected himself into the affair.

What happened is best explained by Hansen, as quoted

During his short tenure on the boards with Buffalo Bill Cody (right) and Texas Jack Omohundro (center), Wild Bill's improvisations brought laughs, crowds.

Buffalo Bill and Wild Bill went 'way back as pals and buffalo shooters. Both were spicy characters.

by James D. Horan in *The Authentic Wild West/The Gunfighters:*

On this occasion, in fact at this very moment — Hickok decided on a course which in this case was so successful that he followed it the remainder of his life on the frontier. It was to shoot to kill on his first suspicion of a physical encounter or personal danger.

From his concealed position behind the curtain he shot McCanles, using the rifle McCanles had left at the Stage Station. This shot was not fired in the heat of a conflict or in self defense, but was deliberate and calculated and well aimed and pierced McCanles in the heart...

McCanles fell backward from the doorstep to the ground. His son, Monroe, who was standing by him when he was shot, says: "Father fell to the ground on his back. He raised himself up to an almost sitting position, took one last look at me as tho he wanted to speak, and then fell back dead." The shot was entirely unexpected as Mc-Canles had at no time made an effort to protect himself from rifle fire. He would never have taken his twelve year old son, Monroe, to the door or to the cabin with him had he expected any gun play. He had never in his life on the frontier used a gun nor threatened to use a gun on any man. If, or when, he fought, he fought fair and never with a deadly weapon of any kind, but with his bare fists.

Woods and Glenn, hearing the shots, came running to the cabin, when Hickok came to the door and fired two shots at Woods from a Colt's revolver, wounding him

severely. Woods ran around to the north of the cabin, followed by Wellman who had a heavy hoe in his hands.

Meanwhile Glenn turned and ran to get away from the gunfire and Hickok fired two shots at him, wounding him. Wellman had succeeded in dispatching Woods by crushing his skull with the heavy hoe, and, running around the house where young McCanles was kneeling over his father, stupefied at the awful horror of the things taking place around him, struck at young McCanles with the hoe yelling "Let's kill them all." Monroe dodged the blow and ran terrified away, chased by Wellman, but outran his pursuer, and, familiar with every foot of the ground, found a hiding place in the ravine south of the Stage Station.

Mrs. Wellman, who was the common law wife of Wellman, stood in the doorway when the chase began, screaming: "Kill 'em all, kill em all." Glenn, altho severely wounded, had succeeded in getting into the brush about 80 rods (400 yards) down the creek away from the cabin, where he fell exhausted from loss of blood. He was followed by the Hickok crowd and while he begged for his

Some historians try to couple Wild Bill and Calamity Jane in (or out of) wedlock, but there's no proof. Calamity at Wild Bill's grave just before her own death. She sought glory by burial close to Hickok.

THE GUN DIGEST BOOK OF SINGLE ACTION REVOLVERS

"Wild Bill — J.B. Hickok, killed by the assassin Jack McCall in Deadwood, Black Hills, August 2, 1876, Pard we will meet again in the happy Hunting ground to part no more — Colorado Charlie C.H. Utter" reads wooden tombstone on Hickok's first burial place.

life, was finished with a load of buckshot fired from Brink's shot gun, thus completing the triple murder by the butchery of two of the wounded victims...

To cap the grisly tale, Hickok and friends pleaded self-defense in a trial at which Monroe was denied testimony, while Mrs. Wellman's testimony was sought. The three men were released and news of the killings spread.

Some years later Hickok was interviewed by Colonel George Ward Nichols for a story that appeared in the February 1867 issue of *Harper's New Monthly Magazine.* Now known as Wild Bill — a nickname he earned by backing down a bar full of hostile teamsters in Independence, Missouri — Hickok "prettied up" his version of the Rock Creek Station episode for Nichols' pen and it was accepted without question for sixty years, until Hansen's story. This is what Wild Bill told Nichols:

You see this M'Kandlas was the Captain of a gang of desperadoes, horsethieves, murderers, regular cut-throats, who were the terror of everybody on the border, and who kept us in the mountains in hot water whenever they were around. I knew them all in the mountains, where they pretended to be trapping, but they were there hiding from the hangman. M'Kandlas was the biggest scoundrel and bully of them all, and was allers a-braggin' of what he could do. One day I beat him shootin' at a mark, and then threw him at the back-holt. And I didn't drop him as soft as you would a baby, you may be sure. Well, he got savage mad about it, and swore he would have his revenge on me some time.

This was just before the war broke out, and we were already takin' sides in the mountains either for the South or the Union. M'Kandlas and his gang were border-ruffians in the Kansas row, and of course they went with the rebs. Bime-by he clar'd out, and I shouldn't have thought of the feller again ef he hadn't crossed my path. It'pears he didn't forget me.

It was in '61, when I guided a detachment of cavalry who were comin' in from Camp Floyd. We had nearly reached the Kansas line, and were in South Nebraska, when one afternoon I went out of camp to go to the cabin of an old friend of mine, a Mrs. Waltman (Wellman). I took only one of my revolvers with me, for although the war had broke out I didn't think it necessary to carry both my pistols, and, in all or'nary scrimmages, one is better than a dozen ef you shoot straight. I saw some wild turkeys on

David McCanles, bullying landowner shot down by J.B. Hickok at Rock Creek Station. True story of grisly affair differs from baloney dealt to public.

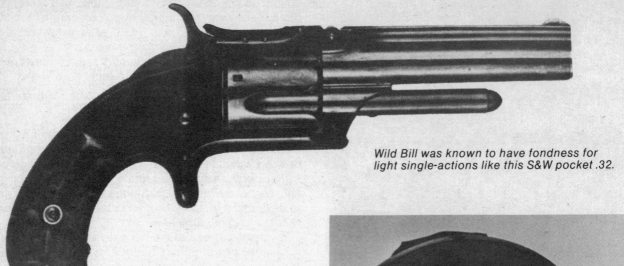

Wild Bill was known to have fondness for light single-actions like this S&W pocket .32.

General George Armstrong Custer, who was to make history at the Little Big Horn, and his wife thought highly of Wild Bill the scout. Hickok earned $5 a day scouting for the Army — big money back then.

the road as I was goin' down, and popped one of 'em over, thinking he'd be just the thing for supper.

Well, I rode up to Mrs. Waltman's, jumped off my horse, and went into the cabin, which is like most of the cabins on the prarer, with only one room, and that had two doors, one opening in front and t'other on a yard like.

"How are you, Mrs. Waltman?" I said, feeling as jolly as you please.

The minute she saw me she was turned white as a sheet and screamed: "Is that you, Bill? Oh, God! They will kill you! Run! run! They will kill you!"

"Who's a-goin' to kill me? said I. There's two can play at that game."

"It's M'Kandlas and his gang. There's ten of them, and you've no chance. They've jes gone down the road to the corn-rack. They came up here only five minutes ago. M'Kandlas was draggin poor Parson Shipley on the ground with a lariat around his neck. The preacher was most dead with choking and the horses stamping on him. M'Kandlas knows yer bringing in that party of Yankee cavalry, and he swears he'll cut yer heart out. Run, Bill, run! — But it's too late; they're comin up the lane."

While she was a-talkin' I remembered that I had but one revolver, and a load gone out of that. On the table was a horn of powder and some little bars of lead. I poured some powder into the empty chamber and rammed the lead after it by hammering the barrel on the table, and had just capped the pistol when I heard M'Kandlas shout:

"There's that d--d Yank Wild Bill's horse; he's here; and we'll skin him alive!"

If I had thought of runnin before it war too late now, and the house was my best holt — sort of fortress, like. I never thought I should leave the room alive.'

The scout stopped his story, rose from his seat, and strode back and forward in a state of great excitement.

"I tell you what it is Kernel," he resumed, after a while, "I don't mind a scrimmage with these fellers round here. Shoot one or two of them and the rest run way. But all of M'Kandlas's gang were reckless, blood-thirsty devils, who would fight as long as they had strength to pull a trigger. I have been in tight places, but that's one of the few times I said my prayers."

"Surround the house and give no quarter!" yelled M'Kandlas. When I heard that I felt as quiet and cool as if I was a-goin to church. I looked round the room and saw a Hawkins rifle hangin over the bed.

Plaid-lined cape, checkered trousers, rolled-brim fedora, necktie, vest and tailored coat — Wild Bill of newspaper fame. He "prettied up" truth.

afterward holding tight to his rifle, which had fallen over his head.

His disappearance was followed by a yell from his gang, and then there was a dead silence. I put down the rifle and took the revolver, and said to myself: "Only six shots and nine men to kill. Save your powder, Bill, for the death-hug's a-comin!" I don't know why it was Kernel, continued Bill, looking at me inquiringly, but at that moment things seemed clear and sharp. I could think strong.

There was a few seconds of that awful stillness, and then the ruffians came rushing in at both doors. How wild they looked with their red, drunken faces and inflamed eyes, shouting and cussing! But I never aimed more deliberately in my life.

One — two — three — four; and four men fell dead.

That didn't stop the rest. Two of them fired their bird-guns at me. And then I felt a sting run all over me. The

"Is that loaded?" said I to Mrs. Waltman.

"Yes," the poor thing whispered. She was so frightened she couldn't speak out loud.

"Are you sure?" said I, as I jumped to the bed and caught it from its hooks. Although my eye did not leave the door, yet I could see she nodded "Yes" again. I put the revolver on the bed, and just then M'Kandlas poked his head inside the doorway, but jumped back when he saw me with the rifle in my hand.

"Come in here, you cowardly dog!" I shouted. "Come in here, and fight me!"

M'Kandlas was no coward, if he was a bully. He jumped inside the room with his gun leveled to shoot; but he was not quick enough. My rifle-ball went through his heart. He fell back outside the house, where he was found

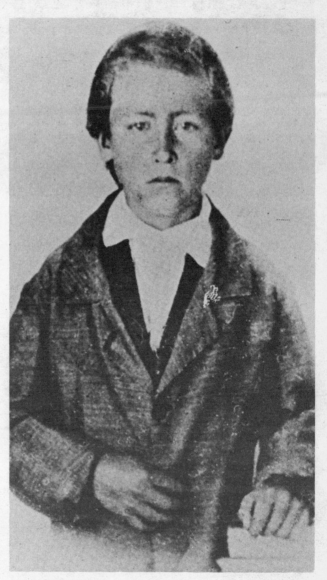

Young William Monroe McCanles was present at Rock Creek Station and witnessed macabre events. Boy missed being killed and was denied chance to testify.

Wild Bill (second from left), Buffalo Bill (center), and Texas Jack (second from right) pose with other cast members during days they performed plays for bug-eyed Easterners susceptible to Wild Bill's extraordinary exploits.

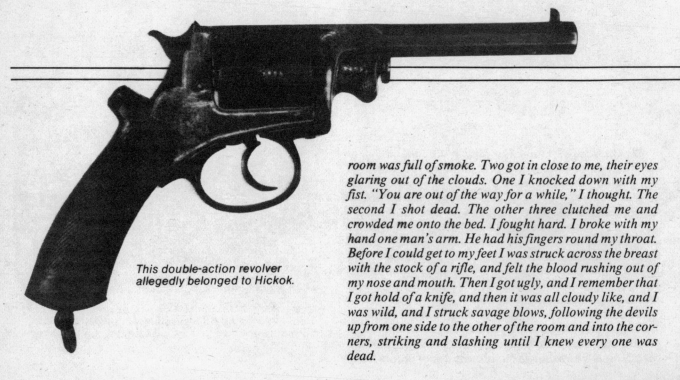

This double-action revolver allegedly belonged to Hickok.

room was full of smoke. Two got in close to me, their eyes glaring out of the clouds. One I knocked down with my fist. "You are out of the way for a while," I thought. The second I shot dead. The other three clutched me and crowded me onto the bed. I fought hard. I broke with my hand one man's arm. He had his fingers round my throat. Before I could get to my feet I was struck across the breast with the stock of a rifle, and felt the blood rushing out of my nose and mouth. Then I got ugly, and I remember that I got hold of a knife, and then it was all cloudy like, and I was wild, and I struck savage blows, following the devils up from one side to the other of the room and into the corners, striking and slashing until I knew every one was dead.

THE GUN DIGEST BOOK OF SINGLE ACTION REVOLVERS

Extraordinary moustache and shoulder-length hair were two of Wild Bill's calling cards. He had more photographs made than most legendary figures.

old Dr. Mills pulled me safe through it, after a bed siege of many a long week."

This story was later retracted by *Harper's New Monthly Magazine,* but the legend had begun and was embellished by subsequent stories.

After Rock Creek Station Hickok hired out as a civilian scout with Union forces and just a month later participated in the Battle of Wilson's Creek. He then worked as a wagonmaster out of Sedalia, Missouri, and in other capacities for the Union forces until mustered out June 9, 1865. He meandered to Springfield and tangled with Davis K. Tutt, an Arkansas gambler, whom Wild Bill shot dead at seventy-five yards while the townsfolk watched. As Tutt shot first Hickok's plea of self-defense was upheld.

He then drops out of sight for a couple of years. From 1867-69 he worked as a deputy U.S. marshal out of Ft. Riley, Kansas. He scouted with William F. "Buffalo Bill" Cody for the Army during the Indian wars, and gave his first interviews to Colonel Nichols and Henry M. Stanley,

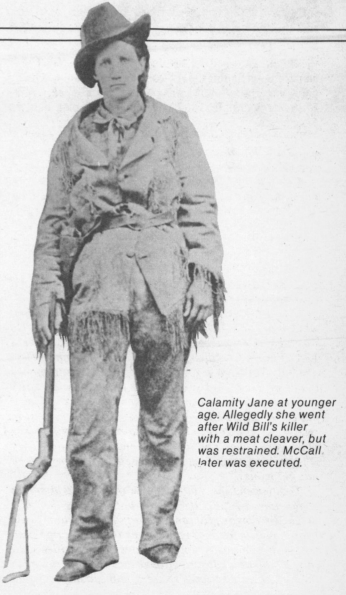

Calamity Jane at younger age. Allegedly she went after Wild Bill's killer with a meat cleaver, but was restrained. McCall later was executed.

All of a sudden it seemed as if my heart was on fire. I was bleeding every where. I rushed out to the well and drank from the bucket, and then tumbled down in a faint.

Breathless with the intense interest with which I had followed this strange story, all the more thrilling and weird when its hero, seeming to live over again the bloody events of that day, gave way to its terrible spirit with wild, savage gestures. I saw then — what my scrutiny of the morning had failed to discover — the tiger which lay concealed beneath that gentle exterior.

"You must have been hurt almost to death," I said.

"There were eleven buck-shot in me. I carry some of them now. I was cut in thirteen places. All of them bad enough to have let the life out of a man. But that blessed

Agnes Lake Thatcher, Wild Bill's soon-to-be-widowed bride. She ran a circus.

the latter renowned for his line, "Dr. Livingston, I presume?" upon finding the African explorer. Stanley's interview, excerpt to follow, was printed in the *Weekly Missouri Democrat* in 1867 and shows Hickok's bent to exaggeration:

The following verbatim dialogue took place between us: "I say Bill, or Mr. Hickok, how many white men have you killed to your certain knowledge?"

After a little deliberation, he replied, "I would be willing to take my oath on the Bible tomorrow that I have killed over a hundred a long ways off."

"What made you kill all those men; did you kill them without cause or provocation?"

"No, by heaven! I never killed one man without a good cause."

"How old were you when you killed your first man, and for what cause?"

"I was twenty-eight years old when I killed the first white man, and if ever a man deserved killing he did. He was a gambler and counterfeiter, and I was in a hotel in Leavenworth City then, as seeing some loose characters around, I ordered a room, and as I had some money about me, I thought I would go to it. I had lain some thirty minutes on the bed when I heard some men at the door. I pulled out my revolver and Bowie knife and held them ready, but half concealed, pretending to be asleep. The door was opened and five men entered the room. They whispered together, 'Let us kill the son of a b—h; I bet he has got money."

"Gentlemen," he said further, "that was a time, an awful time. I kept perfectly still until just as the knife touched my breast; I sprang aside and buried mine in his heart and then used my revolvers on the others, right and left. Only one was wounded besides the one killed; and then, gentlemen, I dashed through the room and rushed to the fort, procured a lot of soldiers, came to the hotel and

captured the whole gang of them, fifteen in all. We searched the cellar and found eleven bodies buried there — men who had been murdered by these villains."

Turning to us he asked, "Would you have not done the same? That was the first man I killed and I was never sorry for that yet."

Hickok went back to scouting against warring Indians and in 1869 took a Cheyenne lance through a thigh; he was forced to recuperate back home in Troy Hills. He then was appointed sheriff of Ellis County, which included in his jurisdiction the tough town of Hays City. Before he was voted out of office, Hickok was seen making the rounds with twin pistols hanging from his waist, a Bowie knife in a boot, and a shotgun cradled in his arms. He's reported to have killed a couple of roughnecks in his official capacity, and a couple of cavalrymen unofficially before skedaddling for St. Louis to "meet many old friends among the members" of the legislature. He was something to see: plaid cape, checkered pants, long-tailed frock coat, embroidered vests and leather boots. For good measure, he sometimes wore a scarlet sash around his waist. He was every inch the frontier legend with long hair and wild moustache.

Hickok then drifted to Abilene, Kansas, and hired on as marshal of the railhead cowtown where Texas drives concluded. He kept the peace with pistols, derringers under his coat, a rifle or shotgun in his hands and Bowie in his belt. He was respected as "a killer" by such hard-bitten characters as John Wesley Hardin, who drank with Hickok although a warrant was standing for the outlaw from Texas.

When relieved of duty, Hickok drifted through the West as a gambler or lawman, and was respected for his shooting ability with his favorite handgun, a double-action .44 Colt he tucked into his waistband, or the other sidearm he carried. What he could do with a pistol was recorded by an early editor of *Outdoor Life*, Robert A. Kane, in June 1906:

When we arrived at his hotel Mr. Hickok treated us with great courtesy, showed us his weapons and offered to do a little shooting for us if it could be arranged for outside the city limits. Accordingly, the early hours of the afternoon found us on the way to the outskirts of the city. Mr. Hickok's weapons were a pair of silver plated S.A.-44 Colt revolvers. Both had pearl handles and were tastefully engraved.

He also had a pair of Remington revolvers of the same calibre.

Jack McCall stepped inside the Deadwood tent where Hickok and friends were playing poker, then shot Wild Bill through the back of the head with this .22.

The more showy pair of Colts were used in the stage performance. On reaching a place suitable for our purpose, Mr. Hickok proceeded to entertain us with the best pistol work which it has been my good fortune to witness.

Standing on the railroad track, in a deep cut, his pistol crackling with the regularity of an old house clock, he struck and dislodged the bleaching pebbles stuck in the face of the bank at a distance of fifteen yards.

Standing about thirty feet from the shooter, one of our party tossed a quart can in the air to the height of about thirty feet. This was perforated three times before it reached the ground, twice with his right hand and once with his left.

Standing between the fences of a country road, which is four rods wide, Mr. Hickok's instinct of location was so accurate that he placed a bullet in each of the fence posts on opposite sides. Both shots were fired simultaneously.

Located between two telegraph poles he placed a bullet in one of them, then wheeled about and with the same weapon planted a bullet in the second. Telegraph poles in that part of the country are about thirty to a mile, or one hundred and seventy feet distant from each other.

Two common bricks were placed on the top board of a fence, about two feet apart and about fifteen yards from the shooter. They were broken with two shots fired from his pistol in either hand, the reports so nearly together that they seemed as one.

His last feat was to me the most remarkable of all. A quart can was thrown by Mr. Hickok himself, which dropped about ten or twenty yards distant. Quickly whipping out his weapons he fired alternately from left to right. Advancing a step with each shot, his bullets striking the earth under the can, kept it in continuous motion until his pistols were empty.

No matter how elusive the target, even when shooting at objects tossed in the air, he never seemed hurried. This trait was of course natural and in part due to his superb physique, which combined and supplemented by his methods and practice and free wild life in the open, developed in him that perfect coordination of hand and eye which was essential to the perfect mastery of the one-hand gun.

Marriage certificate reads: "This is to certify that Mr. James Butler Hickok of Cheyenne in the State of Wyoming and Mrs. Agnes L. Thatcher of Cincinnati in the State of Ohio were by me joined together in Holy Matrimony on the 5th day of March 1876..."

Wild Bill, the long-haired storyteller, knew his race was about run when his vision started to go. Records indicate glaucoma, blindness soon after.

In 1872 Wild Bill helped stage The Niagara Falls Buffalo Hunt, a modified Wild West show that was a financial disaster, then slipped back to Kansas where he spent one season in two plays with Buffalo Bill and Texas Jack Omohundro. He then guided parties of wealthy Englishmen on hunting excursions until his sight began failing.

According to Mari Sandoz, citing records she examined called the Medical History of Camp Carlin, Wyoming, War Records, National Archives, Washington, D.C., Hickok was examined by the post surgeon at Camp Carlin. In the biographical notes of Horan's The Authentic Wild West/The Gunfighters, it's claimed Hickok went to see the Army doctor "in preference to a civilian doctor because it must not be known how nearly blind he was; he had too many enemies who would shoot him down if they knew how little he could see. The doctor examined Bill's eyes and diagnosed the case as advanced glaucoma, with total blindness in both eyes only a matter of short time."

Wild Bill married circus owner Agnes Lake Thatcher on March 5, 1876. After less than six months of marriage, Hickok was shot dead while playing poker in Deadwood, Dakota Territory.

On August 2, 1876, for the first time Hickok sat with his back to the open door, not against a wall. A 25-year-old drifter named Jack McCall was looking to be a famous gunfighter. He stepped behind Hickok and sent a .22 slug through Wild Bill's head and out his right cheek. Hickok died instantly, dropping the cards he'd just picked up: ace of spades, ace of clubs, two black eights and the jack of diamonds — thereafter called a "Deadman's hand."

Jack McCall was first acquitted on a charge of murder, but later arrested and convicted of killing Wild Bill. He was executed on March 1, 1877.

Wild Bill Hickok was dead at age 39. His body was buried in Deadwood but his legend — fact or fiction? — lives on.

BILL TILGHMAN

Fifty Years A Crime-Fighter, Bill Helped Clear The West Of Notorious Outlaws

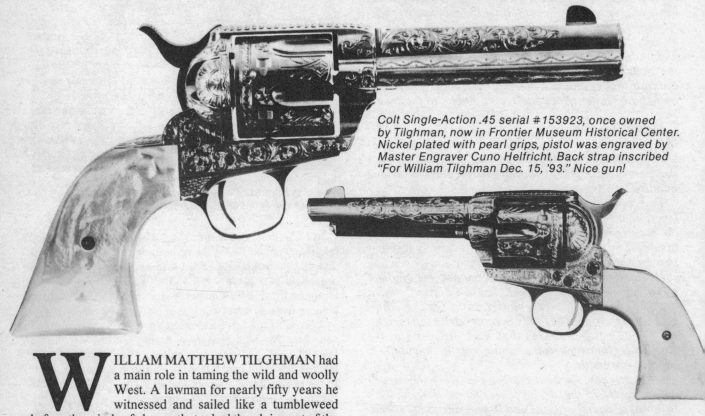

Colt Single-Action .45 serial #153923, once owned by Tilghman, now in Frontier Museum Historical Center. Nickel plated with pearl grips, pistol was engraved by Master Engraver Cuno Helfricht. Back strap inscribed "For William Tilghman Dec. 15, '93." Nice gun!

WILLIAM MATTHEW TILGHMAN had a main role in taming the wild and woolly West. A lawman for nearly fifty years he witnessed and sailed like a tumbleweed before the winds of change that raked the plains out of the East. As a buffalo hunter Bill Tilghman hastened their demise. As an Indian fighter he quelled hostiles, then the whites who then claimed chunks of Cherokee Strip and Oklahoma Territory. As a lawman he terminated the existence of many infamous desperadoes. He saw the horse replaced by the automobile. He saw the criminal element worsen and petty crime in the West evolve into narcotics traffic. The silver boom of his early years was replaced by black gold fever and, as an elderly man devoted to calming these oil boomtowns, he gave his life in the line of duty.

When Bill Tilghman's father went off to the Civil War and returned blind, the 8-year-old youth had to fill the family larder. His family name, "Tilgh-man" means "tiller of the soil" and described how "Willie", as he then was known, accomplished a mean task. He supplemented vegetables with game and one lucky occasion bagged four fat honkers — then almost drowned retrieving them.

During this period Willie Tilghman met Wild Bill Hickok and from that time Hickok was his idol. He read of Wild Bill's firearms feats and determined to emulate them with a pair of cap 'n ball revolvers. Tilghman practiced shooting instictively with both hands and honed his skills until he could hit a rabbit in the head from thirty yards.

Tilghman recounted the fast-draw technique employed by pistoleros of the period, set down by widow Zoe A. Tilghman, in *Marshal of the Last Frontier — Life and services of William Matthew (Bill) Tilghman for 50 years one of the greatest peace officers of the West:*

How did the marksmen of the Old West perform their wizardry? Now and then one sees in a picture a man extending his arm full length. It never was done that way. While the amateur stretched, the expert gave a flip of his wrist, and his bullet was in the other's anatomy before that creature had his gun poised.

The technique of this shooting was timed and coordinated muscular movements measured to a perfect efficiency. Not an inch of lost motion, nor one-tenth second of time. The gun, whether in belt scabbard or shoulder holster, was placed ready to hand. It leaped from the scabbard by an upward flick of the wrist, with perhaps a slight "following" motion of the forearm, with the long-barreled cap-and-ball pistols, such as Wild Bill Hickok used.

With the famous Colt's forty-five, the wrist action often was sufficient to move it clear. Either type, as it came out, described an arc, until the muzzle pointed nearly straight

Photograph of Tilghman at height of his fame, when he arrested Bill Doolin, ended reign of many outlaw gangs.

up. Then, a second flick of the wrist and the gun fell in an outward-downward arc, to a horizontal position, pointed straight in front. In the same half-second the elbow slipped to a pivot on the hipbone.

No muscle moved to draw back the hammer. As he grasped the gun the forefinger crooked about the trigger, the thumb rested on the hammer. The weight of the gun barrel in its descent drew away from the hammer, and by the time it reached the horizontal position the gun was cocked. The slightest pressure of the trigger finger, and it fired. If he wanted to shoot quickly, his finger tightened in the last tenth-second of the arc, with such perfect timing that the bullet sped at the exact instant the muzzle came into line.

The marksman could swing the gun in a half circle, holding it steady by the brace of his elbow on the hip. At any point of the arc, a pressure of the finger would send a bullet crashing forth. The gun thus moving would travel only half as far — and take half the time — as one moved from the shoulder. Also, the full-arm movement could not hold the gun steady without special effort which slowed it up.

The two-gun motion was exactly the same, but performed simultaneously. The gun aimed from the hip, level with or just above the belt, would be certain to strike some vital organ. The heavy slug of the forty-five, too, would either kill instantly or produce a shock to put the enemy

Closeup of engraving on barrel of Bill Tilghman's .45 Colt shows fine detail. How much use he gave gun is uncertain.

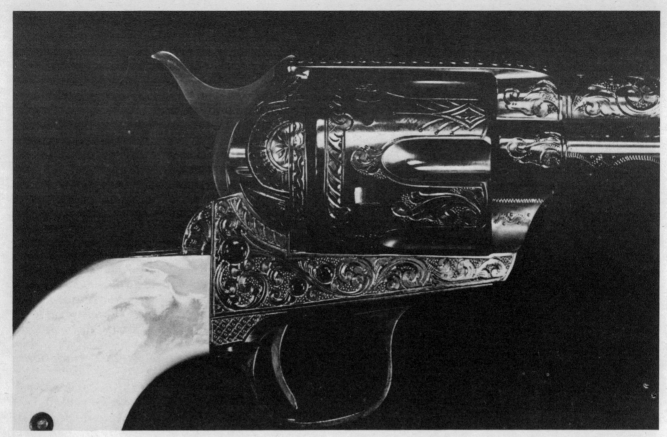

Detailed look at cylinder and trigger assembly of handsome revolver once owned by premier lawman of the West. With Heck Thomas (below) and Chris Madsen, Bill Tilghman completed the trio known as the "Three Guardsmen."

out of commission. "You shoot a man with a small bullet and he may kill you before he dies. But with a forty-five, he's done with," said Bill.

In time, Willie's father regained sight in one eye sufficient that he decided his 14-year-old son should undertake formal schooling in Atchison, Kansas, near the farm. The youth was a prankster and lasted just a couple of years at school, but was tutored by his mother before leaving home for adventure out West at age 16.

Tilghman and various compadres — including Bat Masterson — became buffalo hunters, supplying towns hungry for meat and a fashion industry temporarily infatuated with the skin of the plains' dull-witted behemoth. Tilghman reckoned he killed 7500 of his 11,000 buffalo with a Sharps .40 caliber buffalo gun with set trigger and octagonal barrel. He put so much lead through the Sharps that he had it rebored to .45/60 caliber, then wore out this barrel.

"The rifle load was 120 grains of black powder, with an inch and a quarter patched bullet," writes Zoe Tilghman in Bill's biography. "Bill's outfit, and many others, bought their powder and lead, and loaded their own shells. They used three different charges of powder; for short range, 100 yards; 200-250 medium; and beyond that the long-range load. Bill's shoulder would often be lame and sore from the kick of the gun, and the use of the lighter charge made an appreciable difference, as well as economy. Some hunters carried shoulder pads..."

Bill Tilghman spent the next seven years of his life —

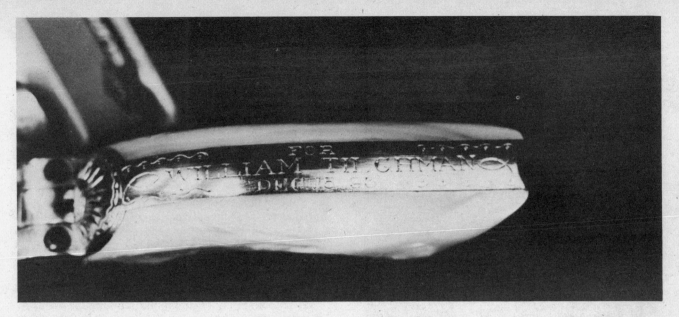

Value of historic firearms is enhanced considerably when positive ownership can be substantiated. Engraving does so.

until age 23 — hunting buffalo or Indians as a scout with the Army. He had many narrow escapes and once was arrested for murder of a white man slain by Indians using a knife Tilghman had lost. He was saved from vigilante justice by a timely attack of the hostiles on the town.

In 1878 he hired on as assistant to Dodge City Marshal Larry Deger. His companions in service were Ed, Jim and Bat Masterson, Wyatt Earp, and Neal Brown, among others. Bill was revered similar to Ed Masterson and both preferred talk to shootouts. Zoe Tilghman reports that well-known Texas rancher, William Clayton, wrote of Bill at this time:

"Bill was a fine-looking youth, the friend of every Texan. When my boys got drunk Bill would handle them with good humor. I remember many time when Bill would come riding out to camp with one of the boys roaring drunk. There was something about Bill Tilghman that commanded respect. When he walked down Front Street, he showed warmth — with kindliness.

"There were a few characters who thought they could run over him. They usually found themselves lying in the dust when they tried it. If anybody had tried to dry-gulch Bill Tilghman, a hundred Texans would have riddled him with bullets. My boys would fight anybody who tried any tricky stuff on Tilghman. Bill didn't need our help. He was the fastest man I ever saw with a gun, but I only saw him use his gun twice. Each time he wounded his opponent rather than kill him."

Tilghman expounded on his philosophy to fellow lawman Fred Sutton, as reported by E.A. Macdonald in *Hands Up!:* "Never try to run a bluff with a six-gun. Many a man has been buried with his boots on because he foolishly tried to scare someone by reaching for his hardware. Always remember that a six-shooter is made to kill the other fellow with and for no other reason on earth. So always have your gun loaded and ready, and never reach for it unless you are in dead earnest and intend to kill the other fellow.

"A lot of inexperienced fellows try to aim a six-shooter

Tilghman near age 70 in Cromwell, Oklahoma. Distinctive badge, hammered from two $20 gold pieces was recognized throughout West as lawful authority.

Bill poses with Danish-born fellow "Guardsman" Chris Madsen. Coordinated attack on criminal bands in the Indian Territory led to rapid passage of outlaw era.

must learn to point the barrel of your six-shooter by instinct. If you haven't that direction-instinct born in you, you will never become an expert with the six-gun."

After two years in Dodge City, Tilghman moved on to become deputy for Pat Sughrue, sheriff of Ford County, Kansas, of which Dodge City is county seat. Bill stayed with Sughrue for four years and spared no hardship in his official duties. An example: traveling two thousand miles to capture a horsethief who'd fled to Texas.

George Snyder stole a horse near Dodge City and rode the 350 miles to Texas. To get proper warrants and permission to arrest Snyder, Tilghman had to travel to Topeka for a requisition from the governor, then to Kansas City and down the MKT railroad to Fort Worth and Austin to present his papers to the Governor of Texas, on by train to Gainesville and to his destination by stage. The return trip racked up more than two thousand miles — but he captured Snyder and thus reinforced his reputation as a lawman who always got his man.

As time went on Tilghman did scouting for the army against the warring Northern Cheyenne, dabbled in horse breeding with Chant, a winner of the Kentucky Derby, and chased the lawless throughout Oklahoma Territory. He formed one-third of the famed "Three Guardsmen" with Heck Thomas and Chris Madsen who brought down the Doolin Gang and some of the Dalton Gang, from which the Doolin band was splintered.

Bill Doolin was one bad hombre who ruled a lawless band of thieves and murderers for four years. A combination of wife, son and rheumatic bones led to his capture by Tilghman, who affected a minister's garb to surprise the wary Doolin at an Arkansas hot springs where the tiring fugitive had sought relief from his rheumatism. Doolin was looking to leave the lawless life and settle down with wife and infant when he went to Eureka Springs to soak. Tilghman learned of his whereabouts and surprised him in a bath house. Some five thousand spectators greeted their arrival in Guthrie, Oklahoma Territory. (Doolin was later to escape and die in a shootout.)

Bill Tilghman was later deputy U.S. marshal of Oklahoma City and, while awaiting an appointment as U.S. Marshal, wrote, directed, and starred with law enforcement contemporaries in a movie called, *Passing of the Oklahoma Outlaws.* He toured the country with his film that did not glamorize outlaws.

In 1924 at 70 years of age Bill Tilghman accepted a post of marshal in the sin-filled oil boomtown of Cromwell, Oklahoma. Tilghman was warned that criminals with integrity were gone; the new breed of outlaw had no scruples.

Tilghman waded into the fray where his main enemy was cocaine. Addicts stole to support habits, big money brought in hard criminal elements and a general dislike of lawmen made Cromwell a real fun spot. Tilghman was making improvements and seeking the big suppliers of the drug trade when shot twice by a corrupt Prohibition enforcement officer named Wylie Lynn during a scuffle. Lynn's acquittal for murder was met with an outrageous howl, silenced only by his death in a shootout with a peace officer eight years later.

Seldom has one man affected history to the degree of William Matthew Tilghman.

by sighting along the barrel, and they try to shoot the other man in the head. Never do that. If you have to stop a man with a gun, grab the stock of your six-shooter with a death grip that won't let it wobble, and try to hit him just where his belt buckle would be. That's the broadest target from head to heel.

"If you point at something, you don't raise your finger to a level of the eye and sight along it; you simply point, by instinct, and your finger will always point straight. So you

GUNS OF THE BAD GUYS

Chapter 5

Time Tends To Soften Viciousness Into Robin Hood Legends

THE ENGLISH-speaking people tend to glorify baddies. No matter how vicious the individual or the type of outlawry he practiced, time has a habit of making a legend and, all too often, a hero of such a villian.

Jesse James often has been compared to Robin Hood and the movies have done more than their share to paint Jesse and brother Frank as victims of society and the railroads rather than two who discovered it was easier to rob trains than to work for a living. However, it must be admitted that the brothers James did introduce one major facet of outlawry to the West. They were the first train robbers and set the trend for decades of similar misadventures by those who came after them.

Billy the Kid was a legend long before Howard Hughes made a film called *The Outlaw*; it made a lot of money for Mr. Hughes and presented Jane Russell's bosom to the world. In this case it was the bountifully endowed lady who became the legend. But again, William Bonney, as he was known legally, was supposed to have been a victim of his peers. The fact that he killed his first man with a knife when 12 years old and had to flee New York City goes ignored or is credited to the misdeeds of society rather than a young punk who probably should not have lived to the age of 21. He was credited with having killed one man for each year of his life, "not including Mexicans," but the record reveals that most of his victims were shot in the back or from ambush.

Some of the good guys didn't do so well either, if you measure them in sociological terms. The United States Cavalry was hardly known for its gallantry, when it came to dealing with the Indians. In more than one cavalry charge, entire villages including women, the aged and children were put to the saber. In another instance, a cavalry commander ordered blankets issued to a tribe of Indians. The fact that said blankets had just been taken from a military hospital and were contaminated with smallpox has made little impression upon historians. At the time, it apparently seemed the logical thing to do.

Gunfighters and their feats have been blown largely out of proportion. In the pages that follow we will note that the so-called legends all too often were psychotics before the term had been invented. They had access to handguns and learned how to use them. Citizens of the Western towns and ranches had the same access and learned how to use their revolvers, too. The situation that resulted is not too far removed from what is happening today. The fact that wherever Wyatt Earp was sheriff he banned the wearing of guns in town did not prevent the shootout at the OK Corral. Banning handguns in today's society cannot prevent crime. It might only make it more simple for the bad guys to become legends, since there will be no one among the citizenry, gun in hand, to challenge the claim.

No matter what may be said, history doesn't repeat itself...it simply continues. That's why that police station in the Bronx is called Fort Apache. The savages are still there. The good guys have just changed geographic locations.

JOHN WESLEY HARDIN

A Life Of Violence, A Six-Gun In Hand, Was This Killer's Way

WHILE HE hasn't today the notoriety — perhaps infamy is a better word — of Billy The Kid, most Western Historians agree that John Wesley Hardin was by far the worse hombre. He was said to have killed thirty-nine men by his twenty-first birthday, while Billy the Kid's total is unclear: He claimed, at age 21, "one for each year of my life," but some folks think the number might have been under ten.

While he isn't so well-known today as is the Kid, John Wesley Hardin in his heyday was a household word. In

Hardin said unflattering things about John Selman to lawman's father, Old John Selman, pictured above. Old John brooded before assassinating son's maligner.

Similarity between the handsome Hardin and his namesake John Wesley ended at the name. A hot-blooded Southern sympathizer, Hardin's Yankee hatred led to big troubles.

many sectors of his native Texas, parents encouraged proper behavior with the threat that "Wes Hardin will get you if you don't watch out!" He was the worst killer Texas ever knew.

John Wesley Hardin was born to the Reverend Joseph G. and Elizabeth Hardin on May 26, 1853, in Bonham, Texas. The second son — his elder brother was named Joe — was christened John Wesley after the founder of the Methodist religion. That's about where the righteousness and godliness finished.

Why John Wesley Hardin chose an outlaw's trail has never been clearly explained, but circumstances surely contributed. He was 12 when the Confederates accepted defeat and became the target of carpetbaggers and freed slaves whom they despised. He was to kill his first of forty-four men three years later. His victim was an ex-slave.

The loose-cylindered cap 'n ball revolver with which John Wesley Hardin shot Mexican trail boss.

dle, Hardin shot him with the Colt single-action percussion he was packing in his belt. "I shot him loose," Hardin was to recall later. "He kept coming back and every time he would start I would shoot him again and again until I shot him down."

His parents were mortified, but advised their 15-year-old son to flee. "To be tried at that time for the killing of a negro meant certain death at the hands of a court backed by Northern bayonets," he wrote in *The Life Of John Wesley Hardin,* published a year before his death at age 42. "... thus, unwillingly, I became a fugitive not from justice, be it known, but from the injustice and misrule of the people who had subjugated the South."

John Wesley Hardin had plenty of kinfolk in central Texas, and had no trouble evading the law. (In a sort of

Old John Selman sports wooly beard in this old photo. Selman was later to die in "fair fight" — perhaps like the one he had with Hardin! He was unarmed when shot.

A sign of what was to come was rendered when the blue-eyed, handsome 14-year-old boy scuffled with an older lad who tauntingly accused John Wesley as the author of a love poem scribbled on the schoolhouse wall. Hardin went for his accuser with a knife and stabbed him twice before they could be disentangled.

He reached that evil fork in the path of righteousness less than a year later. By some accounts he was visiting relatives in Moscow, Texas, in 1868. He got into a wrestling match with an ex-slave named Mage, and bloodied Mage's nose. Hardin was later to write that Mage declared: "No white boy can draw my blood and live." Mage promised revenge.

On his way home Mage "came at me with a big stick," Hardin recounted. When Mage grabbed at the horse's bri-

Wild Bill Hickok befriended Hardin when the young outlaw landed in Dodge City, Kansas. But the pair would surely have had falling out over Hardin's killing of snoring man, so Hardin fled the town red-faced in his nightshirt.

repayment for their hospitality, Hardin was later to participate in a bloody feud between the warring Taylor and Sutton families.) In fact, these Southern sympathizers were only too willing to assist a fugitive from the carpetbaggers.

Such it was that Hardin learned from his brother that Union soldiers were tracking him for the Mage incident. He ambushed the three soldiers and local residents split up their possessions. Thus, before the end of 1868, there were four notches in the 15-year-old Hardin's gunbelt.

During the next two years, according to varied accounts, Hardin moved around Texas and worked as a schoolteacher, cowboy and gambler. He blasted daylight through a couple of Union soldiers trying to arrest him, a gambler and an argumentative circus hand.

In 1870 he was arrested ironically for a murder he truthfully didn't commit. Unable to convince the judge of his innocence, Hardin was jailed in Marshall, awaiting transfer to Waco. He purchased from a cellmate a .44 Colt — don't ask what a prisoner was doing with one — which he tied with string into an improvised shoulder holster. He

Few photos exist of the young man who put more men in Boot Hill than Billy The Kid. John Wesley Hardin has none of typical outlaw hardware showing in this tintype.

Captain John Armstrong of the Texas Rangers allegedly intercepted letter revealing Hardin's whereabouts in Florida, then arrested the outlaw in a railroad car. Hardin was later to plead innocence of any murders.

THE GUN DIGEST BOOK OF SINGLE ACTION REVOLVERS

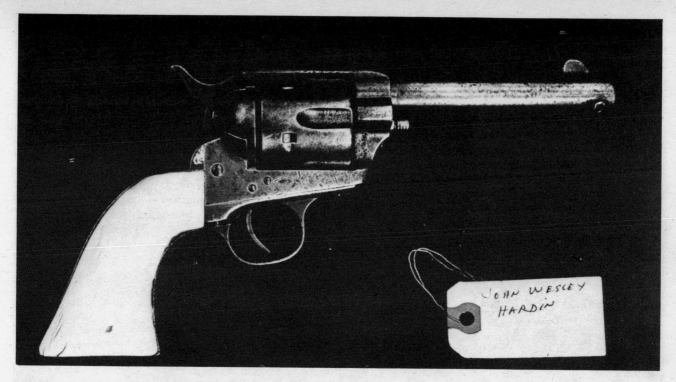

From Frontier Museum Historical Center of John Bianchi comes this ivory-gripped Colt .45 known to have been carried and used by John Wesley Hardin during his infamous career throughout the lawman-scarce Southwest.

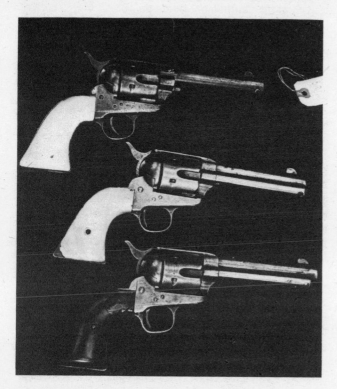

A deadly trio: At top is John Wesley Hardin's pistol, in center is Old John Selman's single-action used to kill Hardin, and at bottom is George Scarborough's Colt that was used in Selman's killing. From Bianchi collection.

also bought a greatcoat to conceal the iron.

He was escorted by one Captain Stokes of the Texas State Police, and a half-breed guard named Jim Smolly. While camped, Stokes left Smolly to guard the 17-year-old fugitive while searching for horse feed. Smolly began to ridicule Hardin, who turned against one of the horses and burst into theatrical tears, simultaneously freeing his Colt. He gunned down Smolly and fled into the night.

He made his way to the safety of his kinfolk, and departed on a cattle drive to Abilene as trail boss. A Mexican herd crowded up behind Hardin's and the cattle became mixed. Hardin and the Mexican trail boss had a heated discussion that evolved into a shooting match. Hardin's hat was perforated, but his loose-cylindered cap-and-ball revolver misfired; he dismounted, steadied the cylinder with his left hand, then shot the Mexican through the leg.

John Wesley Hardin later returned with a better pistol. He killed the Mexican trail boss and another five Mexican cowboys. It's presumed that he took possession of the Mexican cattle and the drive continued to its terminal town, Abilene.

A curious twist is encountered in Hardin's history at this point. The reigning marshal of the Kansas cowtown was none other than James Butler Hickok, better-known as Wild Bill Hickok. Instead of arresting the young killer, Wild Bill permitted him to remain in town so long as there was no trouble. Indeed, Western writer Paul Tractman claims that Wild Bill "drank with Hardin, whored with him and gave advice." When Hardin shot a saloon patron who

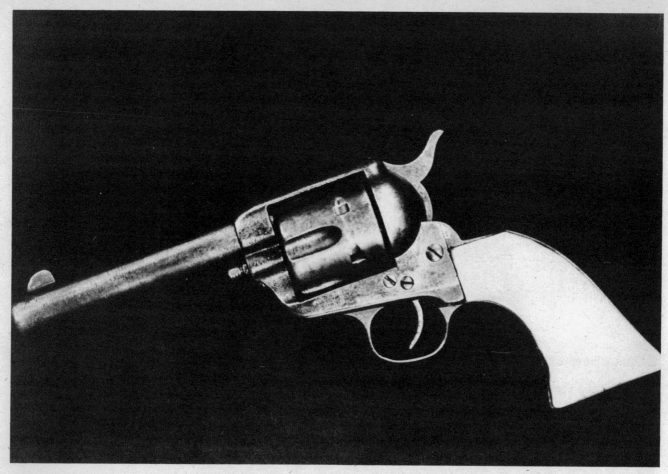

Another view of Hardin's pistol, from Frontier Museum Historical Center. This is double-action, but he packed straight-shooting single-actions throughout his lifetime, even at his death in the Acme Saloon.

objected to Texans, Hickok disarmed Hardin's cronies, but let the outlaw retain his gun.

The heinous crime that drove Hardin from this sanctuary was the killing of a man for snoring. The incident occurred in the American House Hotel, where Hardin lodged. He began shooting through a bedroom wall when disturbed by a stranger's snoring. The first slug eliminated the snoring, and the second eliminated the snorer!

Although Hardin was later to claim he killed the man for attempting to steal his pants, he didn't wait to explain to Hickok. "I believed that if Wild Bill found me in a defenseless condition, he would take no explanation, but would kill me to add to his reputation," he wrote later.

Hardin left behind all of his possesions and, clad only in his nightshirt, departed through a window. He hid in a haystack, then made his way back to Texas on a stolen pony. "I was a sorry spectacle," he recounted, "...bareheaded, unarmed, red-faced and in my night-clothes."

He was again partially clad when next he ran into trouble. In Kosse, Texas, he entered a "soiled dove's" room. Almost immediately, her enraged boyfriend burst in. In his book Hardin explained what happened:

"The fellow told me he would kill me if I did not give him $100. I told him that I only had about $50 or $60 in my pocket, but if he would go with me to the stable I would give him more, as I had the money in my saddle pocket...He said, 'Give me what you have first.' I told him all right, and in so doing, dropped some of it on the floor. He stooped down to pick it up and as he was straightening up I pulled my pistol and fired. The ball struck him between the eyes and he fell over, a dead robber."

After his return to Texas Hardin married Jane Bowen, his longtime sweetheart. In the six years they spent together before his arrest, she bore him two children and "was as true to me as the magnet of steel," he once said.

Hardin spent long periods away from home, as when

helping the Taylor family in their feud with the Suttons of DeWitt County, Texas. Hardin shot to death several Suttons and their gang before moving on.

During one of his forays Hardin hankered to see his wife. He writes in his autobiography, "I was at Banquetto, Texas, and feeling relatively safe. There I got to thinking that I had one of the prettiest and sweetest girls in the country as my wife. The more I thought of her, the more I wanted to see her.

"So one night about 10 o'clock I started from Banquetto for Gonzales County, a hundred miles away. I got home about 4 a.m., but forever ruined a good horse worth $50 doing so. The sight of my wife recompensed me for the loss of Old Bob."

A shootout in Comanche, Texas, on Hardin's twenty-first birthday would cost him twenty-five years of his life. Brown County Sheriff Charlie Webb knew Hardin was in Comanche, and was determined to arrest him. When Webb arrived he learned that Hardin had enjoyed phenomenal success at the local races. He'd won $3000 cash, a string of fifteen saddle horses, fifty head of cattle and a wagon. Hardin was celebrating around the watering holes of Comanche when Webb approached him.

"I turned and faced the man whom I had seen coming up from the street," Hardin wrote in his autobiography. "He had on two six-shooters and was about fifteen steps from me, advancing. He stopped when he got to within five steps

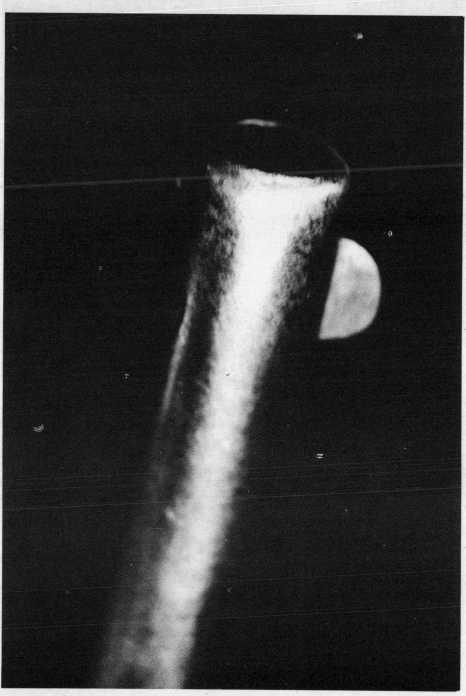

Museum curator Frank Boyer says wear on exterior of gun's muzzle resulted from continued drawing from inside coat breast pocket, where gun was carried grip-down. Grasping muzzle with finger and thumb, gun was extracted easily, ready for business in free hand.

After a fun night of drinking and carousing, George Scarborough terminated the person known as Old John Selman. Scarborough was a U.S. Marshal at the time.

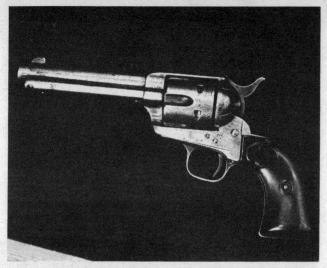

Scarborough's piece was a non-embellished Colt .45 single-action with black factory grips. He was a tough hombre.

of me...and scrutinized me closely, with his hands behind him. I asked him:

"Have you any papers for my arrest?"

"He said: 'I don't know you.'"

"I said: 'My name is John Wesley Hardin.'"

"He said' 'Now I know you, but have no papers for your arrest.'"

Hardin then invited the lawman into the saloon for a drink, and Webb accepted. "As I turned around to go in the door, I heard someone say, 'Look out, Jack.' It was Bud Dixon and as I turned around I saw Charles Webb drawing his pistol," continued Hardin "He was in the act of pre-

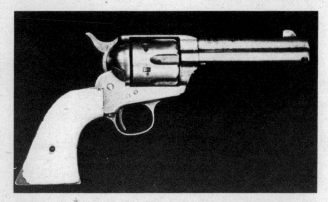

This was Selman's iron, with which he concluded Wes Hardin's infamous existence. It was not found on Old John's body when he was gunned down in a "fair fight."

senting it when I jumped to one side, drew my pistol and fired.

"In the meantime, Webb had fired, hitting me in the left side, cutting the length of it, inflicting an ugly and painful wound. My aim was good and a bullet hole in the left cheek did the work. He fell against the wall and as he fell he fired a second shot, which went into the air."

He was Hardin's thirty-ninth victim.

Hardin then fled Texas with his wife and hid in Alabama, Georgia and Florida for three years. He was finally captured by Captain John Armstrong of the Texas Rangers and returned to Gonzales for trial.

Hardin protested his innocence and addressed the jury: "Gentlemen, I swear before God that I never shot a man except in self-defense. Sheriff Webb came to Comanche for the purpose of arresting me, and I knew it. I met him and defied him to arrest me, but I did not threaten him...I knew it was in his mind to kill me, not arrest me...Everybody knows that he was a dangerous man with a pistol...

"People will call me a killer, but I swear to you, gentlemen, that I have shot only in defense of myself. And when Sheriff Webb drew his pistol I had to draw mine. Anybody else would have done the same thing. Sheriff Webb had shot a lot of men..."

After deliberating ninety minutes, a verdict of guilty of second-degree murder was returned against the 25-year-old Hardin. He was sentenced to spend twenty-five years at hard labor in the Texas State Penitentiary at Huntsville.

Hardin was non-repentent in his first years in jail, and spent much time in solitary for fighting and attempted escapes. He settled down somewhat and studied algebra, theology and law, and one time taught the prison Sunday School.

He was released after sixteen years, and received a full pardon from the governor in 1894. Although his wife had died two years earlier he returned to Gonzales and established himself as a lawyer at age 41, then moved to El Paso.

He spent much time in the watering holes of El Paso, got

Markings on barrel of Hardin's piece tell maker — Sam'l Colt of Hartford, Connecticut. A superior product.

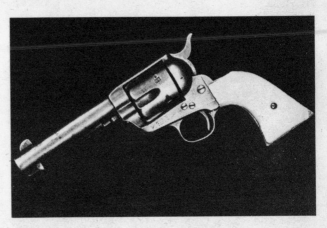

Thirty-nine recorded victims came up against the wrong end of Hardin's shooting iron, before he was shot from behind with this pistol. In his claim of self-defense, Selman said Hardin must've seen him in bar mirror.

Wes Hardin spent sixteen years behind bars, during which time his wife died. He was issued this pardon in 1894.

involved with the buxom wife of an outlaw on the lam. John Selman, a local policeman, one night arrested Hardin's girlfriend. John Wesley Hardin was incensed, and said some unflattering things about the boy to Old John Selman, an El Paso constable, who was the policeman's father. Old John didn't like what he heard, and on August 19, 1895, strode into the Acme Saloon to square things.

John Wesley Hardin was rolling dice for drinks with the bartender, Henry Brown. Looking down at his roll he announced, "four sixes to beat." At that moment Old John Selman sent a pistol bullet into Hardin's brain, killing him instantly.

Old John Selman was acquitted of murder by the defense that he was sure Hardin had spotted him in the bar mirror, and was drawing his gun. Therefore, Old John had to shoot.

Old John Selman was later dispatched to Boot Hill by a Deputy U.S. Marshal, George Scarborough, at the end of an evening's drinking and revelry at the Wigwam Saloon. Scarborough claimed it was a fair fight, but no gun was found on the deceased. Someone suggested that a trophy collector must have removed it while Selman was dying.

Jim Younger (left) was a bloody mess after he was captured following Northfield raid. The younger Younger brother, Bob, is shown at right.

THE JAMES-YOUNGER GANG

Cole Younger had eleven wounds not counting his closed eye when taken into custody by posse after Northfield (left). The Youngers were more fortunate than compadre Charlie Pitts (right). Wound in center of his breast was fatal one.

The Most Famous Of All Banditti — Were They Saints Or Sinners?

WAS JESSE JAMES hero or murderer? Was the James-Younger gang a band of murdering cutthroats or decent men driven to desperate deeds by forces of the times? Were the Youngers and Jameses Robin Hoods who stole from the rich to give to the poor, or merely hoods who stole — period?

Probably both. It's a subject on which Western writers cannot agree; in fact, most discredit all others and insist *their* particular version is the only one worth a stamp.

You'll not get that here. What follows has been compiled from works previously published and no claim is made for authenticity of fact. Where there's dispute it is noted without judgment.

For example, the idea Jesse Woodson James and his outlaw band were Nineteenth Century Robin Hoods: Carl W. Breihan's *The Complete And Authentic Life of Jesse*

Photographed in death are Bill Chadwell/Stiles (left), and Clell Miller. They died in attack.

Frank James was never convicted of a crime and during later years joined with Cole in a Wild West show. He carried this Colt Bisley model, caliber .32-20, with 5½-inch barrel, as a prop gun. Grips were black.

Frank James' Remington .44-40 (left) with wood grips was a present for backwoods doctor who treated the ill outlaw and didn't divulge his whereabouts.

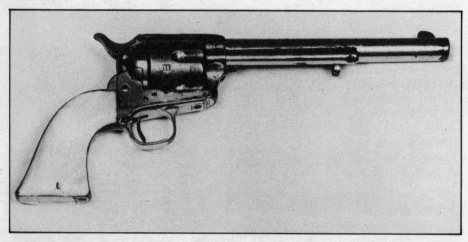

This Colt .45 single-action with 7½-inch barrel and pearl grips, serial number 19242, is said to be a Cole Younger gun. Perhaps

James builds on this theme, discounted by James D. Horan's *The Authentic Wild West: The Outlaws.* Breihan credits Frank and Jesse, first two children born to preacher Robert James and domineering wife Zerelda Cole James, as helping establish a school for Negro children in Missouri. "J. Milton Turner, a noted Negro educator, was seated on the porch of his home one day with a friend, discussing means of financing a school," says Breihan in his 1953 hardback. "Two riders appeared suddenly, tossed a bag upon the porch, and rode away without identifying themselves. Over their backs they shouted, 'Use the gold to start your school!' The educator's friend was of the opinion that one of the riders was Jesse..."

Jesse is alleged to have helped the penniless widow of a Quantrill confederate in Breihan's book. As Carl tells it: "...This woman, poor and alone on a small farm in the Tennessee mountains, was expecting the sheriff and a loan shark to foreclose the mortgage on the farm. By a coincidence, on the day this distressing event was to take place Jesse and a companion rode by the place, had lunch with the widow, and inquired concerning her obvious despondency. Jesse, so the story goes, gave her the $500 she needed to pay off the mortgage, and went on his way with his companion, after cautioning the widow to be sure and get a receipt for the money and a release of the mortgage. Several hours later Jesse held up the sheriff and the banker as they returned from their visit to the widow, and the money used to pay off the mortgage found its way back into Jesse's pocket..."

According to James D. Horan: "He will always be the boy eternal, the merry-eyed outlaw who rides across the western plains on a magnificent bay, the bag of gold stolen from the hated railroads slung across his saddle horn while behind him, helplessly outclassed, comes the lumbering posse. He steals only from the rich to help the poor. Minutes after the sneering landload takes the last dollar from the weeping widow, he is robbed by Jesse, who gallantly returns the previous dollars to the grateful woman as her children look on, their shining faces filled with love and admiration...It's the stuff of a nation's myth and legend, and while attractive, it is distorted and without foundation. In reality, Jesse was a thief and a callous killer. His unarmed victims included bank cashiers, citizens caught on the street during a robbery, a train conductor, a young stone cutter shot in the back..."

Get the picture? He's revered or reviled; doubtless there's some truth on both sides.

The James-Younger story has its roots in the bloody soil of Clay County, Missouri. Abolitionist and pro-slavery antagonism gave rise during the Fifties and Sixties to violence repaid in kind. Abolitionist "Jayhawkers" persecuted Southern sympathizers who banded behind leaders like William Clarke Quantrill and William "Bloody Bill" Anderson to seek vengeance. Osceola, Missouri, was raided by Jayhawkers, so Lawrence, Kansas, was destroyed by Quantrill.

Frank James joined Quantrill in '62 and served with Thomas Coleman Younger. Jesse joined "Bloody Bill"

Zerelda Samuel, mother of Jesse and Frank, was a domineering woman with acid tongue who helped to turn public sentiment in sons' favor by consistent vitriolic harangue at Pinkerton's National Detective Agency. Their raid crippled her, killed young son.

Anderson's unit after being harassed by Federal forces that jailed his mother and sister for a month, and through the Civil War saw horrible combat. He also participated in the slaughter of twenty-five unarmed Union soldiers captured from a train.

After Lee's surrender raiding bands had difficulty returning to life on the farm. Many like the James and Younger boys turned to crime.

The first of up to seventeen robberies attributed to the James boys was in Liberty, Missouri, in mid-February 1866. The band escaped with $57,072.64. A college student on the street was shot dead following this first daylight robbery in America.

Thus began a series of similar stickups involving known James-Younger compatriots, if not the outlaws themselves: October '66 — Lexington, Missouri, $2000; May '67 — Richmond, Missouri, $4000 and three citizen fatalities; March '68 — Russellville, Kentucky, $12,000 and one citizen wounded; and December '69 — Gallatin, Missouri, one citizen killed, unknown amount stolen.

After the last robbery a posse tracked the two criminals to Clay County, then to the James place near Kearney. Frank and Jesse fled after exchanging shots and began life on the run.

Jesse's Robin Hood character was created by *Kansas City Times* publisher John Newman Edwards, a Southern sympathizer to whom Jesse addressed letters to the editor denying guilt in the Gallatin and subsequent affairs. Jesse

also wrote to Missouri Governor McClurg offering to surrender if he could be guaranteed a fair trial and not "mob justice." He usually proferred the names of respectable citizens who would swear to the band's alibi — but these were largely discounted because citizens were friends or relatives for the most part.

Their fame spread through subsequent heists: a bank job in Columbia, Kentucky, in April '72 in which the cashier was killed and a July '73 train robbery at Council Bluffs, Iowa, during which an engineer was scalded to death and the James-Younger gang collected $2000 plus passenger valuables. A robbery atttibuted to the gang and disputed by many was theft of $10,000 in gate receipts from the Kan-

During the sixteen years Jesse (right) was on the scout, he masterminded schemes that produced an estimated $200,000 — fabulous wealth for the time.

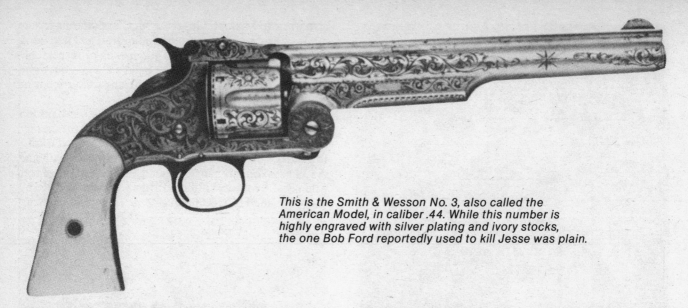

This is the Smith & Wesson No. 3, also called the American Model, in caliber .44. While this number is highly engraved with silver plating and ivory stocks, the one Bob Ford reportedly used to kill Jesse was plain.

sas City Fair, and the stickup of the St. Genevieve, Missouri, bank in '73. Gang members Jesse and Cole hotly denied involvement and perhaps other bandits perpetrated the crimes and cast the blame on the James-Younger Gang.

After the Iron Mountain Railroad at Gad's Hill, Missouri, was plundered in January '74, the Jameses and Youngers quieted. Jesse married his cousin, Zerelda (also called Zee or Josie), who had nursed a war gunshot wound in his right breast for months. Frank married Annie Ralston the same year in Omaha, Nebraska, Leavenworth, Kansas, or Independence, Missouri.

In 1875 authorities struck back and turned public sentiment in favor of the Jameses. During the night of January 26, 1875, men of the Pinkerton Detective Agency set fire to the James home and threw in a thirty-two-pound iron illuminating flare either filled with kerosene or wrapped with kerosene-soaked rags set alight. Dr. Samuel kicked the bomb into the fireplace where it exploded. Zerelda Samuel's right arm was mangled and later amputated, and 8-year-old son, Archie, was killed by shrapnel in the stomach. The outlaws were not in Kearney and newspapers led by John Newman Edwards fairly roasted the Pinkertons.

While makeup of the gang changed, the Youngers — Cole, John, Jim, and Bob — and the two James lads formed the nucleus until the catastrophic Northfield, Minnesota, raid on September 7, 1876. The gang members were perceived by the public to be dead shots, but author Horan claims otherwise. "His (Jesse's) marksmanship...never came up to the reputation," he writes. "...Dick Liddil, one of Jesse's favorite riders, described how Jesse fired six unsuccessful shots at a man who apparently didn't care to be robbed, missed a point-blank shot at a cashier, and during the Gallatin train robbery fired three times at a conductor and missed..."

There are myriad "authentic James guns" in collections around the country; maybe they are. Two with good histories repose in the Frontier Museum Historical Center in Temecula, California. One is Frank's Remington .44-40, serial number 5116, presented in gratitude to a Dr. A.H. Conkwright of Sedalia, Missouri, for nursing Frank with-

out disclosing his whereabouts. A second is a Colt .32-20 Bisley with 5½-inch barrel, serial number 304918 with black grips that Frank carried when he joined Cole Younger's Wild West Show many years after giving up outlawry.

Younger was a fancier of Sam Colt's product in .45 caliber. He once used a single-action black powder model with 7½-inch barrel and walnut stocks. Another said to have belonged to Cole is a .45 with 7½-inch barrel and ivory grips. Allegedly at Cole's request, the sheriff of Northfield sent this pistol to Belle Starr, who subsequently gave it to Texas Jack. (This would be odd, since Cole acknowledged in prison he knew her, but denied romantic involvement or that he fathered Belle's daughter, Pearl.)

At the early stages of their outlawry, Frank (left) and Jesse posed in typical bandit fashion — with arms. Frank's war years were spent with Youngers.

THE GUN DIGEST BOOK OF SINGLE ACTION REVOLVERS

William Pinkerton, founder of the National Detective Agency bearing his name, was allegedly followed by Jesse through Chicago as outlaw sought retribution for night attack on Samuel farm. James didn't succeed.

One of the earliest photos of Jesse Woodson James. The youth fought with Bloody Bill Anderson and other guerrilla forces during the Civil War, then turned criminal. Was he forced into life of crime? Hm...

Still another Younger gun is a .45 Colt single-action with 7½-inch barrel, nickel plating, ivory grips and missing ejector assembly.

His guns helped little during the attempted bank heist in Northfield. Involved were three Younger brothers — Cole, Jim, and Bob — Jesse and Frank James, Charlie Pitts, Clell Miller, and William Chadwell, also called William Stiles.

Split into three groups, the James-Younger gang approached the bank. The heist misfired when cashier J.L. Heywood refused to open the safe — which was already unlocked but closed — and gang members outside came under fire from citizens who used any weapons, including rocks. In the fracas medical student Henry M. Wheeler killed Miller and wounded Bob Younger in the elbow. Shopkeeper Anselm R Manning wounded Cole Younger, killed Chadwell/Stiles and killed one outlaw horse. Cashier Heywood was pistol-whipped, then executed by a bullet in the brain as he struggled to his feet.

The gang fled and was pursued by a huge posse. The Jameses and Youngers split up when Jesse demanded they abandon or kill the wounded Bob Younger, and after two weeks of dodging in the frigid Minnesota countryside the Youngers and Pitts were bailed up in Medalia, 150 miles from Northfield. They pleaded guilty to murder in Faribault and were granted life sentences in Stillwater penitentiary. Jesse and Frank escaped back to Missouri.

On the "scout," Jesse drifted to New Mexico where it's alleged he met Billy The Kid, then returned to Missouri to rob trains in '79. Leading a new band comprising brother Frank, Jim Cummins, Ed Miller and Dick Liddil, Jesse coldly killed a train conductor with two shots in the back as he raided the passenger compartment, shot dead an unarmed stone mason, and pistol-whipped to unconsciousness an express messenger during a train holdup near Winston, Missouri. The band got just $200 in a later train robbery in which Jesse savagely beat the express messenger.

Things were just too hot and Jesse and Frank had rewards up to $25,000 on their heads. The gang split up and several were arrested. Jesse drfted into Kansas City and St. Joseph with his family, posing as a horse dealer named Tom Howard. Frank turned to farming in Tennessee.

Jesse was planning to knock over the Platte City bank and recruited brothers Charlie and Bob Ford to assist. But the brothers schemed to kill Jesse for the reward, and Bob Ford sent a slug through Jesse's skull as the outlaw stood on a chair without his guns to straighten a picture. Most accounts claim Ford used a Smith & Wesson No. 3 American Model in .44 caliber, nickel-plated, with 6½-inch barrel and serial number 3766. George Virgines, in his *Saga of the Colt Six-Shooter*, says some folks think the gun used was a Colt single-action .45, serial number 23960, with 7½-inch barrel and checkered ivory grips with nineteen notches cut into them.

Following Jesse's death Frank wrote to Missouri Governor Thomas T. Crittenden and offered to surrender for a fair trial. Accompanied by newspaper champion John Newman Edwards, Frank unbuckled his gunbelt carrying forty-two cartridges and a .44 caliber Remington 1875 Model and handed them to the governor, saying: "Governor Crittenden, I want to hand over to you that which no living man except myself has been permitted to touch since 1861, and to say I am your prisoner."

Frank was subsequently tried and acquitted of crimes and in later life joined with pardoned Cole Younger in a Wild West show that lasted a few years. (Bob Younger at age 33 died in prison of tuberculosis and Jim Younger committed suicide when his parole board would not let him marry.)

Frank died in 1915 and Cole a year later, both of old age. Thus ended the James-Younger gang of Robin Hoods.

THE DEADLY DALTONS

Factory-engraved Colt single-action .44-40, serial number 83073, originally carried by Emmett Dalton. It's in the Los Angeles County Museum, presented as a memorial.

Train Robbers, Kin Of The Youngers, Desperadoes After Places In History

... last of the Doolin gang to go.

Little Dick West, shown in mortuary, caused mayhem with Bill Dalton in Doolin Gang. He proves Emmett's statement about the result of crime. See text for more.

WHILE THE James-Younger outlaw band survived for sixteen years, the crime-filled careers of the brothers Dalton and friends spanned less than two. What was lacking in time was compensated in ferocity, as if these outlaws were driven by an uncontrollable urge to earn a place in history.

Five of the fifteen children born to James Lewis and Adeline Lee Younger Dalton sought careers in which firearms were required. All gained familiarity with shooting at early ages, and Emmett's first weapon was a "musket with the kick of a cannon" for which he'd traded some 'coon skins. The boys revelled in stories of the James-Younger gang, since they were cousins to the Youngers of Lee's Summit, Missouri, and their beliefs were likewise forged in the fires of discontent raging between Southern and Yankee camps.

Emmett quit the family farm for cowboying on the Bar X Bar near Pawnee, Indian Territory, where he was to meet his future compadres in crime. With him on the cattle spread were Bill Doolin — later to form his own gang after the massacre at Coffeyville, with whom Bill Dalton rode to his death; George Newcomb — better-known to history as

After his release from jail, Emmett Dalton and Charles M. Martin worked together on Dalton book. In gratitude, Emmett is seen giving pistol on page 110 to Martin, at left in this old photo.

the handsome "Bitter Creek"; Charlie Bryant — alias "Black-Faced Charlie," so dubbed because of powder burns on his face and whose voiced wish to "get killed in one hell-firin' minute of smoking action" was granted by a lawman; and Dick Broadwell, Charlie Pierce and Bill Powers.

While Emmett was chasing beeves, brothers Gratton, "Grat", and Frank were chasing moonshiners and rustlers as Indian policemen throughout the Indian Territory. Frank was the first Dalton to die, cut down by a whiskey smuggler. His job then was assumed by Grat, Bob and Emmett, who combined chasing criminals for fees with a little rustling, bribery and whiskey smuggling of their own.

When the Indian Territory became the Oklahoma Territory, the Dalton trio turned in their badges. Grat went to visit ranching brothers in California, while Bob and Emmett drifted into trouble by robbing a faro dealer they claimed was cheating. Bob lit out for California, while Emmett rode back to the lawless Oklahoma Territory.

On the night of February 5, 1891, the Southern Pacific train bound for Alila, California, was stopped and robbed. The fireman was killed and the Wells, Fargo messenger wounded. Bob and Grat were arrested for the crime. Bob was acquitted and Grat convicted, then sentenced to twenty years' jail. Both Daltons refuted the charge and, when Bob returned to home range near the Oklahoma/Kansas state lines, the brothers decided to seek revenge on the express companies that they felt had erroneously wronged them. They also might have thought train robbery a damn sight easier than punching cows for a living.

Thus began a series of train stickups in which the Dalton boys were enormously successful, aided by their saddle pals of the cowcamps. Near Wharton, Oklahoma Territory, a Santa Fe train was relieved of $14,000; the Missouri, Kansas and Texas Railroad lost $19,000 near Wag-

Seeking fame to surpass even the James-Younger gang, Daltons planned simultaneous holdup of two banks in Coffeyville, Kansas. A real war shot up windows.

goner; the Daltons let a dummy train filled with deputies pass and bushwhacked another Santa Fe near Red Rock in the Cherokee Strip, earning $11,000; in July '92, the boys boarded the Missouri, Kansas and Texas train at Adair, took $17,000 and wounded three deputies before quitting the train ahead of a detective ambush waiting farther down the line.

Meantime, every train holdup during '91-'92 was blamed on the Daltons. A pair that would have been magical occurred one thousand miles apart on the same night — in St. Charles, Missouri, and El Paso, Texas — yet the Daltons were wanted for both!

Lawmen were hot to collar the bunch and had eliminated Black-Faced Charlie. Grat had escaped to join the boys who decided on one more raid before quitting the life, a raid to be even more spectacular than the James-Younger holdups. They decided to simultaneously plunder the two banks in their hometown of Coffeyville, Kansas. They would make their mark in history, then vanish to settle down in South America.

As the six outlaws — Doolin, Emmett, Grat, Bob, Broadwell, and Powers — approached town, their carefully rehearsed plan started to fall apart. Doolin's horse went lame and he figured to steal another and rejoin the group, but he never did. Then the quintet discovered road repairmen had removed the hitching rail outside the two banks, which meant they had to leave the horses in an alley a half-block away. Bob and Emmett were wearing false beards, but were recognized by townsfolk who discovered the heist and spread the alarm. In the manner of Northfield, Coffeyville townfolk grabbed Winchesters from the local hardware outlet and waited for the badmen to emerge from the two banks.

Grat, Broadwell and Powers ducked into the C.M. Condon and Co. Bank, while Emmett and Bob crossed to the First National. Inside the Condon Grat was stymied when the cashier informed him the safe was on a time lock that wouldn't open for several minutes. Grat elected to wait — a fatal mistake that gave residents time to arm themselves and take up firing positions.

In the First National, Bob and Emmett emptied $21,-000 into their grain sack and began to exit with tellers and customers shielding them, but came under withering fire and ducked back inside, then dashed out the back door. Bob Dalton used his Winchester to send a bullet through the left breast of Lucius M. Baldwin, approaching with pistol in hand. Bob and Emmett then abandoned their hostages and sprinted for the horses in what was to become known as "Death Alley." En route, Bob and Emmett shot rifle-toting George W. Cubine in the chest, leg and ankle. As Cubine slumped mortally wounded, his partner Charles T. Brown scooped up his weapon. Another four shots from fifty yards dropped him alongside Cubine. Tom Ayres took a Bob Dalton slug through the cheek below the left eye, severely wounding him as they made Death Alley.

In the Condon bank the robbers heard the shooting start and Grat Dalton ordered a retreat with just $1100 in his vest. As they came into the street, Grat and Bill Powers were each mortally wounded before going twenty feet. Both kept firing and Powers took a round in the chest that killed him before he could mount his horse. Grat fired a few more wild rifle shots from under the cover of an oil tank, where he'd sought refuge. Dick Broadwell, wounded in the back, had lain down in the lumber yard and during a short lull in the shooting had reached his horse and put the spurs to him. Before Broadwell had gone twenty feet, he was hit by a rifle ball and shot from a shotgun; he kept the saddle,

Grisly scene: Dead gang members piled in a heap in street.

but was found sprawled dead a half-mile from town.

Grat, meanwhile, had somehow regained his feet and was making weakly for his horse when a rifle bullet tore through his throat and broke his neck.

Bob and Emmett had entered Death Alley and Bob was immediately shot. He staggered across the alley and sat down, then put a rifle bullet into the back of Marshal Charles T. Connelly before taking another shot full in the chest. Emmett had miraculously been unharmed and as he mounted, took bullets in the right arm and left hip and groin. Still clutching the grain sack full of money, Emmett rode to where Bob was lying and leaned over as if to raise his mortally wounded brother into the saddle. Both barrels of a shotgun were discharged into his back, toppling him from the saddle to surrender for trial. The entire episode took fifteen minutes; twelve minutes from the first shot.

Describing the scene in his *Coffeyville Journal,* witness and participant David Stewart Elliot wrote: "The scene that was presented in the 'alley of death' was ghastly beyond human conception. A moment or two passed after the cry went up, 'They are all down!' before anyone ventured to approach the prostrate forms of the dead and dying. Just as soon as their work was finished, the citizens ceased firing, shouldering their guns and gathered around those who had fallen in the alley. Three men lay dead in an almost direct line with each other, a fourth was in the last throes of death, and a fifth was helpless and bleeding from a number of dreadful wounds. Three dead horses, a smoking Winchester, the hats of the fallen, and other evidences of a bloody conflict were scattered over the ground where the bandits made their last stand..."

Emmett was nursed to health and sent to prison for life, but pardoned in 1907 after fifteen years. He became a successful building contractor in California and spent his years condemning the outlaw ways. He also wrote a revealing tome entitled, *When the Daltons Rode,* and makes some telling comments about pistols.:

"Personally, I have met hundreds of bad men, hard men, shooting men, killers, both peace officer and outlaw. And I have yet to see the first notch on any of their six-shooters. I have, however, seen fake bad men ostentatiously file dummy notches.

"Men who killed other men, I observed, did not boast of it. They did not advertise their prowess, aggressive or defensive, by cutting a notch on a gun. It is a fiction writer's elaboration.

"Never did I see a man 'fan' his six-shooter.

"Never did I see any shooting from the hip.

"Never did I see a man waste precious ammunition by using two guns simultaneously. Bob Dalton was accounted one of the best shots in the Southwest, with rifle, pistol or shotgun. Never once did he indulge any of the phony stunts attributed to so many 'master' gunmen of the old border...

"Indeed the six-shooter's deadliness has always been overrated. The number of shots fired, and the net results, in numerous historic frays with this weapon, make an almost ludicrous contrast. How often, in accurate accounts of the 'carnage,' does one come across the phrase, alibiing the short gun, 'It was a miracle that so few were killed!'..."

One of the short guns owned by Emmett Dalton was in 1950 presented to the Los Angeles County Museum by the late Charles Martin, a well-known author and friend of Emmett's. The gun, Emmett wrote, was presented for Martin's help with the written history of the Daltons, but was not carried on the Coffeyville raid. It's a .44-40 Colt Single-Action, serial number 83073, with 5½-inch barrel. It is engraved and equipped with the rare Colt Eagle grips and bears the inscription of the Daltons' names inside the grips.

A .45 Colt single-action allegedly taken from the dead body of Bob Dalton now reposes in the Dalton Defenders' Museum in Coffeyville. It's silver-plated, engraved, with pearl grips and a 5½-inch barrel.

In 1931, six years before his death, Emmett Dalton returned to Coffeyville and the gravesite of his brothers. A reporter accompanying him quoted Emmett, staring at the graves of Grat and Bob: "I challenge the world to produce the history of an outlaw who ever got anything out of it but that," he said, pointing to the grave, "or else to be huddled in a prison cell. And that goes for the modern bandit of the skyscraper frontier of our big cities, too. The machine gun may help them get away with it a little better and the motor car may help them in making an escape better than to ride on horseback as we did, but it all ends the same way. The biggest fool on earth is the one who thinks he can beat the law, that crime can be made to pay. It never paid and it never will and that was the one big lesson of the Coffeyville raid."

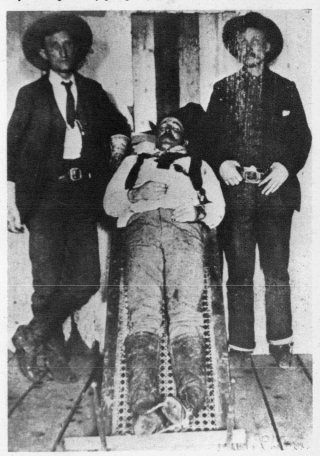

Bill Doolin's horse came up lame en route to the Coffeyville catastrophe, so he formed another gang that included Tulsa Jack Blake, shown dead below. Days of legendary gang exploits were waning rapidly.

BELLE STARR

More Fiction Than Truth Surrounds The Bandit Queen; Hopefully, This Sets Some Of The Record Straight!

BELLE STARR, "The Bandit Queen". The True STORY of the ROMANTIC and EXCITING CAREER Of the DARING and GLAMOROUS Lady Famed in Legend and Story throughout the West As The BEAUTIFUL GIRL Who Would never have WENT WRONG if THINGS HADN'T GONE WRONG. The TRUE FACTS about the DASTARDLY DEEDS and THE COMEUPPENCE Of Such Dick Turpins, Robin Hoods and Rini Rinaldos AS The Youngers, the Jameses, the Daltons, the Starrs, the Doolins and the Jenningses. The REal StORY With court RECORDS and cONtemPoraRY NEWSPAPER ACCOUNTS And Testimony of Old Nesters, here and there, in the Southwest. A VERITABLE Exposee of BADMEN and MARSHALS and Why Crime Does Not Pay!

Not the produce of an alcoholic typesetter, the foregoing is the title page of Burton Rascoe's 1941 book published by Random House. Sex, violence, good and evil — all the sales stimulators are present in Belle's biography, authored by a deputy sheriff of Pottawatomie County, Shawnee, Oklahoma.

In the introduction to his version of Belle's true history, Rascoe jabs a thumb in the eye of Richard K. Fox's *National Police Gazette,* which Rascoe claims originated the fictional history of Belle Starr when caught without prepared background material when Belle was slain. Fox's hungrily received twenty-five-cent paperback was titled, *Bella Starr, The Bandit Queen, or the Female Jesse James.* In it, says Rascoe, you could learn her incorrect name, date, and place of birth, and that's just for starters. But Fox's pulp sure read swell, to wit:

"Of all women of the Cleopatra type, since the days of the Egyptian queen herself, the universe has produced none more remarkable than Bella Starr, the Bandit Queen. Her character was a combination of the very worst as well as some of the very best traits of her sex. She was more amorous than Anthony's mistress; more relentless than

Pharoh's daughter, and braver than Joan of Arc. Of her it may well be said that Mother Nature was indulging in one of her rarest freaks, when she produced such a novel specimen of womankind. Bella was not only well-educated, but gifted with uncommon musical and literary talents, which were almost thrown away through the bias of her nomadic and lawless disposition, which early isolated her from civilized life, except at intervals, when in a strange country, and under an assumed name, she brightened the social circle for a week or a month, and then was, perhaps, lost forever."

Horse-handling expertise gained on her father's farm in Missouri served "The Bandit Queen" well — like when she rode at a gallop through downtown Dallas, sending all types of traffic scurrying for the safer sidewalks!

114

Deputy Rascoe conducted lengthy research and found much input — unfortunately, he says, most were garbled versions of Fox's fabrications. Here's an example typical of what he received:

I have some true happenings in the life of Belle Starr in which my grandfather, unfortunately, participated. All this information came from him. I heard him tell it no less than forty-nine times.

It is a little difficult to write, so I am going to write as if I were writing a book. Note description of Belle Starr's clothes. I thought this was something you might not have.

Chandler, Oklahoma, on June 2, 1894, was like any other day in July — warm and almost sultry. Mr. Blank

(name omitted) wiped the perspiration from his forehead as he entered the city bank's one large room. His law office was on one section off a wooden fence. From the other offices in the bank came greetings.

"Good morning, Mr. Blank," one called. "You seem to be in a big hurry this morning."

"Yes," he answered. "I've got some letters to write. Have to get them off in the early morning mail."

At nine-thirty o'clock that morning the letters were ready for mailing, and Mr. Blank was walking out of the bank. As he stepped out to the sidewalk, he was confronted by one of the most handsome men he had ever seen. Blank recognized the face of Bill Doolin who was leveling a gun at his heart.

One of her lovers was known simply as the Blue Duck, and he's pictured here with Belle when the pair were in Fort Smith, Arkansas. Belle's shackeled paramour had been arrested for murder.

Cole Younger (left), shown with brother Jim, learned murderous lessons from Quantrill service and later was to apply same for personal gain. Cole was about 24 when he wooed Myra Belle Shirley in a consummated courtship resulting in the birth of a daughter, who was christened Pearl Younger. Belle was later to name her bandit hideaway "Younger's Bend" after her lover.

"Keep going, but don't bat an eyelash, or I'll send you straight to hell."

Mr. Blank was so frightened he could scarcely move. He saw four other men with revolvers. Since none of them were masked, and since he had seen many pictures of Cherokee Bill and Lucas, he immediately recognized them.

Carefully putting one foot in front of the other, Mr. Blank thought each step might be his last as he considered his past life. He later reported that it seemed a year before the walk to the end of the block was at an end.

In the middle of the road sat Belle Starr on her brown and white horse. Dressed in a black riding habit and a crisp white blouse, she rode side-saddle, her high-top laced shoes showing beneath her skirt. Her black eyes blazed at Mr. Blank.

Her guns were concealed in the folds of her dress, and Mr. Blank saw them move as he passed by. He felt sure

she intended to kill him then, but at that instant Mitchell, a barber, saw the bank robbers and rushed out yelling, "Bank robbers! Bank robbers!"

Belle Starr stormed, "Get back in there or I'll blow your head off."

He disappeared, then returned, screaming, "Bank...!"

That was his last word, for he fell at the feet of Mr. Blank who was forced to step over his body and continue down the street.

As the robbers were leaving the bank and mounting their horses, Lucas was injured and his horse killed. He fell to the ground. The robbers picked him up and started to take him on with them, but he was so badly wounded, he begged them to leave him. They did that, so Lucas was captured.

Sounds okay, until you consider Rascoe's rebuttal. "My correspondent's grandfather's yarn, although repeated forty-nine times, is entirely fictitious on the face of it. The robbery the narrator tells about is alleged to have taken place in 1894. Belle Starr was murdered on February 3, 1889. Belle Starr *never* participated in the robbery of a bank. There was *never* a warrant out for her charging her with murder."

While the woods are full of antique revolvers that allegedly belonged to the James Brothers, to one of the Youngers or to the Daltons, we know of no collection that claims a genuine authenticated Belle Starr gun.

There has been great conjecture as to what type of revolver the lady of dubious repute might have carried in her adventures. There are those who favor the Smith & Wesson Ladysmith, which was designed for women as a self-defender, but was discontinued when Daniel Wesson, its inventor, found it was the favored tool of prostitutes.

Others say this model was entirely too small and too ladylike for the woman outlaw. Indeed, there were a number of arms available to her, most left over from the War Between the States, but in the one known picture in which she is packing a revolver in a holster, it appears to be the Smith & Wesson American model with ivory grips.

Belle's infamy captivated Europe, mostly through the writings of one Italian Professor Caesar Lombroso and William Ferrero in *The Female Offender.*

The born criminal is rarely inclined to write much. We know of but three instances among them of memoirs: those of Madame Lafarge, of X., and of Bell-Star, while male criminals are greatly addicted to these egotistic outpourings. Madame Lafarge, the woman X., and Bell-Star, particularly the last, were certainly endowed with superior intelligence...

But when by an unfortunate chance muscular strength and intellectual force meet in the same individual, we have a female delinquent of a terrible type indeed. A typical example of these extraordinary women is presented by Bell-Star, the female brigand, who a few years ago terrorized all Texas. Her education had been of the sort to develop her natural qualities; for, being the daughter of a guerilla chief who had fought on the side of the South in the war of 1861-65, she had grown up in the midst of fighting, and when only ten years old, already used the lasso, the revolver, the carbine, and the bowie-knife in a way to excite the enthusiasm of her ferocious companions. She was as strong and bold as a man, and loved to ride untamed horses which the boldest of the brigands dared not mount. One day at Oakland she twice won a race, dressed as a man and once as a woman, changing her dress so rapidly that her ruse remained unsuspected. She was extremely dissolute, and had more than one lover at a time, her admirer en titre being always the most intrepid and daring of the band. At the first sign of cowardice he was degraded from his rank. But, while all the time having — as Varigny writes — as many lovers as there were desperadoes in four States. At the age of eighteen she became head of the band, and ruled her associates partly through her superior intelligence, partly through her courage, and to a certain degree through her personal charm as a woman. She organized attacks of the most daring description on populous cities, and even fought against government troops, not hesitating the very day after one of these raids to enter some neighboring towns unaccompanied, and dress — as almost always — in male attire. Once she slept in the same hotel as the judge of the district without his once suspecting her identity or even her sex... She wrote her memoirs, recording in them her desire to die in her boots. This wish was granted, for she fell in a battle against the government troops, directing the fire to her last breath.

Rascoe gleefully counters with information that Professor Lombroso was the founder of the "science of criminology" at the University of Turin. "When he published his *Criminal Man* in 1876, he set the enlightened world by the ears," digs Rascoe. "He had measured a great number of skulls of the living and the dead, and announced the astounding 'discovery' that a man's career as a criminal was predetermined by the shape of his head! There were some secondary characteristics possessed by the criminal type, he wrote, such as short ear-lobes and eyes set close together. He went into the psychological and psychophysical determinants and identification marks, also, giving elaborate case histories. These were probably as imbecile as the above 'case history' of Belle Starr."

All of which attempts to explain the difficulty facing Western historians. The aim here is not to join the howl from one camp or another, but to put before you what's available about this black queen. Fact or fiction, it's still scorchy stuff. Sheriff Rascoe, lead on...

Myra Belle was the youngest of John and Elizabeth Shirley's three children and most likely began her forty-one-year tenure February 5, 1848. She was born in Missouri, but exactly where is unclear — Rascoe doubts Carthage, chiseled into her tombstone, since her parents hadn't settled there by the time Myra joined brothers Preston, 8, and Ed, 6, to complete the Shirley quintet.

John Shirley alternately farmed, bred horses and livestock, owned and operated a saloon/hotel, then repeated the cycle. During the eight years she lived on the 160-acre farm before her dad became innkeeper, Myra Belle learned the horse-handling skills for which she was later to be renowned.

When her parents moved to Carthage and the hotel trade, 8-year-old Myra Belle was probably enrolled in the Carthage Female Academy where for less than $100 per

While Jesse James had frequented Myra Belle's home as a member of Quantrill's cadre, he was not so welcome following the abortive bank stickup that landed Cole Younger in jail. Still, he holed up at Younger's Bend for a spell when Belle was married to badman Sam Starr.

year young ladies studied reading, spelling, grammar, arithmetic, algebra, deportment, Greek, Latin, Hebrew and took instruction at the piano. The latter served Myra Belle well when she pounded a Fort Smith saloon piano all night to celebrate her acquittal on a charge of horse theft.

She also studied at William Cravens' private school in Carthage. As a 10-year-old, she was remembered as "small and dark...a bright, intelligent girl but was of a fierce nature and would fight anyone, boy or girl, that she quarreled with. Except for this trait, she seemed a nice little girl, however. In fact, the entire Shirley family were nice people..."

Not for long. "The bloodiest man in America," William Clarke Quantrill, was the scourge of Kansas and Missouri in the late 1850s, leading his Confederate guerillas who included the Daltons, Youngers and James boys — tied to Belle Starr, and all welcome at the Shirley homes in Missouri, Texas and Arkansas.

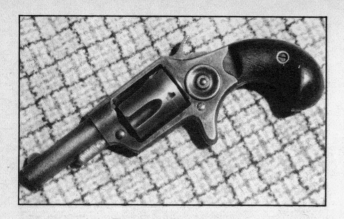 

Typical of the firearms available to both sides of the law were the Marlin (left), 1855 Colt side hammers at right. There is a possibility that Belle Starr carried one of these, as well as the Colt SAA which is identified with her.

Belle's brother, Ed, aligned himself with the Confederate cause but kept busy bushwhacking for personal gain. S.W. Harman, co-author with C.P. Sterns of the 1898 *Hell On The Border,* explains Belle's first flutter from grace thusly:

On her sixteenth birthday, February 3, 1862, Belle was returning from a scout, riding through the village of Newtonia, in the eastern part of Newton County, Missouri, thirty-five miles, as the crow flies, from her home town, Carthage. She was intercepted by a Major Enos who, with a troop of cavalry, was stationed in the village and who had his headquarters at the home of Judge M.H. Richery...

On the day of Belle Shirley's capture...Major Enos had sent a detachment of cavalry to Carthage for the purpose of capturing her brother, Captain Shirley, who was known to be on a visit to his home. Belle, or Myra, as she was then called, had ridden into that section of the country for the purpose of obtaining information that might be of value to her people, and having discovered that men had been sent to capture her brother, was on the point of hastening to warn him when she was arrested and detained. She had been in the habit of riding recklessly where she pleased, and as scarce any Union soldier would think of molesting a woman, especially when the woman chanced to be a beautiful and buxom girl, her plans had not, hitherto, been disarranged. It happened that Major Enos, who had resided in Carthage, was acquainted with both her and her brother as children, and this was why he had ordered her arrest; he rightly surmising that she was about to go to her brother's assistance. The girl was taken to the chamber of the Richery home and guarded by the major himself, who laughed at her annoyance. This served to anger her and she gave expression to her rage in loud and deep curses. Then she would sit at the piano and rattle off some wild selection in full keeping with her fury; the next instant she would spring to her feet, stamp the floor and berate the major and his acts with all the ability and profanity of an experienced trooper, while the tears of mortification rolled down her cheeks, her terrible passion only increased by the laughter and taunts of her captor. At last, believing his men to have had plenty of time to reach

Carthage ahead of her, Major Enos said:

"Well, Myra, you can go now. My men will have your brother under arrest before you can reach him!"

With eagerness, trembling in every lineament, she sprang to the door, rushed down the stairway and out to a clump of cherry bushes, where she cut several long sprouts for use as riding whips. The judge's daughter, now Mrs. Graves, accompanied her.

"I'll beat them yet," said the girl, as with tearful eyes she swallowed a great lump in her throat. Her horse stood just where her captors had left it; vaulting into the saddle, she sped away, plying the cherry sprouts with vigor. A short distance from the house she deserted the traveled road and, leaping fences and ditches without ceremony, struck a bee line in the direction of Carthage. She was a beautiful sight as she rode away through the fields; her lithe figure clad in a closely fitting jacket, erect as an arrow, her hair unconfined by her broad-brimmed, feather-decked sombrero, but falling free and flung to the breeze, and her right hand plying the whip at almost every leap of her fiery steed. The major seized a field glass and ascending to the chamber watched her course cross the great stretch of level country.

"Well, I'll be d——," he ejaculated, admiringly, "She's a born guerilla. If she doesn't reach Carthage ahead of my troopers, I'm a fool."

The major was right; when his detachment of cavalry galloped leisurely into Carthage that evening they were greeted by a slip of a girl mounted on a freshly groomed horse. She dropped a curtsy and asked:

"Looking for Captain Shirley? He isn't here — left half an hour ago — had business up Spring River. 'Spect he's in Lawrence county by this time."

Deputy Rascoe doubts the incident occurred. Maj. Edwin B. Eno (not Enos) of the Federal Eighth Missouri Militia, never mentioned the incident in his normally concise daily reports. Ed Shirley was no captain, and was killed by Federal troops on or about June 20, 1863. Chances are that John, Elizabeth and Myra Belle had sold out and headed for Texas to join Preston before Ed Shirley "bought the farm."

The remaining Shirleys relocated in Scyene, near modern-day Mesquite. It was here that 20-year-old Myra Belle

"Shed not for her the bitter tear, Nor give the heart to vain regret; Tis but the casket that lies here, The gem that filled it sparkles yet" is the flowery prose on her tombstone. Place of birth is probably incorrect. Oh well.

which she kept in the stables back of the hotel, hiring a Negro as her special hostler and groom. She dressed in black velvet, with low flowing skirts when she rode side-saddle, and wore white chiffon waists, a tight black jacket, high-topped boots and a man's Stetson hat turned up in front and decorated with an ostrich plume. The only peculiarity about this costume was that around her waist she wore a cartridge belt from which two revolvers were suspended in holsters. She attended the races, the circus and the county fair. She would enter bars and drink like a man or take her place at gaming tables for a try at her luck at dice, cards or roulette."

Rascoe further reports that Belle would occasionally stir the citizenry of Dallas by changing into a beaded and fringed buckskin outfit and ride at breakneck speed through the streets of the town, scattering everyone to the sidewalk.

After Jim Reed was killed, Belle took a series of lovers, progressively younger, including Jack Spaniard, Jim French, Sam Starr, John Middleton, Jim July, and Blue Duck. She always carried a torch for her first love, however, and named her eighty-acre bandit hideaway in Arkansas "Younger's Bend."

Myra Belle Shirley became Belle Starr after she married an Indian named Sam Starr and set up housekeeping at Younger's Bend. From 1880 to 1882, she masterminded many misdeeds perpetrated by outlaw bands involved with cattle rustling, horse stealing, bootleg whiskey, and robbery. She kept herself out of sight for the most part, and was run up on a few minor charges of larceny. She served her only time in the penitentiary in 1883, being convicted with husband Sam of horse stealing. Both received one-year sentences and served nine-month terms, but the trial attracted press attention and Belle's fame began.

Her attendance at a Fort Smith trial — her own for leading a band of horse thieves and a robbery while dressed as a man — drew attention of news reporters. After entering her plea, she shopped for new "babies" as she called them — pistols. "...she purchased a fine pair of .45-calibre revolvers, latest pattern, with black rubber handles and short barrel, for which she paid $29," reported the *Dallas News* on June 7, 1886. "She showed them to your correspondent, with the remark: 'Next to a fine horse I admire a fine pistol. Don't you think these are beauties?'"

On February 3, 1889, Belle Starr was killed when shot in the back with buckshot while returning to Younger's Bend. Many tried to pin the crime on a neighbor named Watson, for whom Belle had immense dislike. The reasoning was that Belle must have ridden close to her assassin, because she was shot at close range. She would have been wary of a stranger.

Of Belle's lovers, only Cole Younger died of natural causes. Jim Reed was shot by a deputy; John Middleton, with whom Belle was eloping, drowned; Blue Duck, killed by unknown assailant; Sam Starr, killed in shootout; Jack Spaniard, hanged for murder; Jim French, killed during a robbery; and Jim July, alias Jim Starr, killed resisting arrest.

Curiously, there's no record of Belle Starr shooting anyone. She was never charged with murder — but her reputation as a Bandit Queen suffered little for the discrepancy.

was courted, impregnated and abandoned by Cole Younger, who was on the lam with brothers Bob, Jim, and John. A year or two after Pearl Younger was born, Myra Belle either married or set up a common law partnership with a no-account outlaw named James H. Reed.

Before Jim Reed took a slug twixt nose and right eye resisting arrest in 1874, he and Belle made mischief with the James and Younger boys from California to Kentucky. Reed also eliminated a few sworn enemies for Cherokee friends, tortured and robbed a Creek Indian of $30,000 in gold and introduced stagecoach stickups to Texas.

With a portion of the misbegotten loot, Belle bought fancy clothes and lived high in Dallas. Rascoe says she "purchased a horse and buggy, a riding horse and a stud

There has been great conjecture as to what type of revolver the lady of dubious repute might have carried in her various misadventures. There is at least one writer who has suggested that she favored the Smith & Wesson Ladysmith, which was designed and produced as a self-defender for the ladies. However, this seems somewhat unlikely, since the Ladysmith did not go into production until after Belle Starr had been buried!

Indeed, there were a number of arms available to her, most left over from the War Between the States. In one known picture of Belle Starr sitting astride a horse, she is packing a revolver in a holster. Under a magnifying glass, the sixgun appears to be the Smith & Wesson No. 3 American with ivory grips.

She is seen in other photos to be packing a long-barreled revolver that does not resemble the S&W. Doubtless she went through many guns, but the only one of relatively certain origin exists in the collection of Carl W. Breihan, a Western author perhaps best noted for his researches and writings on Jesse James and Cole Younger.

The Belle Starr Colt single-action .45 carries serial number 85272. It sports a five-inch barrel that obviously has been cut down. The original nickel plating has been almost worn away, the ejector assembly is missing and the white bone grips are badly cracked. A star has been scratched into the right side of the frame. This gun is alleged to have been kept by friends upon Belle's demise.

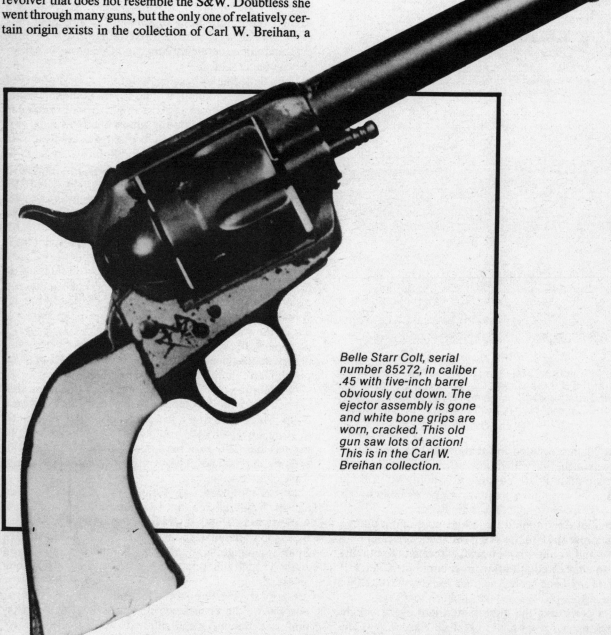

Belle Starr Colt, serial number 85272, in caliber .45 with five-inch barrel obviously cut down. The ejector assembly is gone and white bone grips are worn, cracked. This old gun saw lots of action! This is in the Carl W. Breihan collection.

REWARD
$10,000
IN GOLD COIN

Will be paid by the U.S. Government
for the apprehension

DEAD OR ALIVE
of

SAM and BELLE STARR

Wanted for Robbery, Murder, Treason
and other acts against the peace
and dignity of the U.S.

THOMAS CRAIL
Major, 8th Missouri Cavalry, Commanding

Confusion and disagreement between Western historians is shown in this reward poster. According to
Burton Rascoe, there never was a warrant out for Belle Starr charging her with murder. Who can say?

Chapter 6

THE COPY CATS

Today, They Are Called Replicas; Once They Were Patent Infringements!

One of the early designs aimed at circumventing existing patents was the pin fire self-contained cartridge in which a blow from the hammer drove the protruding pin down into the cup of fulminate to ignite the explosive. Device was used extensively in France, Belgium.

THERE IS an ancient tale concerning Christopher Columbus. Following his discovery of the New World, the adventurer was at the Spanish Court during a dinner, listening to his detractors who downgraded his voyages, claiming the discovery of America really had been quite simple.

Finally, Chris had had enough and quietly looked around the table, asking, "Can anyone here balance an egg on its small end?"

The others accepted the challenge and raw eggs were handed to each of those present. All tried to stand an egg on end to no avail. Finally, they looked at the explorer and demanded he try it. Chris picked up his egg, gently cracked one end to flatten it and stood it on the table, allowing the egg white and bits of yoke to run where they may.

"That's so simple," one of his detractors declared. "You made it easy!"

"Discovering the New World is easy, too, after I showed you how," Christopher Columbus is said to have agreed.

Moore front-loader teat fire was based upon patent of 1864 by one D. Williamson. It was circumvention of the Rollin White patent. The hammer struck a teat of fulminate on the end of cartridge to fire.

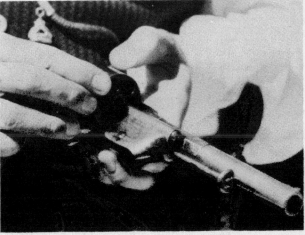

There were numerous means of installing cylinders and removing them, most of them meant to circumvent Colt's patents. (Below) Plant front-loading revolver was one of those aimed at the military market without any success.

There is little doubt that Samuel Colt must have experienced similar feelings. No sooner had he issued his first percussion revolver than others began infringing upon his patents.

Among the infringers, as indicated earlier, were Smith & Wesson. Through court action Colt was able to halt their production of near copies of his patents as well as the production of other companies. Still others managed to turn out percussion revolvers that were close or direct copies, but it may be that their production was so minor that Colt tended to feel that it would hardly be worth the trouble to haul them into court.

However, all had been waiting impatiently for the day when Sam Colt's patents became public domain. Some manufacturers already were tooled up, ready to flood the market with competitive handguns based upon his earlier designs. There were literally dozens of such makers, most of them concentrated in Connecticut, parts of New York

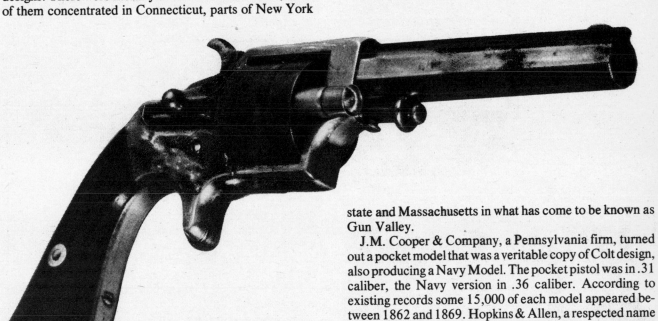

state and Massachusetts in what has come to be known as Gun Valley.

J.M. Cooper & Company, a Pennsylvania firm, turned out a pocket model that was a veritable copy of Colt design, also producing a Navy Model. The pocket pistol was in .31 caliber, the Navy version in .36 caliber. According to existing records some 15,000 of each model appeared between 1862 and 1869. Hopkins & Allen, a respected name of the era, turned out what they called the Dictator model in .36 caliber during ten years of the 1860-1870 period.

Considered a crime by collectors, these Rogers & Spencer percussion models have been reworked with modern accessories in an effort to improve potential accuracy.

But the most obvious plagiarizer of design was the Metropolitan Arms Company of New York City. Between 1864 and 1866 this firm turned out more than 6000 Navy Models that were an absolute copy of the Colt Model 1851.

The same manufacturer produced another Navy model in the last days of the Civil War that was a direct copy of the Colt Model 1861. Fewer than fifty of these guns are believed to have been made, however. Both of the models loaded six rounds and the cylinders of both were roll engraved with the same scene from the Battle of New Orleans. During the same period, Metropolitan produced a Police Model that was a carbon from specs for the Colt Model 1862. Some 2750 of these were turned out. The Colt products, in each case, were better made and better advertised, so the company eventually found itself unable to compete, as happened with many others.

Eli Whitney was one of Colt's early backers, but when their partnership dissolved Whitney continued to produce revolvers. About 1000 units of the Protection pocket model are known to have been produced; although the identity of the maker is somewhat vague, some reason that these were made by Whitney, closely following the Colt patents which expired virtually on the evening that the Protection model appeared in 1857.

Based upon Civil War needs, Rogers and Spencer also turned out an Army model that held a more than vague similarity to Colt patterns. Some 5800 of these single-action percussion revolvers were made under contract, but were delivered too late for use on the battlefields. Francis

The Navy Colt influence is obviously apparent in this model made during the Civil War era by H.E. Dimick of Mississippi.

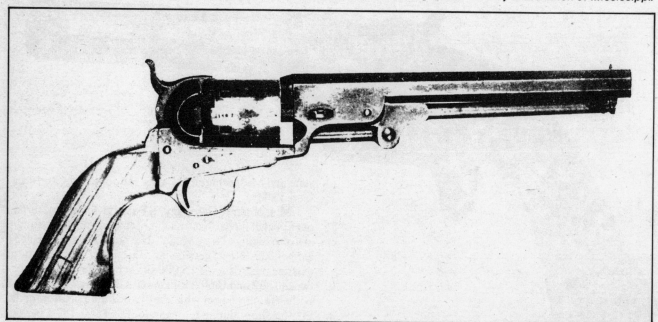

Bannerman, the first war surplus dealer, took control of the entire lot in 1901, selling them from his castle on the Hudson.

While they bear little outward resemblance to Colt products of the era, Springfield Arms Company of Massachusetts turned out a series of .40 caliber six-shot Dragoon models in 1851; only a hundred-plus were made before Colt attorneys brought a halt to production. The same maker made several hundred Navy revolvers, as well as other variations on their original design; these too were caught in the cease-and-desist order from the courts.

The list is virtually endless, including such names — known and forgotten — as Starr Arms, Aaron Vaughn, James Warner, Edwin Wesson and Manhattan Arms.

With the advent of the self-contained cartridge, Colt found other competitors as did Smith & Wesson, which had been the first on line with a cartridge revolver.

One of the first into this particular arena of competition was Marlin, which began handgun production with a series of Derringers during the Civil War, then graduated to the Little Joker pocket model. About five hundred of these were made in .22 rimfire between 1871 and 1873. The Marlin single-actions were improved with a new model almost annually until 1887, when the firm introduced its first double-action. This gun was made until 1899, when the firm withdrew from the handgun business.

Remington had made its early name with longarms, but was another that had been waiting on the sidelines for Sam Colt's original patents to expire. In 1857 Philo Remington, a descendent of the founder, was ready with the First Model Remington-Beals pocket revolver, making about 4000 of them in two years of production. Later came second and third models before the Remington-Rider dou-

The progression of gun development based upon the Colt patents is illustrated with Colt Third Model Dragoon (bottom) Remington single-action percussion (center) and Austin T. Freeman Army Model made in 1863-64 era. Of the last gun mentioned, only 2000 were manufactured.

ble-action pocket revolver was introduced in 1860. It was built until 1873, with factory conversions to cartridge loads being made in the final years of production.

During the Civil War years Remington went through a host of revolvers designed for Army and Navy use, reaching its percussion era peak with the Remington New Model Army revolver, which was made from 1863 to 1875. Popularity of this model is reflected in the fact that this .44 six-shooter sold some 140,000 units!

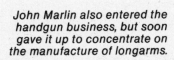

John Marlin also entered the handgun business, but soon gave it up to concentrate on the manufacture of longarms.

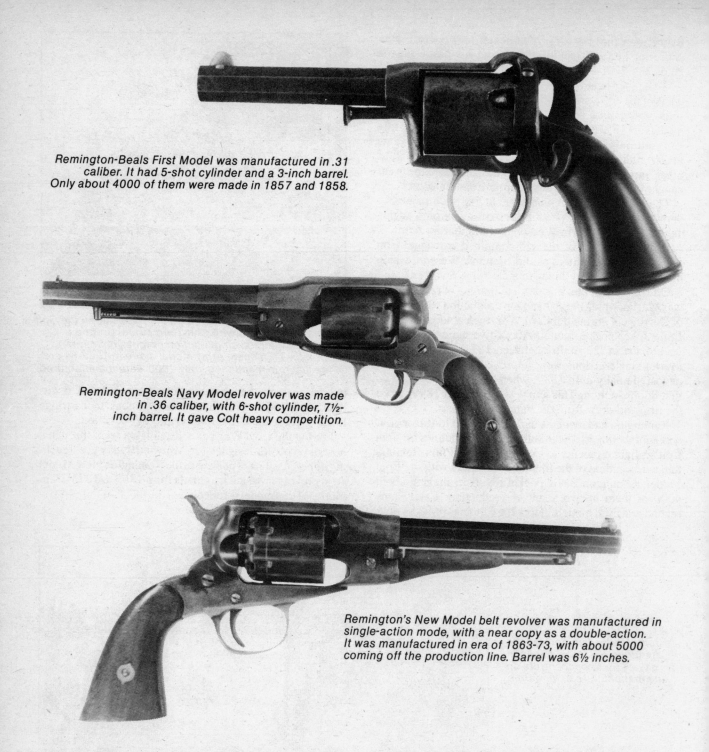

Remington-Beals First Model was manufactured in .31 caliber. It had 5-shot cylinder and a 3-inch barrel. Only about 4000 of them were made in 1857 and 1858.

Remington-Beals Navy Model revolver was made in .36 caliber, with 6-shot cylinder, 7½-inch barrel. It gave Colt heavy competition.

Remington's New Model belt revolver was manufactured in single-action mode, with a near copy as a double-action. It was manufactured in era of 1863-73, with about 5000 coming off the production line. Barrel was 6½ inches.

At about the time that S&W was introducing cartridge arms and Colt was starting to utilize the Richards conversion, the folks in Ilion were producing the Remington-Smoot revolver, which went through four different models. There were lesser offerings from the company such as the Remington Iroquois pocket pistol, with 10,000 marketed in 1878-1888 in .22 rimfire.

Remington's ultimate in the single-action cartridge revolver is considered to be the 1875 Single Action Army model. Originally made in .44 Remington center-fire, it also was produced in .45 Government and .44-40 calibers. The last single-action produced by the boys from Ilion was the 1890 Single Action Army, which bore a startling resem-

blance to the Colt SAA. Only 2000 were made, all in .44-40; it would appear that buyers decided they might as well have a Colt as a look-alike. Remington produced several single-shot pistols, all based upon the rolling block action, as late as 1901 before banishing handguns from the line until the introduction two decades ago of the XP-100.

Frank Wesson, the younger brother of Daniel Wesson, also entered the handgun field, starting with single-shot arms before joining with Gilbert Harrington to form Wesson & Harrington, the forerunner of today's Harrington & Richardson. The first offerings from this firm were .22 rimfire guns which were made between 1871 and 1879. A .32 version was manufactured from 1874 to 1879. Soon after

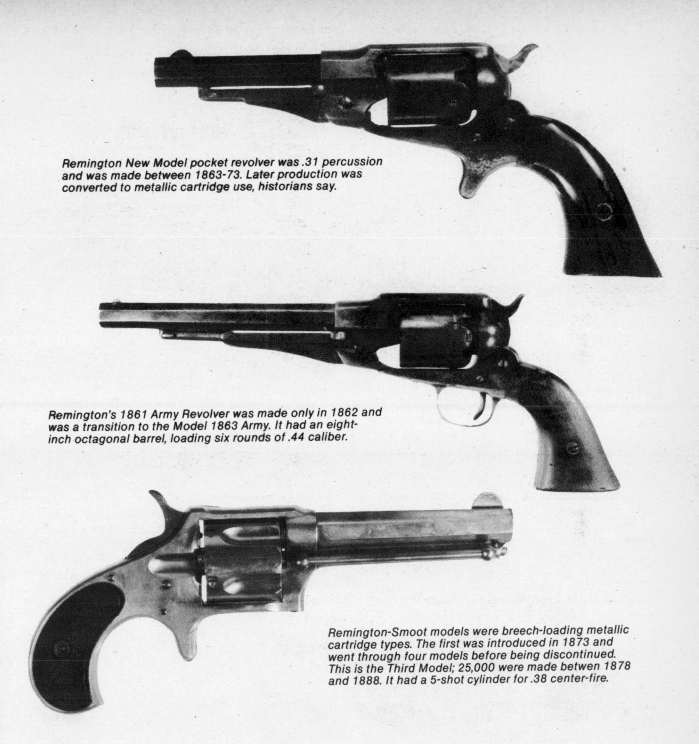

Remington New Model pocket revolver was .31 percussion and was made between 1863-73. Later production was converted to metallic cartridge use, historians say.

Remington's 1861 Army Revolver was made only in 1862 and was a transition to the Model 1863 Army. It had an eight-inch octagonal barrel, loading six rounds of .44 caliber.

Remington-Smoot models were breech-loading metallic cartridge types. The first was introduced in 1873 and went through four models before being discontinued. This is the Third Model; 25,000 were made betwen 1878 and 1888. It had a 5-shot cylinder for .38 center-fire.

the firm became known as Harrington and Richardson, the trend was in favor of double-action handguns and this is what the firm has pursued for the most part to the present day. It must be said of Frank Wesson that his designs may have been based upon the Colt principle, but the designs were truly his own.

Another firm that attempted to take advantage of Civil War Arms needs was the Bacon Manufacturing Company of Norwich, Connecticut. This maker came up with a Navy Model .36 caliber in the early years of the war; only a few hundred were made, since the Navy showed little interest. Baker's next offering, a revolver featuring a swing-out cylinder, was made immediately after the Civil War. It

apparently was before its time; only a few hundred were made.

Still seeking a design that would mean success, the firm produced several pocket models in the 1860s that had definite Colt line, but none did well in the marketplace. Only a few were made. The later versions were cartridge models for the .32 rimfire.

When one looks at the records of gun manufacturing in the last half of the Nineteenth Century, dozens of names rise to the historical surface and disappear into the well of bankruptcy. Most of those products were based upon older Colt or Smith & Wesson patents. The Connecticut Arms Company, for example, made a pocket revolver in the mid-

The Remington Model 1875 Army model was manufactured 1875-89, with some 25,000 produced. Nickel-plated versions were used by the Indian police on nation's reservations. It was made in .44-40, .45 Government.

Some 10,000 Remington Iroquois pocket pistols were made in the ten years following its introduction in 1878. Cylinder held seven .22 rimfire rounds.

Sixties that front-loaded a .28 cup-primed cartridge in each of its six chambers. The design was an attempt to circumvent the Rollin White patents being used by Smith & Wesson. The Cummings & Wheeler pocket revolver, manufactured from 1870 to 1880 in .22 rimfire with a seven-shot cylinder, was a virtual steal on the S&W Third Model revolver.

Forehand and Wadsworth was a company to be reckoned with following the Civil War. Starting with a line of single-shot Derringers, a few years later they came up with a single-action Army revolver. At first glance it appears to be a cross between the S&W Model 3 and the Remington percussion Army model. It was made in .44 Russian caliber and allegedly was issued to the California militia, although there was no major military buy. Undaunted, the Massachusetts firm announced what is called the F&W

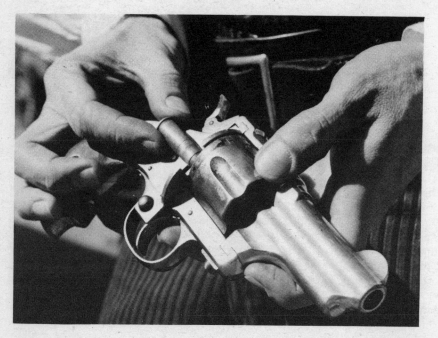

Merwin Hulbert Pocket Army model was sold by this firm, but manufactured for the sales company under contract at the factory of Hopkins and Allen.

The so-called "baby" Merwin Hulbert pocket pistol was made in 1880 for .32 and .38 center-fire cartridges. It is compared for size with Colt SAA and .44 S&W American. Only a few of these guns were made and are valued today.

New Model Army revolver. Only a few hundred were made into the 1880s in .44 Russian center-fire. The lines tend to resemble early Remington revolvers.

Merwin Hulbert & Company is a name frequently seen in handgun collections, but this firm was not a manufacturer. Instead, they served strictly as a marketer operating out of New York City; the guns they sold were produced by Hopkins & Allen. They marketed a line of what they called Army revolvers in .44-40 and .44 M&H center-fire calibers. These guns were made primarily in the Eighties, aiming at a government contract without success. There were numerous design changes in an effort to interest the Army, including a double-action. The guns were made between 1876 and 1880 and bore a startling resemblance to the Smith & Wesson Model 3. Knowing a good thing, in the late Eighties they came up with a .22 revolver that is a virtual screw-by-screw, spring-by-spring copy of the Smith & Wesson First Model, Third Issue.

Although literally thousands of Colt revolvers were used by the Confederacy during the Civil War, there still was a military market among the Rebels, who were short of armament. Thus the war spawned gun factories throughout the South, most making copies of Colt revolvers for sale to Jeff Davis' undersupplied forces. The guns were created primarily by hand with only a few hundred being made by each manufacturer.

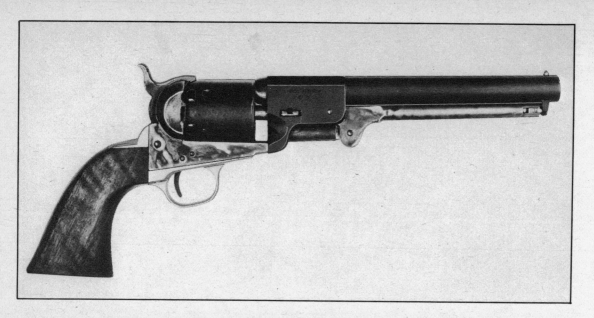

Literally a copy of a copy is Navy Arms replica of Model 1863 Leech & Rigdon Confederate percussion. (Below) Dixie Gun Works was another to enter the replica field with copy of 1860 Colt Army model. In the early days of replica manufacture, most of the guns were manufactured in Italian gun works.

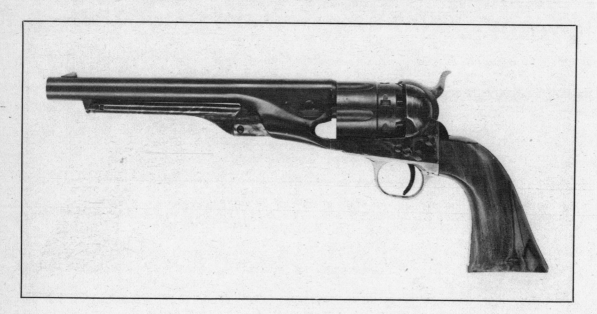

The August Machine Works in Georgia turned out about a hundred revolvers copied directly from the Colt 1851 Navy model. Like the original, it was in .36 caliber with a six-shot cylinder.

Another Georgia firm, Columbus Fire Arms, also copied the Colt 1851 Navy to turn out about a hundred .36 revolvers for the Confederacy between 1863 and the end of the war. Griswold and Gunnison, also of Georgia, copied the same Colt design, making about 3700 revolvers between 1862 and 1864. Oddly enough, Samuel Griswold, a partner in the firm, had learned the gunmaking business in his home state of Connecticut before moving to Georgia and adopting Rebel ways.

Other Confederate firms that reproduced the 1851 Navy Colt were Leech and Rigdon of Mississippi, Rigdon,

Ansley and Company of Georgia, and Schneider and Glassick of Tennessee.

The Virginia firm of Thomas W. Cofer designed a revolver based upon the Whitney Navy model. It was in .36 caliber with a six-round cylinder. Spiller and Burr of Atlanta turned out a .36 revolver copied from the Whitney Navy model also, while Tucker, Sherrard & Company of Lancaster, Texas, produced Dragoon and Navy models based upon Colt patents. All were in .44 caliber.

The Dance Brothers of Columbia, Texas, turned out a percussion Dragoon in both .36 and .44 caliber for the Confederacy. While these Colt copies have elicited a great deal of interest from collectors, the makers were not that prolific. Fewer than five hundred guns were made in the four years of the war in spite of the fact that the governor of

Another replica that has been manufactured in recent years is the Rogers & Spencer .44. The original was based on expired Colt patents. (Below) A number of marketers of replicas made copies of various Remington percussions.

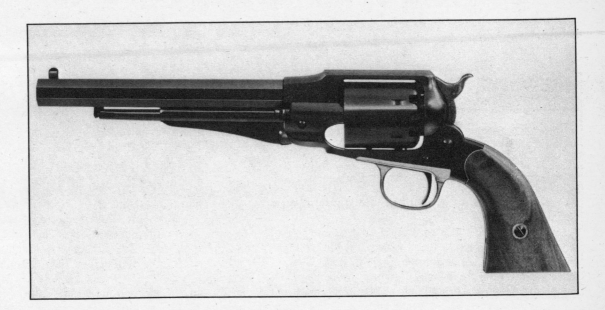

Texas exempted Dance employees from military service.

In the decade-plus between the turn of the century and the start of World War I, the firearms companies sorted themselves out. Many went bankrupt or merged. Most that survived settled on patents that allowed them a specific niche in the firearms market. When the Kaiser decided he wanted to own Europe, the major firms became involved in war production. When the war ended, it was back to business as usual, until World War II, when history repeated itself and four years of military production resulted in a lot of war surplus.

In the post-WWII period there still were many single-action handguns about, but they rapidly were becoming collector items. A young veteran named Val Forgett, who had learned arms and demolitions courtesy of the United States Army, became a name in the antique arms business when he contracted to dismantle Bannerman's Island in the Hudson River. His reward was the hordes of old weaponry stored in the ancient structure that had disintegrated to the status of a veritable bomb.

Forgett founded Navy Arms Company on the arms obtained from the Bannerman estate. He was selling Civil War relics, while other war surplus dealers were peddling the remnants of World War II.

But even then Forgett and a few others such as Turner Kirkland of the Dixie Gun Works in Tennessee were looking ahead. Both realized the supply of antique weapons would not long supply the market that suddenly found a growth in black powder shooters. Entering the field in the

Nacy Arms reproduced a replica of 3d Model Dragoon with a so-caled Buntline barrel, although lengths were made long before Ned Buntline made claim. Detachable stock and carrying holster also were available as part of the set.

same era was Early and Modern Firearms, a West Coast outfit.

Forgett and Kirkland apparently tread the same ground to learn they could have exact copies of the old Colt percussion models made at a proper price in Italy. Most of these guns were made in Italian factories in the begining, not only for these two firms, but for EMF, Centennial and a host of other who sought to take advantage of what, in reality, was a new business: the replica.

The quality was good, the price right and things went along charmingly. Forgett, for example, produced an entire line of replica arms from the last century, most of them from Colt patterns, but he also branched off into replicas of several Colt-inspired Confederate-made revolvers, recreating them in exacting detail. Thus, he made copies of copies.

There was some fear in the early days of replica manufacture that these look-alike reproductions could be reworked by less scrupulous gunsmiths and sold as originals. Forgett felt — and still contends — this was not likely, with

Navy Arms introduced this replica of 1875 Remington Army in .45 Long Colt, .44-40 and .357 magnum. It was available in nickel plate.

the differences in steels and manufacturing techniques. Such shenanigans may have taken place, but certainly not among knowledgeable gun collectors.

This reproduction of black powder arms was going well, when others beside Bill Ruger began to take note of this nation's nostalgic affair with the Colt SAA. It was not long before replicas of the old Model 1873 Colt Army began to dribble in from the factories in Italy as well. There also were lesser versions in .22 caliber. One which I owned in the early Sixties was a mail-order item prior to the changes in the law. For about sixty bucks you could order it with engraving. It was pretty to look at, but it didn't shoot worth a damn. In fact, the one for which I plunked down those sixty 1962 dollars — when those bucks still bought groceries and gas in wholesale quantities — had to be totally reworked by a gunsmith before the cylinder would align properly and not shear off lead at the cylinder to sprinkle shooters on each side of me on the firing line. This little

gem, of course, didn't stay long in the marketplace.

Colt had discontinued the Colt SAA with the advent of World War II and the single-action revolver seemingly had come to be considered a dinasour as far as other major firearms companies were concerned. From the turn of the century, Harrington & Richardson, for example, had made only one model, the Model 199, which was introduced in 1933 and dropped in 1951. High Standard, with a growing line of revolvers, carried no SA at all.

Yet this was the infancy of network television and the film cowboys were riding high, first in old films, then in the new half-hour series made specifically for the home screen. William Boyd made a whole new career with reruns of Hopalong Cassidy. The B Western had become a thing of the past in movie theaters, but was in multiple reruns on the home screens. Most of those white-hatted heroes carried single-action revolvers.

A California firm known as Great Western Arms —

Great Western Arms, no longer in existence, reproduced the Colt SAA in minute detail in the Fifties. It was a favorite with Hollywood film studios, who wanted to use single-actions without paying full collector price.

Iver Johnson had various configurations of Colt SAA made in Europe for several years, importing them on the basis of the continuing popularity of the model.

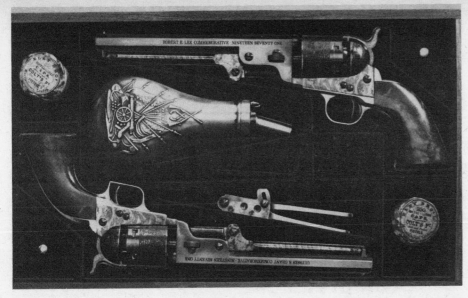

During the 1970s, Colt returned to black powder percussion making, but contended their production was not a replica, but simply a continuation of original Colts.

since absorbed by Early & Modern Firearms — saw a need for an American-made copy of the Colt SAA. They began turning them out in a San Fernando Valley plant. Many were purchased by the studios, which didn't want to plunk down the collector price money for an authentic Colt. Bill Ruger also had come upon the scene with his first .22 rimfire single-actions which would soon grow bigger in caliber as well as fame.

Val Forgett, through his Navy Arms, introduced an Italian-made copy of the Remington Model 1875 cartridge gun. In addition to .45 Colt, this one was chambered for .44-40 and .357 magnum. Introduced in 1955, production continues to this day. In the 1970s Forgett took a look at some of the Colt cartridge models and settled on a Navy Arms replica of the long-barreled Buntline, featuring a 16½-inch barrel. This was chambered for .357 magnum and .45 Colt. Shorter-barreled models of what he called the Navy Arms Frontier also were available in calibers ranging from .22 LR through .22 magnum, .357 magnum and .45 Colt.

A young man named George Hawes also had been smitten with the popularity being accorded the single-action Colt Army as a result of television exposure. A former Marine pilot, with a flair for salesmanship, he arranged for Sauer & Sohn of West Germany to turn out a line of Colt copies. The first of these was the Hawes Western Marshal, introduced in 1968. It proved so successful that there soon was a line of other Marshals from Montana, Texas, Silver City, ad infinitum. In all, there were eleven variations of the same gun. Each was slightly different than the others by the addition or subtraction of some feature. The Montana Marshal, for example, was the same as the Western Marshal, except for a brass grip frame; the Texas Marshal differed only in its pearlite grips and nickel finish.

By 1980, however, the entire line had been dropped and the Hawes firm disappeared from the major sporting goods scene.

Interarms contracted with Hammerli to manufacture the Virginian model in the maker's European plants between 1973 and 1976. The only difference between it and the basic Colt SAA is that the Hammerli version boasted a base pin safety feature. However, when Interarms opened its own factory in the Virginia hinterlands in the late Seventies, they began making this model themselves, calling it the Virginia Dragoon. It is, of course, still in production.

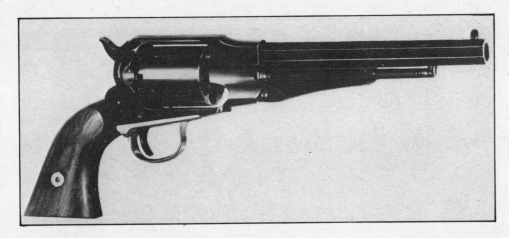

Lyman also foresaw sales in black powder market and reproduced a version of Remington percussion.

A BIT ON A KIT

You Can Legally Build Your Own Replica Of The Single Action Army With This Package

Chapter 7

JACK MITCHELL's question after examining EMF's Single Action Revolver Kit known as the *California* was "Why?" He admits, however, the more he thought about it the more sense it made. The California, a Colt SAA look-alike, is a quality-made steel six-shooter with brass backstrap and trigger guard chambered for the venerable .45 Colt cartridge.

Customizing the EMF California is an intelligent and practical alternative to doing the same work to a Colt. First, the price tag on the 5½-inch-barreled California is a couple hundred dollars cheaper than a new or even used Colt. It retails at this writing for about $200.

Doing a custom job on a vintage Colt also destroys the collector value, which can be a considerable chunk of change these days. Building the EMF version of the single-action revolver allows the buyer the luxury of finishing it to his own tastes — and abilities — and actually increasing its value over the original purchase price.

The California Single Action Kit built by Mitchell arrived with a 7½-inch barrel. This was a sample from the factory. At the present time, The California Kit is available with 5½-inch barrel only.

The brochure from EMF pertaining to the California Model states, *All machine operations have been performed and only de-burring, fitting, polishing and bluing remain to be done. Fit the action to suit your taste, and*

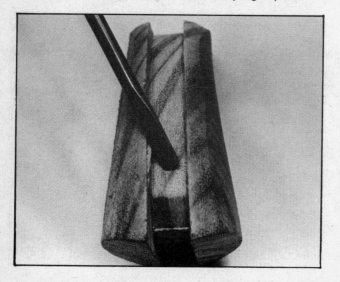

The brass back strap must be fitted to the grips before it can be mated to the frame of the gun. Inletting black is applied to the back strap to locate any high spots.

Seating the back strap deeply into the grip slot reduces later need to grind down brass for perfect fit. High spots are removed with a file of diameter to match slot.

polish and blue it in the manner you consider most attractive. With patience and care you can produce a smooth-shooting gun, hand fitted to precision accuracy and superior in many respects to production-line models.

"After completing the work on this gun I'd agree with the folks from EMF, but I'm a gunsmith. I assume EMF aimed those words more to the professional than the amateur," Mitchell says.

There are literally hundreds of kit guns available on today's market. Some are quite simple, even for the less than mechanically proficient. There also are a few kits that would tax the patience and skill of the top-notch professional gunsmith. The California would be best left to the

pro, but it is still a good buy for the amateur gun tinkerer.

A fellow wanting a custom single-action revolver could have his favorite gunsmith buy the California for him. He then could have the gunsmith polish and blue the gun to a custom finish, smooth up critical internal parts, shape, fit, and finish the grips to individual specs for under $200 in labor. The owner now would own a functional and attractive custom revolver for less money than it would have taken to buy the least expensive used Colt Single Action floating around the gun show circuits commonly called in the trade, "a beater." And attempting to restore abused or

To ensure brass back strap is seated fully in the slot a rawhide hammer is used. It prevents scratching of brass.

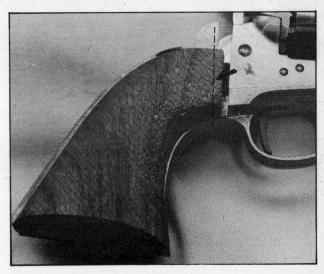

With trigger guard attached to frame, the next step is to fit the back strap to the frame and to front strap. Arrow indicates excess wood to be removed for mating.

Use of inletting black on the frame, along with patience to remove high spots on front of the grips with small files, garnet paper should insure tight mating between the two gun elements.

Arrow indicates slight gap between left grip and frame. Gap may be filled by mixing sawdust from grips with five-minute epoxy to build up low spot, remate to the frame. (Right) With back strap attached to frame, front strap is mated to grips by draw filing to achieve proper fit.

Excess wood (indicated by arrows) must be filed, sanded to mate with front strap, base of back strap with units attached to the frame. (Right) Cast brass trigger guard comes from EMF in an unpolished condition. Combination of much elbow grease and special tools are a necessity to finish this brass to a mirror finish.

neglected single-action revolvers can get highly expensive.

Purchasing this particular kit gun and having a qualified gunsmith build it is not only a less expensive alternative to buying the more expensive used or new Colt, it should function as reliably and perhaps be finished better than a factory gun.

"That may sound like heresy, but let me explain," says Mitchell. "The qualified private gunsmith can spend more time tuning, timing and customizing a firearm than the factory worker. He can build the grips to fit the owner and add any type of desired finish, inlays with initials, checkering or other personalized touches. It's an excellent opportunity to have a custom shooter at great savings."

However, an amateur can build this kit, if successful kit-building means getting it to function. Necessary tuning and timing already has been done at the factory. Removing enough wood from the front of the grips will allow the kit-builder to screw the parts together and have a working firearm.

"But a file or stone in the hands of an inexperienced person will almost assuredly result in major problems if he attempts to work on the sear, trigger, hammer, hand or bolt," Mitchell cautions. "Removal of too much metal will result in the gun being out of time which can make it inoperable and even dangerous."

EMF's instructions to *polish and blue it in the manner you consider most attractive* is much easier said than done

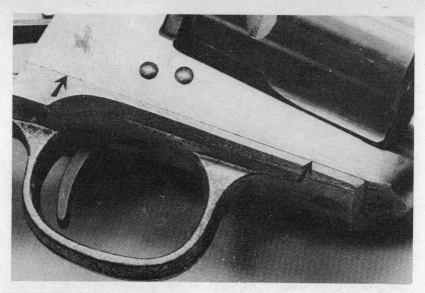

Trigger guard should be attached to frame to properly shape, mate both into a single pleasing line. Use of 180-grit wet-and-dry paper with flat wood backing handles the soft brass adequately, the author found.

Variable-speed Dremel tool with its sanding drum is excellent to remove casting lines and for rough shaping. Caution must be exercised to prevent the removal of too much of the metal.

Round India stones (below), and abrasive cords from E.C. Mitchell Co., are an aid in polishing, shaping small rounded areas such as trigger guard, adjoining corners.

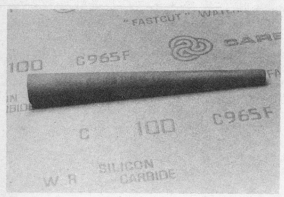

Shaping, polishing contours of frame housing, barrel and around the cylinder base pin latch hole are facilitated with Dremel tool and sanding disc. (Right) Area where the frame mates with the loading gate is rough at delivery.

for most amateurs. Single-action-style revolvers have few flat spots that allow the polisher to use wet-and-dry paper with a wood block to prevent ripples in the metal. Polishing with progressively finer grits of paper in an area like the flutes in the cylinder will only highlight machine marks from the factory. Eliminating these marks before sanding using various Cratex bobs attached to a Dremel tool or rotary die grinder should be a first step. The region in front of the cylinder on the frame that houses the barrel and around the base pin must be polished using wet-and-dry paper wrapped around a wood dowel. With such tools a great deal of care and patience is required to remove scratches and pits without altering the classic single-action contours. When polishing the flat lower portion of the frame the screws should be in place to prevent "running" the screwholes. The brass trigger guard also should be attached to mate the guard to the frame.

Polishing is accomplished more easily with polishing and buffing wheels than exclusively by hand. The wheels used for the polishing of steel parts should never be used to polish brass and vice versa. Brass particles get caught in the polishing compound (called loading up) and will cause scratches in the steel from which you are trying to eliminate scratches. Hence, two sets of wheels should be available.

While shaping the brass trigger guard, back strap and

Polishing the loading gate area is not necessary for proper function, but does add custom touch to gun.

The Cratex polishing bob, available through industrial supply outlets, is excellent for the removal of machine marks in cylinder flutes and on sighting plane of the frame.

A rough spot on the cylinder and in the cylinder flute was removed with the use of a Cratex polishing bob.

The sighting plane of the frame also needed cleaning up and the same bob was used to accomplish this neatly.

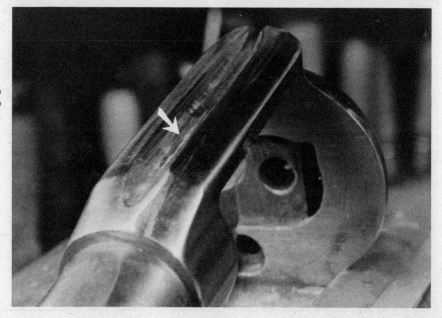

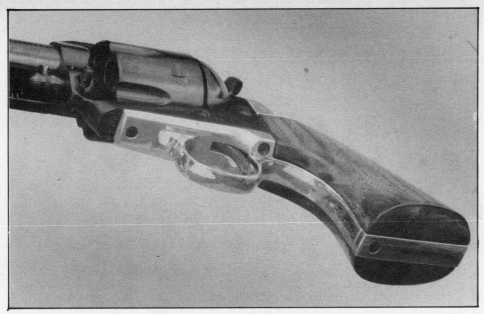

Trigger guard has been brought to custom finish using wet/dry paper in various grits, then buffed on a 600-grit wheel.

wooden grips, the gun should be assembled. The first step is to fit the grips to the frame. Removal of wood from the front of the grips is necessary before the back strap can be screwed to the frame. Next the grips are shaped to individual tastes and brass back strap and front strap are mated to the grips by filing and then polishing.

After all polishing is completed and the desired finish on metal parts obtained (ranging from 240 grit to 600 mirror finish) it is time to blue the steel parts, springs excluded, of course. If the amateur wants just a blue or black gun with no further regard for appearance, he can cold blue it with any of the products available on the market. However, cold blue is primarily used by the trade to touch up spots and to blue screws and other small parts, It is not as durable as hot bluing and certainly not as attractive. However, it will help prevent rusting to a certain degree.

"If an amateur does build this gun and takes the time and effort to do a good polishing job I would highly recommend he then take it to a professional and let him hot blue the firearm. This service — if all polishing is complete — should be less than $25. Such a finish is considerably more durable and much more attractive,"Mitchell says.

The EMF California Single Action Revolver is the first smokeless powder kit gun we've seen since the Great Western of two decades ago. If you are an amateur gun enthusiast and want to put in some time and effort, it is an excellent opportunity to own one of the classic style firearms chambered to the excellent .45 Colt cartridge. If you've always hankered to own and shoot a custom single-action, the price of the EMF California and the cost of customization by a professional afford one to do so at a fraction of the normal price. For more information write EMF, Incorporated, 1900 E. Warner Avenue, Suite One-D, Santa Ana, CA 92705.

Care, patience and experience can produce an EMF revolver of fully custom quality, but the author feels such final work is not for talents of amateur.

Chapter 8

RELOADING FOR SINGLE-ACTIONS

At First Glance, Almost Anything Will Fire In The Old Hawgleg, But Use A Bit Of Care!

Several of the larger cartridges for which single-action revolvers have been chambered: (1) .38 S&W, (2) .38 Short Colt, (3) .38 Special, (4) .357 magnum, (5) .41 Long Colt case only, (6) .41 magnum, (7) .38-40 WCF, (8) .44 S&W Russian, (9) .44 Special, (10) .44-40 WCF, (11) .44 magnum, (12) .45 ACP, (13) .45 Colt, (14) .445 Eley. The 9mm Parabellum/Luger is not shown here. The .455 Eley case seldom occurs Boxer-primed; no data listed.

IF YOU ENJOY shooting your single-action revolver you can do a lot more of it by reloading the empty cases. That assumes you're working with center-fire cartridge calibers rather than rimfire numbers since the latter cannot be reloaded. It helps immensely if the spent cartridge cases you plan to reload are of the Boxer-primed type rather than Berdan-primed. It is possible to reload the latter, but vast amounts of complexity and difficulty are involved.

When it comes to Boxer-primed center-fire cartridges reloading is a pleasantly easy and simple operation, widely practiced by a great many people. That is a development of comparatively recent times. Thirty years ago reloading was a mystic art performed by the dedicated few. Today reloaders turn out more rounds of ammunition per year than all of the major ammo makers combined.

Let's pause briefly for a few definitions for the sake of avoiding confusion. A *cartridge* is the complete round of ammunition, ready to be put in the gun and fired. A *bullet* is the projectile that starts out in the front end of the cartridge and goes zipping out the muzzle when the cartridge is fired. A *case* is the rear portion of the cartridge, also the item that remains in the chamber after firing. A great many people persist in referring to cartridges as bullets, thereby generating lots of confusion.

A rimfire cartridge carries its priming compound in the hollow outer rim of the case so that the off-center firing pin of such guns crushes the rim against the edge of the chamber to set off the priming compound and ignite the powder.

A center-fire cartridge is readily identified by the presence of a primer in the center of the case head, likewise

From left, .32 S&W, .32 S&W Long, .32 Long Colt, and .30 GI carbine. Note the .32 LC is a bit smaller in diameter than the two S&W numbers. The .32 Short Colt isn't shown.

Approximate operator's-eye view of a typical reloading bench set up with Pacific's OO-7 loading press and items for reloading the .44 mag' with equipment clamped down.

Unless tungsten carbide resizing die is used, cases must be lubed before sizing. Here lube has been applied to an uninked stamp pad and cases are laid out to be lubed.

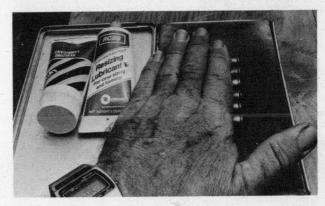

As in photo at top of page, the cases are rolled back and forth a few times with the palm of the hand to coat sides lightly with lube, which must be removed after resizing.

This illustrates the essential differences between the rimfire case (top), Boxer (left) and Berdan priming systems. Note the single central flash hole of the Boxer case and twin off-center holes of the Berdan case. Text discusses the significances of the difference.

illustrated. In the Boxer priming system, each primer is a hollow cup with its own anvil and the wafer of priming compound is located between the tip of the anvil and the inner surface of the primer cup.

The Berdan primer differs in that the anvil is an integral part of the head of the cartridge case and the primer consists solely of the cup and wafer of priming compound. Berdan-primed cases are easily identified after firing by the fact that you can see two small holes in the case head when you look into the case mouth. A Boxer-primed case after firing will show a slightly larger single hole in the center. Reloading Boxer cases is greatly simplified by the fact that a single decapping pin goes into that flash hole to expel the fired primer for convenient replacement. The difficulty of a comparable approach for the Berdan lies in aligning

Absence of ejector housing usually indicates a SA Colt for black powder only. This happened to one when it fired a smokeless powder load. If in doubt, check with a good gunsmith!

Hogdon #23 Manual, above, and Hornady Handbook #3, left, are but two of many excellent sources of data for reloading the more popular of the modern cartridges.

two decapping pins with the two off-center holes in the case head. Berdan primers can be removed by a sharp pronged tool operating on the edge of the spent primer from the outside. Once removed a special primer is needed for repriming, as well as a priming punch to fit it, and both are difficult to obtain. For that reason the remainder of the discussion will be concerned with reloading Boxer-type center-fire cartridge cases.

The usual reloading procedure involves a reloading press, a set of reloading dies for the intended cartridge caliber, a

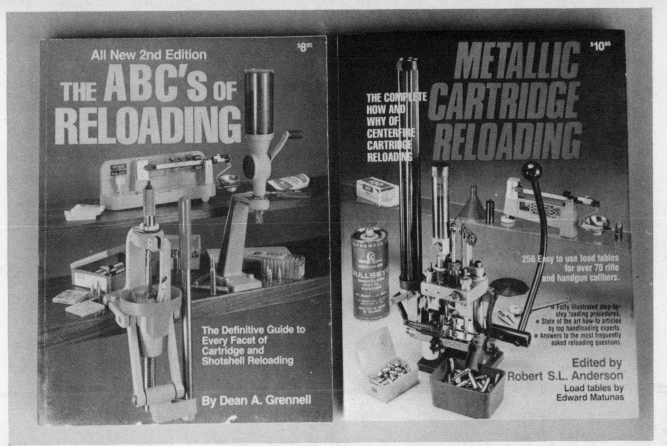

Available from DBI Books, publishers of this book, are several other titles pertaining to reloading cartridges. They carry information to considerably greater details than space permits in the book at hand. In the discussion here, effort has been made to supply suggested loads for several of the obsolete cartridges no longer covered in any or all of the other contemporary data sources by reason of the fact that such cartridges are seldom reloaded.

shell holder to fit it and one of two sizes of priming punch, plus the necessary reloading components and some suitable device for dispensing the powder in uniform and correct quantities.

The components consists of empty cases, primers, powder and bullets. It is possible to buy empty cases in the popular calibers from the more well stocked gun stores if you do not have an adequate supply left from firing factory loads. Some of the older cartridge calibers have been discontinued by the commercial ammomakers because of sagging sales. Obtaining a supply of cases for the .41 Long Colt, .44 S&W Russian and similar obsolete numbers may prove difficult. It is possible to make up some of these cases by trimming or modifying cases still readily available. For example, the .44 S&W Russian can be produced by trimming a .44 Special or .44 magnum case to a length of .950-inch as measured from head to case mouth.

That brings up a further consideration however. Most if not all of the original .44 S&WR cases had the balloon head configuration rather than the modern solid or web head, as illustrated. The balloon head was weaker, but it gave a case with somewhat greater capaity. When reloading such a case, published charge weights should be reduced by at least ten percent if the cases are produced by trimming web-head cases such as the .44 magnum. The two head types are easily recognizable by looking into the neck of an empty to see if it has the raised area around the central flash hole that distinguishes the balloon head type, as illustrated here.

Primers come in two types and two diameters for a basic choice of four possibilities. There are rifle primers and pistol primers and both are to be had in small (.175-inch) and large (.210-inch). Thus we have small pistol, small rifle, large pistol and large rifle. Some makers of primers also offer the four just listed in a further choice of standard or magnum, thereby opening the choice to eight more or less different primers.

Rifle primers have thicker primer cups and slightly greater amounts of priming compound; they should not be used in making up reloads for single-action revolvers because the handgun might not be able to set the primer off reliably and because the hotter priming charge would be quite apt to result in higher, probably dangerous peak pressures.

As for the magnum primers, they are used for the magnum cartridges such as .357, .41 and .44 when using those powders that are more difficult to ignite, specifically the W-W Ball powders and the Hodgdon Spherical ones. Thus we'll be using the standard small pistol or large pistol primers for the loads discussed here with the few exceptions noted by an asterisk (*) following the charge weight to denote a magnum primer.

There are some of the older single-action revolvers that are not safe to fire with cartridges loaded with smokeless powder due to the substantially higher pressures developed by the modern powder. If you have any reason to won-

While it is certainly true that extreme care and caution must be employed in making up and firing reloads in old guns — many dubious in condition, design and/or workmanship — the same applies to the use of old corroded factory loads with appearance such as illustrated here. These .32 S&Ws are probably more than fifty years old!

der if a given gun is safe for smokeless powder loads, have it checked by a reliable gunsmith. It is the owner/shooter's responsibility to make certain regarding that point. An accompanying photo shows the unpleasant consequence of firing a smokeless load in a revolver designed solely for use with black powder. Such calamities are worth going to considerable bother for the sake of avoiding!

There are a number of excellent books on reloading, several from the publisher of the book at hand and others from makers of bullets or reloading equipment. Several such are shown and one or more are recommended to the interested would-be reloader as the source of in-depth details that are apt to be helpful and beneficial. Extensive coverage of details would take more space than is available here and the intent is to provide at least a few typical listings of load data for the scarce old cartridge calibers, Along with a few suggested loads for the modern, high-performance numbers. The field of single-action cartridges runs a gamut from the feeblest to the most robust calibers and quite a few of the older numbers are no longer listed in present-day manuals or handbooks. Insofar as possible black powder charges will be listed for those cartridges with their origins in the black powder era. Be ad-

vised however that even black powder loads can be damaging to a gun in poor condition or shoddy in materials and/or workmanship. Again, if you've doubts, check with a good local gunsmith and heed his advice.

.30 M1 GI Carbine — Sturm, Ruger & Company introduced a .30 Carbine version of their popular Blackhawk revolvers in the Sixties. Prior to that a few single-action revolvers such as the Colt Bisley Model had been converted to the cartridge by bushing the chambers and relining the bores. The conversion is a dubious approach as pressures run quite high in the military loads of the .30 Carbine. Loads quoted here are for the Ruger Blackhawk and are not recommended for conversions.

The 110-grain Speer JHP known as the Varminter is a good choice for pest control. If expansion is not desired, the Sierra 110-grain round-nose FMJ works nicely and the same maker offers a round-nose JSP as well. The .30 Carbine is a tapered case and usually requires full-length resizing. Small rifle primers should be used and the magnum type is suited for the powders for which the charge weight is followed by an asterisk.

Reloading presses such as this Model OO-7 from Pacific develop a tremendous amount of leverage to force the cases into and out of reloading dies to return them to the proper dimensions to accept the next bullet and replace the spent primer with a fresh one for next shot.

Bullet Weight	Powder	Charge	Velocity (fps)	Energy (fpe)
110	680	16.0*	1210	358
	296	14.2	1310	419
	H110	14.2*	1366	456
	Herco	9.7	1400	479
	2400	10.7	1196	349
	IMR-4227	14.0	1334	435

Heavier bullets are not recommended; data can be used with lighter bullets.

.32 Short Colt — This cartridge has been around for nearly a century and the brass cases should be inspected critically before reloading. The old black powder load was 7.7 grains of FFFg behind an 80-grain lead bullet and that should not be exceeded if you've reason to doubt the strength of the gun in question. Ancient factory loads should not be fired if they show signs of serious corrosion. Cases from the era of mercuric primers may be dangerously weakened by the effect of mercuric residue. In a gun judged to be of competent design and in good condition, 1.5 grains of Bullseye behind an 80-grain lead bullet will deliver about 790 fps/111 fpe from a three-inch barrel. Check bore diameter and size cast bullets to not over .001-inch larger than groove diameter. Use standard small pistol primers.

.32 Smith & Wesson — Observations just given for the .32 Short Colt generally apply to the .32 S&W as well. The .32 S&W can be fired in guns chambered for the .32 S&W Long. Take care to match sized bullet diameter to bore dimensions as previously noted. With an 85-grain lead bullet, 1.4 grains of Bullseye will deliver about 725 fps/99 fpe in a three-inch barrel. As a black powder load for the same bullet, 7.4 grains of FFFg is suitable. Use standard small pistol primers.

.32 Long Colt — This straight-sided case is substantially smaller in diameter than the .32 S&W Long or .32 Colt New Police. Fairly recent factory loads measure about .315-inch case diameter, unfired, as compared to about .334-inch for a .32 S&W Long. With an 80-grain lead bullet sized not more than .001-inch larger than groove diameter, 2.1 grains of Bullseye will deliver about 770 fps/105 fpe. General observations on the other caliber .32 cartridges apply. Use standard small pistol primer.

.32 S&W Long/.38 Colt New Police (NP) — These two cartridges are virtually identical. The principal difference was that the .32 S&WL carried a round-nose bullet while the .32 Colt NP had the flattened tip preferred by Colt at the time of its introduction. The .32 S&WL remains readily available to the present and it can be fired in guns chambered for the .32 Colt NP or vice versa. Reasonably modern guns work well with cast bullets sized to .313-inch diameter, but it is always well to check bore dimensions of the gun at hand, holding bullet diameter to not more than .001-inch over groove diameter of the bore. Hornady recently introduced a lead semi-wadcutter in .314-inch di-

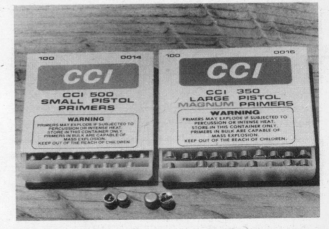

The small primer has a diameter of .175-inch while the large size measures .210-inch. Shown here are two of each, with the LP size in magnum-type, as discussed.

A shell holder and three-die loading set for the .44 magnum with an empty case positioned in the shell holder. The die at left on the box is the full-length resizing die, here with an insert of tungsten-carbide to eliminate the need for applying lube before sizing and removing it afterwards. Although its top is threaded internally, no inner assembly is used with the resizing die, customarily. Center die is decapper/expander, bullet-seating die at right.

ameter at 90 grains for the .32 S&WL/Colt NP; their index #3250. Alberts Bullets has an excellent hollow-base wadcutter (HBWC) at .313-inch diameter and 100 grains; index #2905. Hornady suggests these loads; velocities taken in a three-inch Model 31 S&W revolver; a Winchester #1-½-108 standard small pistol primer was used for all loads quoted:

	Velocity/Energy				
Powder in grains	550/60	600/72	650/84	700/98	750/112
700-X	1.4	1.6	1.7	1.8	1.9
HP-38	1.4	1.6	1.7	1.9	—
Bullseye	1.6	1.7	1.9	2.0	—
Red Dot	1.5	1.7	1.8	2.0	2.1
Green Dot	1.7	1.9	2.1	2.2	—
Unique	1.7	1.9	2.1	2.3	2.5
231	1.8	2.1	2.3	2.5	—

Alberts Bullets says their 100-grain HBWC does best with 1.9 grains of Unique, delivering about 680 fps in a three-inch barrel. Note: Hornady data was developed in their test facilities under controlled conditions, using pres-sure barrels. As components and conditions may vary, the reloader should approach maximum loads with extreme caution. Hornady Manufacturing Company, as well as the writers and publishers of this book, disclaim all responsibility for mishaps of any nature that might occur from the use of this data.

.32-20 Winchester, .32-20 Winchester Center-Fire, .32 WCF, .32-20 WCF — Primarily designed as a rifle cartridge, the Colt SAA was chambered for this round, perhaps others as well. In an earlier time before the .357 magnum came upon the scene the .32-20 was regarded as a most noteworthy round and a hotrod handloader's delight. In modern times the fickle public has ignored the cartridge so assiduously that it's no longer listed as a loaded round or empty case in catalog sections devoted to handgun ammunition. Remington lists a .32-20 load in their rifle section, made up to the latest — 1977 — specifications for the .32-20 handgun and likewise usable in rifles. Winchester offers empty brass and loaded ammo suitable for use in handguns but listed in their rifle section. The .32-20 has not been listed in any of the regular manuals or handbooks on reloading since an early Pacific edition of 1969, although a few suggested loads are given in books such as Barnes' *Cartridges of the World*. Ammunition made up for exclusive use in rifles is considered hazardous for use in handguns and random rounds separated from their original carton should be

The set of Pacific Durachrome .44 magnum t-c dies on the facing page is shown with center assemblies removed from the decapper/expander and bullet seater. The case has been removed from its shell holder to show it clearly.

viewed as suspect. Cartridges with jacketed soft point (JSP) bullets can be assumed to be loaded at rifle pressures and unsuitable for use in revolvers.

Typical diameter for sizing cast bullets to load for the .32-20 is .311-inch, but it's best to check actual bore diameter of the gun at hand, holding sized diameter to not more than .001-inch larger than groove diameter.

100-grain cast bullets
3.4 grains Bullseye	970 fps/209 fpe
5.5 grains Unique	1065 fps/252 fpe

115-grain cast bullets
3.1 grains Bullseye	850 fps/185 fpe
4.5 grains Unique	925 fps/219 fpe

It is rather unusual to achieve an exceptional degree of accuracy with the .32-20 cartridge in revolvers. Although some sources specify use of the small rifle primer, most prefer the small pistol primer.

9mm Parabellum (Luger) — Although it may seem an unlikely load for a SA revolver, Ruger's .357 magnum Blackhawk was made available with a factory-fitted auxiliary cylinder to handle the 9mmP and it performed quite well. The Blackhawk's ejector rod poked out the empty rimless cases with no problems. Groove diameter of the Blackhawk bore is tailored to the .357- to .358-inch bullet diameter of the longer cartridge, but it is not unusual to find the .355- to .356-inch bullet diameter customarily used for the 9mmP delivers surprisingly acceptable accuracy in the slightly oversized bores. Many of the usual problems of loading 9mmP can be ignored when working with the Blackhawk since it obviously requires no minimum amount of power to work the action. Cartridge overall length need not be held to a minimum for the sake of feeding through a magazine and so on. This affords an unusual degree of flexibility in making up loads and the longer barrel — usually 7½ inches — more than offsets velocity loss from cylinder gap leakage. Thus, nearly any of the 9mmP loads given in manuals or handbooks work well in the Blackhawk and some work quite a bit better. Hercules Herco powder is a good performer in the 9mmP and often does exceptionally well in the Blackhawk at charges of 7.7 grains for 90-grain bullets to 7.0 grains for 115-grain bullets. The quoted loads should be regarded as maximum and approached with caution.

Cases for the 9mmP show unusually large dimensional variations from maker to maker so it's best to sort them by headstamp for best results. A secure grip of the case neck against the bullet base is especially necessary in the revolver to prevent bullet migration forward due to recoil stresses, thus requiring a careful match of die dimensions case neck thickness and bullet base diameter. The 9mmP cases uses the small pistol primer.

.38 Short Colt/.38 Long Colt — Both loaded rounds and unfired cases for this pair have been off the market for a long time. The Short was an outside-lubricated cartridge and the Long was used by the army during the Spanish-American War with notable dissatisfaction. It should be noted that many of the revolvers for the .38 Long Colt had chambers without the usual restriction at the front. When the .357 magnum was introduced, a few intrepid souls discovered that the longer cartridge could be chambered in some guns for the .38 Long Colt and made the highly ill-advised experiment of firing a round of the vastly more powerful cartridge, thereby blowing the gun to smithereens. Trying that is among the poorest of all policies!

Many of the guns chambered for either the Short or Long

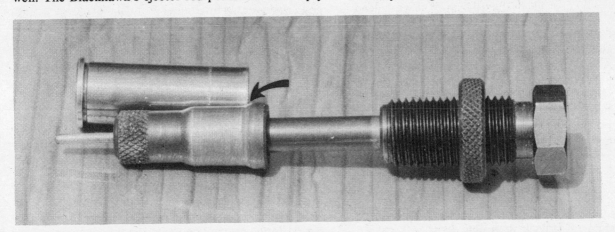

A closer look at the decapper/expander stem: Arrow indicates tapered area that puts a slight flare in the case neck. The area just to the left of that is slightly smaller than bullet diameter to assure expanding neck just enough to provide a secure and uniform grip of the case neck upon the bullet base. That aids reliability, improves accuracy.

This pair of Boxer-primed cases have been cross-sectioned to illustrate the older folded or balloon-head case design at left as compared to the modern solid or web-head construction at right. The new type is much stronger, but the balloon-head case has slightly greater internal capacity, requiring reduction of loads intended for it if they are to be made up in web-head cases. If this precaution is not observed, dangerous pressures are apt to be produced.

Colt are bored large enough to accept cartridges with the .379-inch body diameter of the .38 Special case. As a result, it may be possible to make up reloads by suitable sizing and trimming of the .38 Special case, meanwhile using loads at the Short or Long Colt levels.

A 130-grain bullet can be loaded for the .38 Short Colt with 2.5 grains of Bullseye for 745 fps/160 fpe in a six-inch barrel: Approach that with caution and do not exceed it.

The .38 Long Colt can be loaded with a 148-grain lead bullet ahead of 3.0 grains of Bullseye for 810 fps/216 fpe, also in a six-inch barrel. The same cautions apply as given for the Short.

In either example, bore dimensions must be checked and lead bullets sized to not more than .001-inch larger than groove diameter. Both lengths use the standard small pistol primer.

.38 Smith & Wesson/.38 S&W/.38 Colt New Police (NP) — This is a shorter cartridge, slightly larger in diameter than the extremely popular .38 Smith & Wesson Special and the similarity of the names has produced endless confusion. Bullet diameter for a given gun varies broadly, from .354- to .360-inch, perhaps beyond in extreme examples. Verification of bore dimensions for the given gun should be regarded as mandatory for that reason. The usual procedure of holding diameters of sized lead

bullets to not more than .001-inch larger than groove diameter definitely applies here. Maximum cartridge case length is .775-inch; maximum overall cartridge length with bullet seated is 1.180 inches.

Most current manuals and handbooks carry listings of data for use with both jacketed and lead bullets, both being applicable if the bullet diameter matches the groove diameter of the bore as noted. It will be necessary to seat 148-grain wadcutters with a suitable amount of the bullet nose exposed ahead of the case mouth. The usual factory load bullet weight is 146 grains in a round-nose design; not a common item as a bullet alone in commercial channels. If loaded with the more readily available lead bullets at 158 grains, these are suggested loads, with additional listings in most manuals/handbooks:

158-grain lead bullet — of proper diameter as noted:

2.3 grains Bullseye	661 fps/153 fpe
2.9 grains Unique	657 fps/151 fpe
2.5 grains Red Dot	712 fps/178 fpe

In theory this cartridge should be capable of respectable accuracy. In actuality, few of the guns chambered for it are capable of realizing its potential in that respect. It uses the standard small pistol primer.

.38 Special/.38 Smith & Wesson Special/.38 Colt Spe-

cial; also .38/44 — A refined development of the .38 Long Colt, the .38 Special is actually a scaled-up counterpart of the .32 S&WL/Colt NP discussed earlier and, like its smaller progenitor, it is capable of outstanding accuracy, given the proper gun. The .38 Special in its turn begat the .357 magnum and it has only been in recent years that the .357 has shown signs of supplanting the .38 Special as the most popular of all handgun cartridges in this country, if not in the entire world.

Unlike many of the cartridges covered here, load data for the .38 Special can be found in such teeming abundance that a lengthy tabulation would seem rather redundant.

The traditional target load is 2.7 grains of Bullseye with the 148-grain wadcutter lead bullet sized to .358-inch diameter and it would be a severe challenge to estimate how many millions of rounds have been made up to that recipe and fired over the long career of the cartridge. In a six-inch barrel, typical velocities for that load are on the order of 720 fps/170 fpe and since most of them are expended against paper targets, the energy is more than ample for producing holes that are easy to score. With barrels rifled at a pitch of 1:14, accuracy with that load is excellent, but the more gradual twists such as 1:18.75 may prove marginal in stabilization as evidenced by irregular holes in the paper. With solid-base wadcutters, loads for the 148-grain

wadcutter can be increased to a maximum of 964 fps/305 fpe with 4.3 grains of Red Dot to increase bullet spin and enhance stability and accuracy.

The maximum standard working pressure of the .38 Special is 18,900 pounds per square inch (psi) and +P loads have been developed that operate at 22,400 psi for use in the stronger revolver designs. Many data sources list such hotter loads, but the reloader who plans to fire from a SA revolver should stay within the standard loads and approach maximum levels with extreme caution.

The .38 Special uses small pistol primers, standard or magnum as indicated.

The .38-44 cartridge was an earlier version of the +P load made up for use in the revolver that Smith & Wesson built on their .44 or N-frame chambered for the .38 Special. It was a sort of transitional offering that bridged over to the .357 Smith & Wesson magnum. Few if any of the .38-44 cartridges were headstamped with that designation although some of them may be encountered with a primer pocket dimensioned to accept the large pistol primer rather than the small pistol primer customarily employed. If you happen upon any such, they are better diverted to your curiosity collection rather than used for reloading.

.357 Smith & Wesson magnum/.357 Atomic — In the

For the past several years the S&W Long cartridge seemed to be trending toward an orphan of the storm status; regrettable in view of its mild report and recoil coupled with really exceptional accuracy when fired in guns of top-drawer design and workmanship. As noted here, both Alberts and Hornady recently added bullets above.

As discussed here, the .38 Colt New Police is practically identical to the .38 S&W; both somewhat thicker in case diameter than the .38 Special and considerably shorter.

early Thirties, at the suggestion of Phil Sharpe, Smith & Wesson began development of a cartridge intended to exploit the potential of the .38 Special to the limits of its capability. The proposed peak pressures involved approached twice those of the .38 Special and it was rightly decided that some step must be taken to keep the potent new cartridge from being fired in guns woefully incapable of coping with such pressures. The decision was made to increase the case and chamber length by a distance of .135-inch, from the 1.155 inches of the Special case to the 1.290 inches of the magnum case. In effect, that made it impossible to put a .357 load in a .38 gun and fire it.

Regrettably enough, the case length was increased with little or no effort made to increase the length of the cylinder proportionally, resulting in a problem of long standing for the .357 round as to a severely restricted distance that its bullet can project ahead of the case mouth.

Nevertheless, the .357 magnum burst upon the handgunning world in 1935 as a major marvel of the universe to that point. It quickly gathered an aura of folklore about it so glowing that the myths were hard to match in actual performance. It was an excellent cartridge, but its demonstrable capabilities had difficulty keeping pace with the legends that grew up around it.

There is a profuse amount of load data for the .357 magnum supplied in any reloading manual/handbook published over the past thirty or forty years and the reloader who elects to work with this cartridge would be well advised to obtain one or more copies of modern editions of such indispensible works. The more powerful of such loads need to be approached with extreme caution and are far better avoided. Pressure response will vary from one gun to the next, even if nominally of identical make and model, making such cautions absolutely mandatory.

The Lyman #358156 mould turns out a gas-checked cast SWC or Thompson-type bullet that is among the most satisfactory of all such designs for use in the .357 magnum.

With a charge of 14.0 grains of 2400 velocity is about 1180 fps/489 fpe for this 158-grain bullet in a six-inch barrel and accuracy is usually acceptable to excellent. DuPont's Hi-Skor 800-X, recently introduced, shows promise of being an excellent powder for the same cartridge and bullet weight, and DuPont suggests 8.9 grains of 800-X for the 158-grain lead SWC bullet at 1215 fps/518 fpe in a six-inch barrel, quoting the pressure as 36,000 psi.

The Great Western SA revolvers were offered at one time in what they called the .357 Atomic, with loaded ammo from the same source. The cartridge was dimensionally identical to the .357 magnum but presumably was loaded to pressures in excess of the 46,000 psi level established as maximum for the .357 magnum by Sporting Arms and Ammunition Manufacturers Institute (SAAMI). No information remains available as to the loads used in it nor the pressures it developed.

.38-40 Winchester Center-Fire, .38-40 WCF — As with most such hyphenated cartridge designations, the second figure designates the original charge weight of black powder, 40.0 grains in this instance. The derivation of the .38 is somewhat mystifying since the bullet diameter is usually taken to be .400-inch for jacketed or .400-1 for lead bullets. The Lyman #401452 bullet shown loaded in the accompanying photo of the .38-40 was designed for them by Gordon Boser at a weight of about 196 grains. Most loads for the .38-40 are for bullets weighing somewhat less and the tendency in recent years has been to omit listing of it entirely. One of the newer entries shows 4.0 to a maximum of 5.9 grains of Bullseye for a 172-grain bullet, respective velocities of 740 to 965 fps/209 to 356 fpe. For Unique with the same bullet, 7.0 to a maximum of 10.0 grains shows 830 to 1105 fps/263 to 466 fpe. For the 196-grain Boser bullet, 5.0 to 7.0 grains of Unique are suitable, with the higher weight to be regarded as maximum and approached with extreme caution if at all. Typical velocity would be 728 to 890 fps/231 to 345 fpe. Standard large pistol primers should be used with these powders in this cartridge.

Revolvers chambered for the .38-40 cartridge may have groove and bore diameters so oversize that it is impossible to load a bullet of sufficient diameter because it would not fit in the chambers of the cylinder. The futility of pursuing accuracy with such a combination should be obvious.

.41 Short Colt/.41 Long Colt — Long discontinued as factory loads, with empty cases likewise virtually unobtainable, the obstacles for reloading either of these cartridges are quite formidable. Originally, the cartridge was loaded with outside-lubricated bullets of essentially the same diameter in the exposed portion as the diameter of the case. The part of the bullet enclosed by the case mouth was of smaller diameter, known as a step-heel design. At one time Lyman offered moulds of suitable design for use in reloading both lengths. The one for the .41 Short was #386176 and for the .41 Long, #386177. The latter has a nominal weight of 196 grains. Information as to the weight of the shorter bullet is not readily retrievable. A further offering from Lyman was their #386176, a hollow-base round-nose designed for interior lubrication with the intent that the skirts would expand under pressure to seal powder gases in the manner of the Minie ball. The #386178 is listed as 200 grains in weight. It is highly unlikely that any of these moulds can be obtained at present. The sparse data available suggests a maximum charge of 5.0 grains of Unique for the 200-grain #386178 at 880 fps/344 fpe and an identical charge for the #386177 at 196-grain weight for 890 fps/345 fpe. Original bullet weight for the .41 Short Colt factory load was 160 grains. Given avaiability of bullets in that weight, a charge of 2.4 grains of Bullseye should be regarded as maximum at 625 fps/139 fpe. Primers in all examples would be the standard large pistol size.

.41 Remington magnum, .41 magnum

Unlike the .357 magnum or .44 magnum, both produced by elongating the corresponding Special case, the .41 magnum made its debut about 1964 as an entirely new cartridge case. It bears no dimensional relation to the .41 Colt and there has never been a .41 Special to date, although some have voiced a wish that it might appear. The prospects for that seem quite unlikely as the general acceptance by the shooting public to the .41 magnum have been viewed as disappointing in the shooting industry as a whole. It is a regrettable state of affairs since the .41 magnum, when suitably reloaded, is among the finest handgun cartridges ever offered in terms of accuracy and flexible capability across a broad range of bullet weights and velocities.

The Ruger Blackhawk is the most popular SA revolver offered in .41 magnum and it is awesomely capable in both power and accuracy. The test lab at Sierra Bullets, for example, uses a .41 magnum Blackhawk as their test gun for the cartridge in preference to other guns available for it in testing samples of bullet production and the groups it delivers are often so small as to strain credulity.

Lightest cast bullet for the .41 magnum is the #255 mould at 175 grains from Hensley & Gibbs, heaviest is the #410426, the latter initially designed for the .401 Winchester cartridge, weighing about 242 grains in typical alloy. The 242-grain is well regarded by metallic silhouette competitors for the momentum it can deliver to the heavier targets of that sport. The #45 Lyman Handbook takes the #401426 bullet — listed at 240 grains — to a maximum velocity of 1169 fps/728 fpe on 17.5 grains of 2400 powder; a load that should be approached with extreme caution, if at all. Jacketed bullets are available from 170 to 220 grains, the latter a recent offering from Sierra, designed primarily for silhouette competition. The large pistol primer is used with the .41 magnum, standard or magnum as influenced by charactersitics of the powder being used.

.44 S&W Russian, .44 S&WR

Original factory loads for this round carried a 246-grain bullet ahead of 23.0 grains of FFg black powder for 750 fps/307 fpe, the quoted velocity having been obtained with the older corrosive primers. With the same bullet weight, in guns suitable for use with smokeless powder, 5.5 grains of Bullseye delivers 680 fps/253 fpe.

The Lyman #429251 at a nominal 253 grains was designated as standard for the .44 S&WR and early Lyman Handbooks suggested 3.0 grains of Bullseye for 630 fps/223 fpe or 6.0 grains of Unique for 800/360.

In the absence of original .44 S&WR cases, replacement cases can be made by trimming .44 Special cases to a

At left is a typical round of 9mm Parabellum (Luger) with a typical full-metal-jacketed (FMJ) round-nose bullet, as used in auxiliary cylinder for the Ruger .357 mag Blackhawk. At center is the .38 Special, with a .357 magnum cartridge, both with partially jacketed bullets; the .38 has a jacketed hollow point (JHP) while the .357 carries a jacketed-soft-point (JSP) type of bullet.

A vintage Remington-UMC (Union Metallic Cartridge Co.) case for the .44 S&W Russian with bullet from discontinued Lyman #429251 mould. From Special or mag brass, it may be necessary to inside-ream the case neck.

length of .950-inch. Virtually all .44 S&WR cases employed the older balloon head design contrasted in a nearby illustration to the modern solid or web-head design. Although the web-head is much stronger, the added brass occupies internal volume to give it a reduced capacity and it is necessary to reduce balloon-head data correspondingly if cases are fashioned by trimming down web-head brass from the longer cartridges. An initial reduction of twenty percent from web-head data would be prudent and any increase should be made with extreme caution, if at all. The standard large pistol primers are used in this cartridge.

.44-40 Winchester Center-Fire, .44 WCF

— As with the .32-20 and .38-40, this is a cartridge initially designed for use in rifles that went on to inspire production of revolvers to handle it. The terminal 40 of the designation signifies its original charge; 40.0 grains of FFg black powder.

Depending upon bore dimensions of the gun at hand, the .44-40 is loaded with bullets from about .425 to .429-inch. The smaller sizes may be difficult to obtain except by casting and sizing to the required diameter.

The .44-40 requires care and delicacy in reloading since its brass is almost paper-thin at the case mouth and thus is easily damaged, particularly if the bullet is seated incautiously or without the necessary slight flare at the neck. The .44-40 is no longer listed as a factory round by most major makers. Indeed, it is not entirely certain if it remains available as either loaded round or empty case from Winchester-Western.

RCBS suggests their #28 shell holder for the .44-40; the one usually offered for the .444 Marlin rifle cartridge. The same firm can supply die sets for best results with cast bullets and a separate expander die and seater for best results with jacketed bullets. In view of the fragility of the .44-40 case mouth you might find either specialized set worth considering. Although RCBS does not list the .44-40 as a standard set of dies, they are available through their custom die shop.

With the 205-grain cast bullet, suggested loads run from 4.0 grains of Bullseye to a maximum of 6.6 grains; performance 695 fps/220 fpe to 945/407; also 6.0 grains of Unique to a maximum of 11.0 grains at 750/256 to 1100/551.

For the 200-grain jacketed bullet: 5.0 grains of Bullseye to a maximum of 6.7 grains for 790/277 to 965/414; also 8.0 grains of Unique to a maximum of 11.1 grains for 825/302 to 1125/562. The standard large pistol primer is used for these loads.

Caution should be exercised to avoid use of .44-40 cartridges in the revolver if loaded to rifle pressure levels.

.44 Smith & Wesson Special, .44 Special

— While not exactly a scaled-up counterpart of the .32 S&WL or .38 Special, the .44 Special seems to share the excellent accuracy potential of the two smaller cartridges. A generous abundance of load data is offered for the .44 Special in any manual/handbook covering handgun loads and components for its reloading as well as moulds for casting suitable bullets are widely available. In many instances, reloading die sets have the multiple capability of handling both the .44 Special and .44 magnum; an obvious advantage to the reloader working with both cartridges. The same shell holder fits both of those as well as the .44 S&WR.

One of the more capable cast bullets for the .44 Special is the Lyman #429348 which remains on that maker's current list of available moulds. It is a full wadcutter with two rather small grease grooves and the weight as cast is about 175 grains with typical alloys. The #38 Lyman Handbook lists loads for that bullet to velocities as high as 1170 fps/526 fpe, giving its weight as 173 grains; a notably powerful performer for that era. The latest Lyman Handbook — #45, with the upcoming #46 still unseen at press time for this book — lists charges of 7.0 to a maximum of 11.5 grains of Unique for the #429348 — now rated at 180 grains in weight — for respective performance of 877 fps/307 fpe to 1351/730. Standard large pistol primers are used and the maximum load should be approached with extreme caution, if at all. In point of fact, the #429348 often shows outstanding target capability when held to velocities in the 875-1000 fps range and its large flat area at the nose gives it impact capabilities well beyond expectations for the paper ballistics. It is customarily seated so the case mouth crimps lightly just ahead of the front driving band. Other moulds and ready-made bullets are available for this cartridge to maximum weights of about 250 grains and load data is readily available, as noted.

.44 Remington magnum, .44 magnum

— Introduced about 1956 at the urgings of Elmer Keith, this cartridge was developed by lengthening the .44 Special case by .125-inch, perhaps beefing it up at the head to moderate extents. It is usually conceded to be the world's most powerful production revolver cartridge and that sometimes acts as a dubious distinction since many owner/reloader/shooters of the guns feel duty bound to drive each bullet forth at the thin brink of disaster. In point of fact, if charges are held to not much more than the upper .44 Special levels, accuracy is improved, firing enjoyment vastly enhanced and the life expectancy of the gun is usefully lengthened. That consideration should be kept in mind although it's often overlooked.

Jacketed bullets for the .44 magnum are available from 180 grains to the massive 265-grain JSP from Hornady. Moulds for cast bullets range from a low of about 180 — the Lyman #429348 — to around 320 grains, the latter being made up by NorthEast Industrial and distributed exclusively by SSK Industries.

The Ruger Super Blackhawk is probably the outstanding SA revolver available in .44 magnum and many other makers offer comparable SA designs for it. Ruger has also offered their Blackhawk in .44 magnum.

As with any cartridge enjoying endless waves of popularity, load data for the .44 magnum is available by the teeming ream. Any individual gun can be expected to have one or a few specific loads with which it performs at its best. As a general-purpose starting load, 20.0 grains of 2400 behind a 240-grain jacketed bullet is an excellent choice. It is well below maximum, but the usual performance from gun to gun is more encouraging than most. The large pistol primer is used in the .44 magnum; standard or magnum type as suitable for the powder being used.

.45 Automatic Colt Pistol, .45 ACP — Although this may seem an unlikely round for use in SA revolvers, Ruger offers their .45 Blackhawk in .45 Long Colt with an optional factory-fitted cylinder for use of the .45 ACP and it makes a highly satisfactory combination with the ability to use the generously available military load or its commercial counterpart.

Designed for and primarily used in the Colt Model 1911 autoloader, customary factory loads and load data are tailored to the consideration that the auto parks a fair-sized section of its cartridge base unsupported in midair over the feed ramp. That trims permissible pressures down to the SAAMI specifications of 19,900 psi as maximum.

Since the Ruger Blackhawk enclosed the head of the chambered .45 ACP case fully and securely, it might seem logical to assume that the .45 ACP could be loaded to pressures somewhat above the usual manual/handbook listings. No reliable data is available for such loads at present and the practice of loading the .45 ACP to higher pressures for the Blackhawk is a dubious one due to the possibility that such a load might go astray and find its way into one of the auto pistols.

The prudent reloader will reflect that longer barrels such as the 7½-inch common to the .45 Blackhawk will deliver usefully higher velocities with the .45 ACP than those obtainable in the five-inch barrel of the auto, despite pressure loss at the gap between cylinder and barrel.

As with other popular cartridges of the present day, .45 ACP load data is available in quantities so lavish as to hardly justify lengthy listing here. The load with 4.5 grains of Bullseye behind the #68 Hensley & Gibbs cast SWC

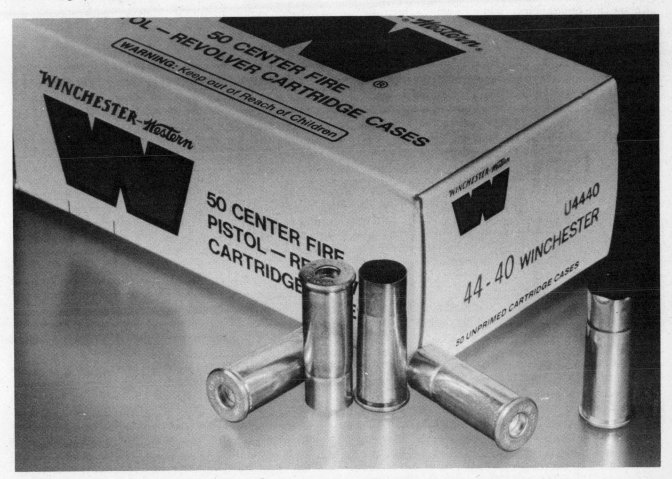

Here is a box of empty, unprimed cases from Winchester-Western in .44-40 WCF; a convenient way to obtain a working supply of empty cases if loaded factory ammunition is not readily obtainable. As noted, case is delicate.

A pair of empty cases for the .45 Automatic Colt Pistol (ACP), of military origin in these examples. Caliber or cartridge designation seldom appears in military headstamps. Case at left was made at Frankford Arsenal in 1941 and it's not readily reloadable since it takes a special .204-inch primer. Nearly all other military .45 ACP brass is reloadable, although some may have stamp-crimped primer pockets that require edge-flaring or reaming to seat new primer.

bullet is notably accurate in the M1911 auto and carries its good grouping abilities over to the Blackhawk virtually intact. In the Blackhawk, performance of the quoted load is about 820 fps/284 fpe with the bullet that casts up about 190 grains in typical alloy. The large pistol primer in standard type is used, magnum primers being seldom required in this case.

.45 Colt, .45 Long Colt — Developed as the military handgun cartridge of this country for use in the Colt Single-Action Army or SAA, this has long been a fairly popular cartridge, although the advent of the .44 magnum in 1956 has hampered its popularity to a considerable extent.

Maximum industry working pressure for the .45 Colt is 15,900 psi; a rather low ceiling that holds the performance of sensible loads to comparatively modest levels.

Many hold the belief that the proper diameter of the cast lead bullet sized for use in the .45 Colt is .454-inch, but that is true only for revolvers made by Colt and a few others prior to cessation of sporting arms production at the entry of this country into WWII. Post-WWII .45 Colt revolvers have bore dimensions of dimensions that respond best to bullets sized to .452-inch. That engenders some amount of dimension variations in loading die sets from the various makers and, coupled with vagaries in case dimension sec-

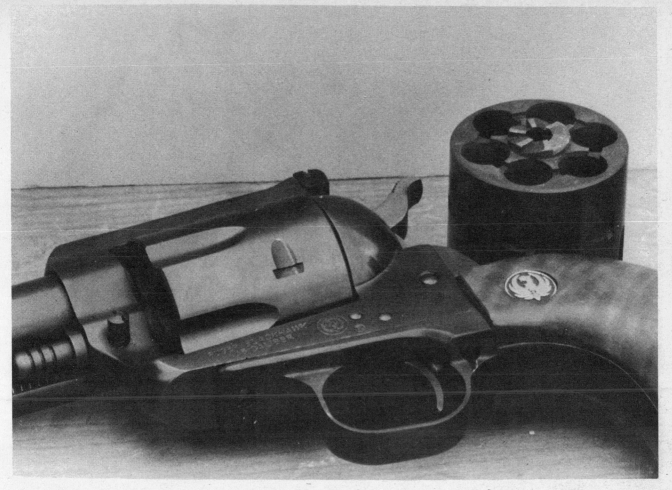

The Ruger Blackhawk in .45 Colt, above, can be supplied with a factory-fitted auxiliary cylinder for use of the .45 ACP cartridge, as in the background here. Due to the strength of the Blackhawk design, some manuals list heavier loads for use in it with the .45 Colt. None at present carry comparable loads for the .45 ACP, nor are they apt to do so.

ond in magnitude solely to those of the 9mmP, it results in the .45 Colt posing occasional perplexities to its reloader.

Sierra offers a 240-grain jacketed hollow cavity (JHC) bullet specifically tailored for use in the .45 Colt case and provides two sets of data listing in their current Sierra Manual, second edition: one for use in conventional revolvers plus a second listing at higher pressures for use exclusively in the Ruger Blackhawk or Thompson/Center Contender. Speer follows the same practice in their tenth edition of the Speer Manual, as does Hornady in the third edition of the Hornady Handbook.

Speer lists their higher Blackhawk listings as not exceeding peak pressures of 25,000 psi. If the more powerful loads are made up, great care must be exercised to avoid firing them in guns (or old, balloon-head cases) incapable of coping with pressures that high. In any event, it must be remembered that the .45 Colt case is of no more than moderate strength making it mandatory that loads be held within sensible pressure levels. The large pistol primer is used with this case, standard or magnum as considered suitable.

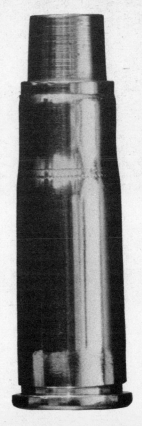

This round of .38-40 WCF carries a cast bullet from the Lyman #401452 mould at 196 grains. Bullet has a broad, flat tip and clean-cutting shoulder for maximum effect.

A single-action .22 may be better than a powder puff in defending your home, but there are many things against such a handgun selection to protect property, person.

Chapter 9

THE SINGLE-ACTION IN SELF-DEFENSE

The Pros And Cons — Mostly Cons — On The Hawgleg As A Personal Protector

The Ruger .44 magnum Blackhawk (top) may have longest barrel of the three guns shown, but the Colt Python in .357 magnum or .45 Government auto are better choice when one is seeking an ideal handgun for self-defense.

I N DISCUSSING the single-action for self-defense, Massad Ayoob and I had a lengthy conversation about the functionability of the single-action revolver as a defensive piece of emergency safety equipment for dealing with life-threatening danger. Ayoob is a recognized expert at that sort of thing, so every time I brought up a point in favor of the thumb-buster revolver for self-defense, I actually was playing devil's advocate.

Ayoob is the author of *In the Gravest Extreme: The Role of the Firearm in Personal Protection,* which has been hailed as the ultimate book on the use of guns in self-defense.

So let's do that same number right here, and check out the claims of people who think a single-action frontier-style revolver is as good to defend your life with now as it was a hundred years ago.

Single-action revolvers have protected Americans for over 150 years — that means they're proven to work great!

"This is true only in the sense that Americans for centuries relied on the horse for transportation, the saddle or the buggy as the only way to go. The single-action revolver, like the horse and surrey, is obsolete for its modern mission, although it still works fine in sporting applications like handgun hunting or IHMSA metallic silhouette shooting. Horses are still neat for riding to the hounds or the Kentucky Derby, but we no longer use them in emergencies where innocent human lives depend on swift expedience. So it is with the frontier six-shooter," Ayoob feels.

The fact that you have to cock the hammer before you

There is no denying that the Colt Single Action Army did much to civilize our Western frontier, but so did the horse and black powder. Today, all are better suited to nostalgia than in an effort to combat modern criminals.

can fire a single-action revolver is a safety feature that could prevent tragedy in a tension-frought armed encounter.

"Wrong again. We find that for every time a person has to shoot an evil-doer, there are fourteen or fifteen times where the law-abiding armed citizen simply places the perpetrator at gunpoint and the thug either freezes or runs for his life. Holding a man at gunpoint is a whole separate exercise from a gun battle. You're talking about someone who is very nervous training a gun on someone he or she must assume is a hardened, violent criminal who still may have an undiscovered deadly weapon concealed on his person.

"If you level your single-action at a man like that and leave the hammer down, there's a good chance you'll be dead meat. Don't assume that criminals are too stupid not to know how single-action revolvers work. If they figure you're going to have to cock the gun before you can blow them away, they may lunge for your weapon. Chances are that they'll have it out of your hand before your thumb even reaches the hammer. We have surveillance photos of prisoners in penetentiary exercise yards practicing how to take revolvers away from police officers.

"If you do cock the gun, you're talking about a very short, light pull to set it off. You are going to be under enormous stress when you place a burglary suspect or whatever at gunpoint. It is human nature for the muscles to contract

Ray Chapman, who now teaches combat shooting, once was a national fast-draw champion with the single-action, but he favors a .45 auto with full magazine for trouble.

involuntarily when the person hears a sudden sound while under great stress. That sound could be an arriving officer or it could be a door slamming as your spouse comes downstairs to see what's going on.

"That convulsive muscular reaction is quite likely to cause your finger to move enough on the trigger of the cocked single-action to make it discharge. Congratulations: you have now 'accidentally' shot an unarmed man who had surrendered to you. They probably won't let you take your

Like the rest of us, police instructor Massad Ayoob has a tender spot for the single-action, but realizes it is not up to the advances of modern firearms for lawmen.

copy of this book into prison, but perhaps your wife can get you a carton of cigarettes a week."

A single action revolver with five full-powered rounds is all you'll need, since statistics prove that the average gun-fight only requires 2.3 rounds fired by each partici-pant.

"That's wrong, too. Those statistics come from places and research systems that don't relate to real 'street gun-fights.' One place that '2.3 shots' figure comes from is an Eastern police department where if an officer is involved in a running gunfight where six shots are fired by each partici-pant at three points in the gunfight — two shots each when they see each other, two shots during the pursuit, and two shots each when the cop corners the punk and drops him — it doesn't go down as a running gunfight with six shots fired on each side. It goes down as three separate encounters, averaging two shots fired by each participant," Ayoob reports.

"You also get some of that '2.3 shots fired' stuff from the annual FBI summary of police casualties. That includes a hefty number of policemen who were shot from ambush and never had a chance to draw and fire their own wea-pons. That skews the statistics considerably. A lot of the cops killed on the job never even had a chance to fight back, and I think it blasphemes their memory when instructors say it only takes 2.3 rounds to survive a gunfight.

"By that standard, the people who lose gunfights are fir-ing 2.3 rounds; an instructor at the Federal Law Enforce-ment Training Center in Brunswick, Georgia, told me that in his interviews of federal agents who had survived shoot-outs, the average was more like six shots fired. And that is probably because by the time the agent had reloaded his empty double-action, the opponent had either run away or been shot down by a brother officer.

"With training you can reload an automatic in one to three seconds, a double-action revolver in three to six seconds. It takes me about thirty seconds to fire six shots, then reload a Colt single-action, and fire six more; the fast-est I've seen that done was by IPSC wizard Tommy Camp-bell, who did it in twenty-four seconds. I can deliver those twelve lethal hits in under ten seconds with a DA revolver and speedloaders, and in ten seconds I've done twenty-two

'kills' on an FBI silhouette with a .45 Colt automatic, including the time for two reloads."

But you can selectively eject empties and reload the single-action's chambers a round at a time, all the while being able to fire the loaded chambers of the frontier-style revolver!

"That only works in Walter Mitty cowboy fantasies, folks. For one thing, it requires a great deal of finger manipulation to empty, then reload a solid-frame single-action revolver. Under the great stress of a lethal-force encounter, when the fight-or-flight reflex takes over and adrenalin dumps into your system, the first thing you lose is 'fine motor coordination.' That means you become mighty clumsy.

"The first time you face lethal violence you'll feel an overwhelming tendency to 'blot it out' with your own gun-fire. In seconds your gun will be empty. I really hope you have something you can reload more swiftly than a single-action revolver.

"In the last century men who carried such guns into mor-tal combat — from Confederate cavalry troops to Wild Bill Hickok — carried multiple handguns, because they knew they could grab another loaded gun far more quickly than they could reload a cap 'n ball sixgun or a cartridge-fed Peacemaker. They were men who understood the realities of the violent human combat they carried handguns to survive.

Everyone knows that single-action fire is easier and more accurate than double-action fire. Doesn't it follow, then, that in a shooting the person with the single-action revolver will fire fewer wild shots?

"Here we have another great theory that works fine on the pistol range, but does not translate to the cold reality of the street. Revolvers are fired single-action in pistol matches where the stopwatches allow plenty of time for the hammer to be cocked and the trigger to carefully be squeez-ed. In a self-defense encounter your time margin between

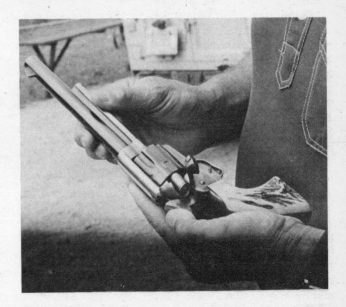

One problem with the single-action revolver in any type of serious shootout is the fact that it takes time to extract spent cases, load new cartridges individually.

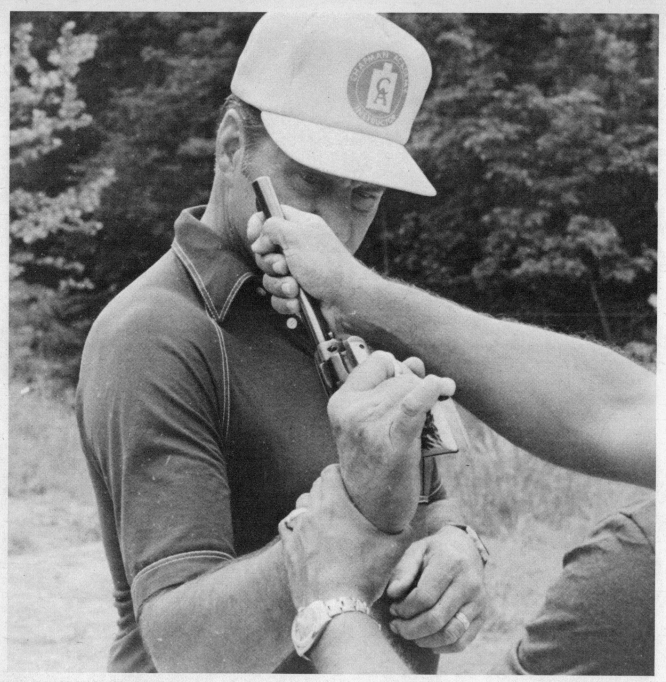

In the instant it requires to thumb back the hammer of the single-action, one can be in serious trouble with a felon who is familiar with the shortcomings of the gun. A double-action revolver is recommended for police use by Chapman, while automatics should be used by experts. Problem of cocking is demonstrated by Chapman, Ayoob.

shots is nil: you're going to be firing about as fast as you can.

"A single-action revolver used in that scenario is a terrible handicap. Not only is there a lot more elapsed time between shots than you need, but the cocking of the hammer forces you to break your hold on the gun, then hastily try to get your fingers back into firing position after the hammer has been brought back. This encourages wild shots. On a firing range, with its backstops and safety directors, a wild shot usually means only a missed target and a few dropped points. But in a self-defense situation, where there's no backstop and precious little time to mentally compute where a bullet will stop if it misses the

antagonist, that sort of wild shooting becomes a grave and present danger to innocent bystanders.

"The single-action revolver was the best threat management tool of its time, which ended in the 1880s. The Model T Ford was a great automobile in 1920, too, but no one today seriously suggests that you use a 'T' for anything but a nostalgia trip. The single-action revolver has better stood the test of time, is still useful for handgun hunting and metallic silhouette shooting. But neither instrument is state-of-the-art if you're looking at efficiency in the intended function of lethal threat management.

"I'm not saying that the single-action revolver is useless in the self-defense mode. A year-and-a-half ago I was rid-

Chapman rapid fires the Colt SAA with 7½-inch barrel. As much as he loves the gun, he knows its limitations. He was able to drop five reaction targets on the Bianchi Cup speed challenge course, however, in a measured 4.76 seconds.

ing with a pair of young black officers in a crime-ridden ghetto, when the radio blurted a call of an armed robbery in progress. No backup cars were immediately available to assist. I opened my hand to receive the 'spare gun' one of the cops passed over to me.

"The pistol was a Walther PPK/S, loaded with seven rounds of .380 hardball. I would normally relate to such a gun the way a surgeon would relate to being handed a Boy Scout knife instead of a scalpel, but it was better than nothing. Yet, if I'd had the choice of that or a single-action Ruger Super Blackhawk .44 magnum, I would definitely have taken the hogleg.

"But I had no choice and that is the point. When faced by a lethal threat, you deal with it using whatever means are available. A person who hunts with a Super Blackhawk or shoots metallic silhouettes with a Virginian Dragoon should be confident and competent to use that handgun under stress, if he's got the rest of his act together.

"If that person does have his act together, though, he probably knows enough about the dynamics of violent conflict with lawless criminals to have armed himself with something better suited to the purpose: a double-action revolver, or a semiautomatic pistol, loaded with good anti-personnel ammunition.

"The nicest thing I can say about a single-action revolver for self defense is that it's better than nothing. In my scale of priorities, the selection of the weapon comes about fourth down on the list of what you need to survive a violent encounter. First, is mental preparedness to deal decisively with life-threatening human violence. Second, comes knowledge and implementation of gunfighting tactics.

Third is skill with the safety equipment, to wit, the defensive firearm. Only when you have all that locked up does it matter much what kind of gun you're using.

"But if you're mentally prepared for a lethal force encounter, I hope you made the decision to use a proper instrument. If you've learned tactics you know that a double-action revolver backed up with speedloaders or a semiauto pistol give you a deadly edge. If you've become skilled with the defensive handgun, you must have learned that the DA revolver and especially the combat automatic were designed with human engineering principles to allow you to use them swiftly, positively and effectively under great stress.

"The single-action revolver doesn't fit into any of that. It's an anachronism. Hoglegs 'won the West' against other men with single-action revolvers...or with knives...or bows and arrows. It was true in 1873 that 'God made men, but Colonel Colt made them equal.' In 1982 that's still a workable statement, but a Python .357 or a Government Model .45 make you a lot more equal than a single-action Peacemaker.

"Good men or women who have their minds and their tactics and their shooting skill together probably can use a single-action revolver to outfight a punk with a fast-shooting modern gun. But if they have their minds, their tactics and their skill together, why should they handicap themselves in the first place?

"For self defense, the single-action revolver is better than nothing. If you care enough about your family to be reading this chapter, I think you deserve something better than that."

Chapter 10

SINGLE-ACTIONS & THE COLLECTOR

Following A Few Whys And Wherefores Can Build A Collection, Avoid Possible Fraud!

This 1849 Colt pocket pistol was found grown into the crotch of a tree in 1914 by a prospector in the Alaskan wilds. According to legend, the skeletons of a man and a bear were found nearby, leading to speculations.

AS INDICATED earlier, probably the most widely recognized firearm the world over is the Colt Single Action Army (SAA) revolver of history and legend. No other American firearm has quite the status as a collectable as the various Colt single-action revolvers. This status was brought about by the combination of a wide range of circumstances not the least of which is the prominence of the single-action Colt in movies and television. Even without TV and movies, the SAA Colt is a classic handgun that saw wide use through the most colorful and glamorous period of American history. It was used by the U.S. Army and such notable historical figures as Buffalo Bill Cody, Wyatt Earp, Bat Masterson, Teddy Roosevelt, and General George Patton, not to mention such famous "bad guys" as John Wesley Hardin, Cole Younger, and Jesse James.

This wide recognition and collectibility has spilled over to many of the Colt SAA's copies to include the contemporary Remington Model 1875 and 1890 revolvers as well as those more modern descendants such as the Ruger single-actions.

This chapter could include everything from percussion revolvers to certain modern S&W K38 target revolvers. Instead this chapter will be limited to the discussion of collecting Colt single-action cartridge revolvers and those revolvers, antique and modern — with emphasis on Rugers — that can be considered copies of it at least in external configuration. We assigned Charles W. Karwan, Jr., an authority on collecting, to research this segment.

"In gun collecting, those guns that cross several areas of collecting interest often are amongst the pieces in the highest demand. This is the case with the very first production of the Colt SAA, the U.S. Army contract .45s adopted in 1873," according to Karwan. "These fit into collections of Colt SAAs, U.S. martial handguns, Colt revolvers in general, Western collections, et al."

These Army Colts are chambered for the .45 Colt cartridge, have a blued finish with a color case-hardened frame, a 7½-inch barrel and one-piece walnut grips. The main thing that distinguishes these military Colts from the civilian variety is the presence of a *U.S.* stamped onto the

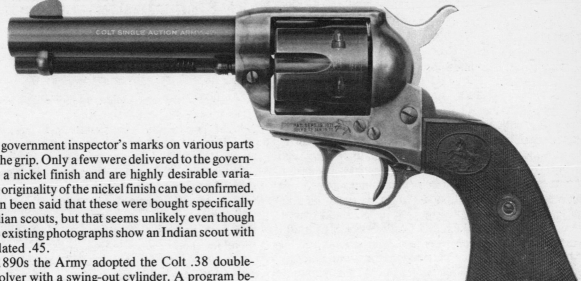

frame and government inspector's marks on various parts including the grip. Only a few were delivered to the government with a nickel finish and are highly desirable variations if the originality of the nickel finish can be confirmed. It has often been said that these were bought specifically for the Indian scouts, but that seems unlikely even though one or two existing photographs show an Indian scout with a nickel-plated .45.

In the 1890s the Army adopted the Colt .38 double-action revolver with a swing-out cylinder. A program began whereby existing stocks of used .45s were refurbished by Springfield Armory and the Colt factory. These guns were rebuilt and refinished to original specifications except that most serviceable barrels were shortened to 5½ inches and unserviceable barrels were replaced with new 5½-inch barrels. This created the other major collecting variation of U.S. Colt SAA. This 5½-inch-barrel variation is inexplicably known amongst collectors as the "Artillery Model" with the 7½-inch barrel variation being called the "Cavalry Model." This is in spite of the fact that both the infantry and artillery were also issued the 7½-inch-barrel version during most of the Colt SAA .45's military career. Curiously when the .38 Long Colt revolvers proved unsatisfactory manstoppers in the Philippines in the early 1900s, 5½-inch Colt SAA .45s were pulled out of stocks and issued primarily to the infantry!

Only a glance at the serial number will tell whether this 4¾-inch Colt Single Action Army was made prior to World War II or after. The pre-war versions are in great demand, increasing in value, among collectors.

The world of civilian Colt single-actions is much more complicated than the few military variations. Generally civilian single-action Colts are divided into two major groups — the pre-WWII SAAs considered by many to be the "original" single actions and the post-WWII Colt single actions.

One approach to collecting these old pre-WWII Colts has been to do it by caliber. It is doubtful that any other

When Springfield Armory and the Colt factory rebuilt these .45s it was done in various batches. It appears that in early batches efforts were made to keep the numbers of the various parts matched so a 5½-inch rebuilt Colt will be found occasionally with all or most of its part numbers matching. This procedure was soon dropped and most subsequently rebuilt Colt .45s were assembled with no regard for the part numbers. This is one case — maybe the only instance in gun collecting — where mixed numbers are considered original and not a detractor. Some authorities have tried to maintain that all 5½-inch rebuilds *should* have mixed numbers. This is not the case, as Karwan has encountered several specimens with all or nearly all matching numbers. U.S. martial Colt SAAs that have low numbers often bring a premium price, because they were in service during such historical events as the Battle of the Little Big Horn.

This Bisley model with 7½-inch barrel has .44 Russian and Smith & Wesson special barrel marking of the era.

handgun in history was ever chambered for as wide a range of cartridges as the pre-WWII Colt single-action. This fact alone is a major attraction of the Colt SAA to collectors.

One problem in this approach is to define what constitutes chambering. Sources that have used Colt records often get confused by Colt's nomenclature which may reflect a barrel marking, special order or different names for the same cartridge — not a different chambering. For instance, most lists based on factory records or letters on the SAA show the .44 Russian and .44 S&W cartridge separately, with some showing .44 S&W Russian as yet another chambering. In fact, the .44 Russian and .44 S&W Russian are the very same cartridge and there is no such separate cartridge as the .44 S&W! It would appear that *.44 S&W* was sometimes used as a substitute name for .44 S&W Russian. To make matters worse, when the .44 Special cartridge was adopted by Colt in 1913 and barrels were marked .44 Russian and S&W Special, Colt still referred to these in their records as being chambered for .44 S&W. Thus it is possible to have a SAA with a factory letter saying it was chambered for the .44 S&W and, in fact, it could be either .44 Russian or .44 Special, depending upon when it was made.

Likewise the .450 Eley and .450 Boxer cartridge are different names for the same cartridge that was adopted in England in 1868 for use in the Adams and later revolvers. Colt records indicate these calibers separately probably because they used whatever designation was used by whoever ordered the particular guns. Examination of the guns shows no difference in markings or chambering for either one. The following includes all the chamberings for the Colt Single Action known to us:

.476 Eley; .455 Eley — These have oversize cylinders with the chambers slightly down slanted to line up with the barrel. In fact the chambers are identical.

.450 Revolver — Listed variously as .450 Eley, Eley long, Eley short, Boxer, and Boxer short.

.45 ACP

.45 Smoothbore — .45 Colt chamber and smoothbore barrel for shot.

.45 Colt

.44-40 WCF — also called .44 Colt rifle and .44 CLMR (Colt Lighting Magazine Rifle).

.44 S&W Special — also listed as .44 S&W.

.44 Russian — also listed as .44 S&W Russian or .44 S&W.

.44 German — virtually identical to .44 Russian.

.44 Rimfire — same as .44 Henry rifle.

.44 Rim and Center-fire — same as .44 RF but two firing pins.

.44 Smoothbore — .44-40 chamber and smoothbore barrel for shot.

.41 Colt — also called .41 Long Colt.

.38-40 WCF — also called .38 Colt rifle and .38 CLMR (see .44-40).

.38 S&W Special; .38 Colt Special — cartridges are interchangeable with identical cases but the chambers on at least some are slightly different; barrel markings for both are the same.

.38-44 S&W Gallery

.38 S&W

.38 Colt — also called .38 Long Colt, two types are encountered; the pre-1904 which are bored straight through and the post 1904 which are identical to the .38 Special chamber.

Note the differences between the hammer, grip frame and trigger of the Bisley (top) and standard Colt SAA model.

These two Bisley single-actions feature changes that detract from their value as collector items. The Bisley at top has been rebarreled with a standard Colt SAA barrel, while one beneath has its barrel shortened.

.380 Eley

.357 Magnum

.32-20 WCF — also called .32 Colt rifle and .32 CLMR (see .44-40).

.32-44 S&W Gallery

.32 S&W — also called .32 S&W Long.

.32 Colt — also called .32 Colt Long.

.32 Rimfire

.22 WRF

.22 Rimfire

Using existing Colt records, the relative rarity of the above cartridges range from two known for the .32 RF and four known for the .380 Eley to 71,391 for the .44-40 and 158,885 for the .45 Colt. By far the most common calibers are .45 Colt, .44-40, .38-40, .32-20, and .41 Colt, in that order. Some calibers such as .450 Eley and Boxer, .455 Eley, and .44 RF were made in substantial quantities of one thousand to three thousand, but virtually all of them were exported. As a result they are even rarer than their production numbers would seem to indicate.

Any caliber other than the aforementioned five most common ones should be considered uncommon to down-

right rare and very desirable as a collectible. Very often the markings on the revolver itself will be of little help in identifying the actual chambering. The barrel marking could just be .38, .38 Special or .45 and not say which one. Likewise many of the earlier ones were marked on the trigger guard as .45 or .44 without saying which one. It can be a rare .450 or .44 German. The revolvers marked on the barrel, *Frontier Six Shooter,* are chambered for the .44-40 cartridge. This was the only caliber designated by such a title. Do not assume anything. If there is any doubt, send $15 for a factory letter to: Colt Industries, Firearms Division, M.S. Huber, Historian, P.O. Box 1868, Hartford, CT 06110.

This Colt-researched letter will supply the available information on the caliber, finish and barrel length with which the revolver was shipped originally. A factory letter is especially important for some calibers such as .44 Special, .38 Special, and .357 magnum, because so many guns were rebarreled and recylindered to these calibers when they became popular.

By far the most common barrel lengths are the 4¾, 5½, and 7½-inch. The factory-shipped guns came with barrels

The Great Western of two decades ago was an exact copy of the Colt SAA and was used as substitute in movies. Unlike many copies, it was manufactured in this country.

ranging from 2½ to 16 inches. Any original barrel other than the three most common could be considered a rarity. Again, be careful and get a factory letter on the odd ones.

The three standard finishes for the Colt Single Action were blue (relatively common), blue with case-hardened frame, and nickel plating. Other optional finishes include silver, gold and copper plate as well as engraved, inlaid and virtually any custom treatment. Copper plate is particularly rare. Anything but blue with a case-hardened frame would warrant a factory letter.

There are four major frame variations for the Colt SAA. These are the standard version, the Flat-top Target, the Bisley and the Bisley Flat-top Target. The Bisley, which came out in 1894, had a radically changed grip frame, hammer and trigger to improve the single-action for off-hand target shooting. It was named after the famous Bisley target range in England. Approximately 359,500 single-actions were produced in the pre-WWII series. The highest number produced was No. 357869, though some numbers were not used. All variations were in this serial number series except about 1800 guns made in .44RF, some of which were later factory-converted to .22RF and one to .32RF. Of the total production slightly more than 44,000 were Bisleys with less than 1000 each of Flat-top Target and Bisley Flat-top Target models. In 1892 the cylinder pin retainer was changed from a screw in the front to a spring-loaded cross-latch that is still used. Another frame variation rarely encountered is the frames that have no position for an ejector housing. These are most commonly found on short-barreled guns called *Sheriff's* or *Storekeeper's* models by collectors. Some Colt SAAs without ejector housings are found with long barrels, even in some cases flat-top target models. Any SAA Colt made originally without an ejector housing is a rare bird.

One subvariant that collectors often seek is the so-called

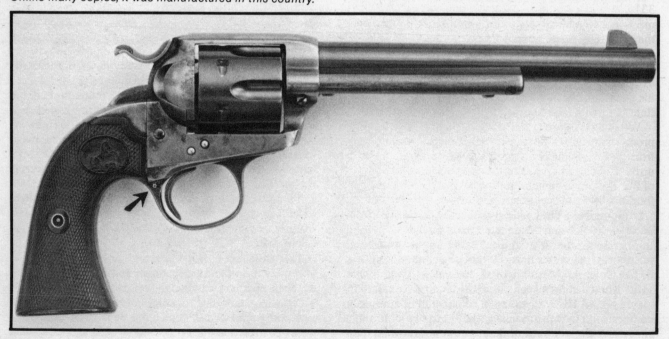

The small six-pointed star at the rear of this Bisley's trigger guard signifies that this single-action had been returned to the fatory for refinishing or other work. It can be an important clue to determine piece's originality.

The Ruger Single Six was the first standard-production single-action to be supplied with two cylinders. One was in .22 LR, the other for .22 WMR. Later versions of this convertible were issued with unfluted magnum cylinder.

"Long Flute" variation. In 1915 Colt decided to use up a substantial quantity of cylinders that they had on hand that were originally for the Double-Action Army Model of 1878. These cylinders had substantially longer flutes than the standard single-action cylinder, hence the nickname. To convert these to be usable on the SAA required only the milling of cylinder bolt notches. Guns originally shipped with these cylinders were serial numbered 330001 through 331379 and include two Bisley models. "These were made in various calibers, but it has been my experience that anything other than .45 Colt is rare. I have never owned a long flute cylinder Colt SAA, but I have owned two of the cylinders," Karwan reports. "One collector was extremely elated when I sold him one of these cylinders for his Colt that was numbered in the proper range for a long flute but had a later short-fluted replacement cylinder."

When WWII broke out and Colt was heavily into war production, the Colt Single Action Army was dropped from the line. Some of the last SAAs produced were bought up by the British Purchasing Commission during the Battle of Britain. Since demand for the SAA averaged less than four hundred guns per year for its last eleven years of pre-war production, the Colt company decided to not bring back the SAA when regular commercial revolver production resumed after WWII. So ended an era of production, but shortly thereafter began an era of collecting interest.

The Colt SAA wasn't in production more than a couple years when a copy hit the market in the form of the Remington Model 1875. It was natural for Remington to try to compete with Colt in this field as they had been Colt's most successful competitor during the percussion revolver era. The 1875 Remington looks and operates virtually identically to the Colt SAA. Its main distinguishing feature is a steel web under the barrel that causes the Remington to look like it has a percussion-type loading lever. This gives it an outline similar to the percussion Remington revolver.

Though an excellent revolver, this model suffered from being too late on the scene. There are no known sales to U.S. military forces, though 1300 were sold to the U.S. government probably for the use of Indian police on Western reservations. With a total production of only about 25,-000, the Remington Model 1875 is equally collectible to the Colt SAA it copied.

Most Model 1875s were chambered for the .44 Remington cartridge, though some were chambered for .44-40 and a very few for .45 Colt. These latter two are particularly desirable and usually bring a premium price.

By far the majority of the M1875 Remingtons had 7½-inch barrels. A few were factory-made with 5½-inch barrels. An original specimen of 5½-inch barrel would be rare, desirable and valuable, but care must be exercised as many barrels were shortened outside the factory. Standard finishes were blue and nickel plate. Nickeled specimens seem the most common.

Though 25,000 were produced, many were exported, including 10,000 to the Egyptian government. Consequently the 1875 Remington is very uncommon and highly collectible.

E. Remington & Sons became Remington Arms Co. about 1889. The reorganized company brought out a variation of Model 1875 called the Model 1890. It is virtually identical to the M1875, except it does not have the prominent web under the barrel and thus looks even more like a Colt SAA. Chambered for the .44-40 cartridge, these were available in 5½ and 7½-inch barrels and had both blue and nickel finish.

As only about 2000 were made in total, the Model 1890

is a rarely encountered single-action and brings correspondingly high prices. Care must be exercised with this model by collectors as many M1875s have been modified to appear to be the rarer M1890. As virtually all the M1890s have the Remington Arms barrel marking as opposed to the E. Remington and Sons on the M1875, this is the first clue for the collector as to the originality of the specimen.

After WWII it became clear to collectors and shooters that the venerable Colt SAA was no more and prices of existing specimens skyrocketed. This situation was aggrevated by a myriad of frontier movies and television Westerns that created even more interest in the single-action Colts.

The first company to step into this void was the now defunct Great Western Arms Company of North Hollywood, California. Great Western started production of Colt SAA copies about 1951. These were virtually exact copies of the Colt with most parts interchangeable with the Colt. The standard finish was blue and most had imitation stag plastic grips. They were offered in .22 LR, .357, .38 Special, .44 Special, .44 magnum, .45 Colt, and .22 Hornet. Barrel lengths were 4¾, 5½ and 7½ inches just like the Colt, with the 5½-inch being the most common. An adjustable-sight version was made for a time, but is uncommon.

The quality of the Great Western revolvers varied from acceptable to poor. Several motion picture celebrities used and endorsed the Great Western, but it never gained a favorable reputation amongst the shooting public. Great Western even tried the promotional gimmick of advertising the .357 Atomic cartridge as one of their chamberings. This was little more than an extra-hot load for the .357 magnum.

In 1956 Great Western revolvers were offered in a do-it-yourself kit form. It took more than a little gunsmithing skill to assemble one of these kits into a well timed, properly working revolver. As a result, these kits did little to improve Great Western's reputation for quality. The company disappeared around 1962. Collector interest in Great Western revolvers is moderate to low at present with most interest centering in California. Total production is

The early Colt Scout, produced after World War II, has become a collector item in its own right, the author says.

These two Rugers, both with ten-inch barrels, are rare. Single-action at top is .357 magnum, other is .44 magnum.

unknown, but they are by no means common. In spite of this fact, values are quite moderate.

The next to attempt to fill the rising demand for Western-style single-actions was the then young Sturm, Ruger & Company. In business only since 1949 with their .22 Standard automatic, Sturm, Ruger introduced their first single-action in 1953 in the form of the Single-Six .22 revolver. This was a revolutionary step forward in the world of single-action revolvers, as Bill Ruger had designed his version to eliminate most of the weaknesses in the more traditional style single-actions by using coil springs and a frame-mounted firing pin. Many innovative manufacturing techniques, such as the use of investment castings, made this excellent revolver moderately priced and an excellent dollar value.

From these humble beginnings came a virtual arms-making dynasty. At the time no one, least of all Bill Ruger himself, could have predicted the huge collector interest that would develop out of the Ruger single-action series. Interest in collecting Ruger guns in general rose to such a peak that a Ruger collecting association was formed. It has grown to such an extent that it is the world's largest specialty arms collectors association in the world. Membership costs $15 per year and the association can be reached at: Ruger Collectors Association, P.O. Box 290, Southport, CT 06490.

The phenomenal interest in collecting Rugers, particularly Ruger single-actions, rises out of several factors. For a start the various Ruger single-actions always have been moderately priced and marketed to shooters. As a result used and/or discontinued specimens, even rare variations, can often be purchased at moderate prices. Collectors who might have been drawn to the Colt single-actions turned to the Rugers out of financial concession. As collectible Colt SAAs became hard to find at any price, the Ruger single-actions were and are a natural alternative.

"Another factor, in my opinion is the fact that the Ruger firm has never let 'well enough' alone. There has been constant changes and improvements, right from the beginning, that create a myriad of variations and subvariations of the various models. For the collector the existence of some variation that he doesn't have just intensifies the search and his enjoyment when he finds a new piece," Karwan opines.

The aforementioned Single-Six was true to the Colt SAA in appearance and function. The grip frame — called by the factory, the XR3 — is exactly the same shape and size as the Colt SAA. Loading, unloading, ejection, et cetera was identical to the Colt. Originally the Single-Six was available only with a 5½-inch barrel. Early production had a flat loading gate, but contoured loading gates started appearing in 1957. In 1959 4⅝- and 9½-inch barrels were added to the line. An aluminum-framed version was produced from 1955 into 1958 with some having aluminum cylinders. Also in 1955 a 6½-inch-barreled version was offered in .22 WMR. In 1961 Ruger offered the Single-Six in a convertible version with two cylinders, one for .22 LR and one for .22 WMR, and in all four barrel lengths.

The Single-Six was replaced by the Super Single-Six in 1965 which was characterized by having a rib-protected adjustable rear sight, the convertible cylinder feature and a redesigned grip frame called the XR3 RED. Barrel lengths were limited to 5½ and 6½ inches. This was replaced by the New Model Super Single-Six convertible in 1972. This model variation, which is still in production, shortly became available in stainless steel and all four barrel lengths: 4⅝, 5½, 6½ and 9½ inches.

The New Model still is in production, but collectors are already eagerly looking for New Model stainless Single Sixes with 4⅝- and 9½-inch barrels as they were discontinued early in New Model production. Also sought are variations with a star on the front of the trigger guard signifying it was made with only one cylinder. "All such 'star' models I have observed have been in 9½-inch stainless. As you can see, a collector could spend a lifetime trying to get all the variations of the Single-Six and what I have reported are just the main variations," Karwan writes.

The Single-Six was a huge success, so Ruger soon turned to a center-fire version called the Blackhawk which they introduced in 1955. Of all the Rugers, the Blackhawk and its variations are the most sought after by collectors particularly the early "flat-top" versions.

The first version of the Blackhawk looked for all the world like a Colt SAA Flat-Top Target model. The XR3 grip, the cylinder and barrel, the flat-top frame all were virtually identical in size and shape to the Colt. The most obvious external difference is that it mounted a micro-adjustable rear sight flush into the frame and a ramp-type front sight. Esthetically, no single-action before or since has quite the clean good looks of these early Ruger Blackhawks. In addition the Blackhawk had all the same improvements of the single-action mechanism that had been pioneered in the Single-Six such as coil springs and frame-mounted firing pin. Initially it was offered only in .357 and with a 4⅝-inch barrel; the 6½-inch barrel was added later.

In 1956 Ruger began production of a Blackhawk with a larger frame and cylinder chambered for the then new .44 Remington magnum cartridge, beating the competition into production by several months. The .44 Blackhawk was initially available only with a 6½-inch barrel, but later in production a few 7½-inch-barreled guns were produced. Both the .357 and .44 Blackhawk were offered with ten-inch barrels in 1959. It is the 7½-inch .44 and the ten-inch

.357 and .44 Blackhawks that are both the rarest and the most eagerly sought after by collectors. A small group of ten-inch .357s, numbering around fifty pieces, was assembled with eight-groove barrels instead of the normal six-groove. These are probably the rarest of the production flat-top variations.

In 1959 a functionally improved variation of the .44 Blackhawk was introduced as the Super Blackhawk. It differed from the flat-top .44 in having a wider hammer and trigger, a larger dragoon-style grip frame with a square-backed guard, an unfluted cylinder and integral sight-protection ribs on the frame top. Virtually all of the Super Blackhawks had 7½-inch barrels though a few were produced with 6½- and 10-inch barrels. These odd barrel lengths get substantial premiums if their originality can be verified. The best approach in such cases is to write the factory to determine whether their records confirm the features of the piece in question. Inquiries should be sent to Sturm, Ruger and Company, Attention: Mr. Vogel, Southport, CT 06490. If you are a member of the aforementioned Ruger Collector's Association, they too have access to the Ruger records and can supply the needed information.

The success of the Super Blackhawk brought about the end of the flat-top Blackhawk series. The sight-protection ribs on the Super became standard on all Blackhawks in 1963. Also the XR3 RED or redesigned grip frame became standard. This new variation is referred to by collectors as the "three screw" or simply the "Old Model" Blackhawk. With these changes came the demise of the .44 Blackhawk, the Super version being the only .44 retained in the line.

The ribbed-top Blackhawks eventually had the .41 mag-

Ruger Blackhawk .44 magnum was the first in this caliber actually marketed to the public, S&W following closely.

The author rates this 6½-inch flat-top Ruger .44 magnum as one of the most esthetically pleasing single-actions.

num, the .30 carbine and .45 Colt added to the chamberings offered as well as two convertibles, the .357/9mm and the .45 Colt/.45 ACP.

In 1958 Ruger added a true miniature single-action to its line called the Bearcat. Available only in .22LR with fixed sights, the only way to describe this piece is cute. It was a dandy revolver for women and children, because of its petite size and was an excellent "kit gun" for the same reason. Originally made with an aluminum frame, a steel-framed version known as the Super Bearcat was offered in 1972. The latter was only produced for a little over a year and is quite difficult to find.

As mentioned in the paragraphs on the Single-Six, Ruger started switching all single-action models over to the New Model action in 1972. This New Model action was a huge change from the traditional Colt-type action. The

The top of the Ruger line is the Super Blackhawk. This is the old model, which has become collector's prize.

motivation for the design was to make a safer single-action, which it did in spades. The New Model Blackhawk could be carried with the hammer down on a loaded chamber, because the hammer cannot touch the firing pin unless the trigger is pulled, thus engaging the transfer bar. In effect the hammer hits the transfer bar which hits the firing pin.

Also, to prevent accidents during loading, the New Model is loaded by just opening the loading gate. This disengages the cylinder bolt allowing the cylinder to turn freely for loading and unloading. Consequently there is no half-cock notch or safety notch on the New Model.

The New Model also does not have the traditional three screws in the frame, using two pins instead. This is why the Old Models are called three-screw models by collectors. The New Model changes were well supported by the gun-writing press and the buyer public though there were more than a few screams of anguish from old-time single-action users.

Ruger Single Six (top) is compared to its little brother, the Ruger Bearcat. Both were made in numerous variations.

The old model Super Blackhawk was called the 3-screw model because of the three screws in the gun's frame. It also was the first Ruger single-action to have the sight-protection ribs which were milled into top strap.

The New Model features were incorporated across the entire Blackhawk and Super Blackhawk lines. The Bearcat fell by the wayside and was discontinued. Also, in the New Model Blackhawk series all calibers are on the same .44 frame. Previously the .357 and .41 magnums were built on the .357 frame. As with the Single-Six, some of the New Model Blackhawk variations became available in stainless steel. Even though the New Model is still in production, some variations are no longer made and are highly sought by collectors. One such is a small run of stainless .357/9mm convertibles.

Two other factors will affect the future collector values of many New Models. In 1976 Ruger marked all the guns they made with the marking: *Made in the 200th Year of American Liberty*. These Liberty models are starting to bring a slight premium over a run-of-the-mill New Model. Likewise when Ruger changed the barrel marking on the New Models to read, *Before using gun — read warnings in instruction manual available free from Sturm, Ruger & Co., Inc., Southport, Conn U.S.A.*, they made the preceding models the "Pre-Warning" variation. Shooters and collectors alike, are paying a slight premium to not have the unsightly warning on their guns. So it goes in the world of collecting.

Ruger's single-action success wasn't lost on Colt. In 1956 Colt reintroduced the SAA. This version was very true to the pre-WWII version in every way. About the only

Differences between the old model Single Six (top) and the New Model are evident, other than the stainless steel, in the profile of the hammer and the trigger. Also the New Model does not have the three screws in the frame.

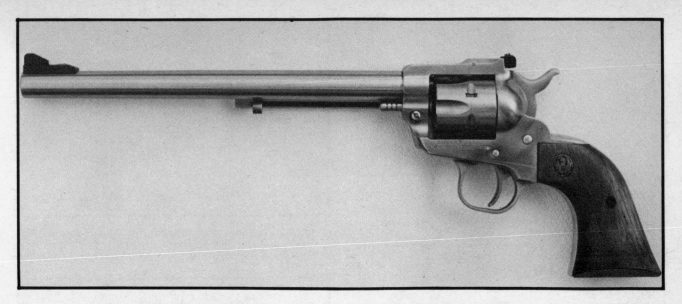

This particular 9½-inch stainless steel New Model Single Six was shipped with two cylinders, one for .22 RF, the other for .22 WRF. If a star is stamped just ahead of the trigger, it means gun was shipped with one cylinder.

obvious difference was the addition of an SA after the serial number. The resurrected Colt SAA eventually became available in 4¾-, 5½-, and 7½-inch barrels in .38 Special, .357 magnum, .44 Special, and .45 Colt. Finishes were blue with case-hardened frame or nickel. A twelve-inch Buntline model was introduced in 1957 probably due to interest brought about by the TV program, *Wyatt Earp*. There was also a limited group of 503 three-inch-barreled Sheriff's Model SAAs with no ejector rod made for one dealer. These have SM after their serial numbers. Many variations in this post-WWII SAA series are desirable due to their limited production. The nickeled .44 Special SAAs are particularly hard to find, but care must be taken that the nickel is original. If there are any doubts, get a factory letter.

Due largely to the success of Ruger's Single-Six, Colt entered the single-action .22 market with their own version, the Frontier Scout .22. This revolver series was true

Note the two frame pins in the New Model Blackhawk .357. The New Model utilizes these pins instead of 3 screws.

New Model Blackhawk differs in appearance from the old model with a larger frame, different profile of hammer and trigger and two pins replacing three frame screws.

Colt New Frontier version (beneath) is direct descendent of the Colt SAA flat-top target models of the 1880s. The difference between it and standard Colt SAA are obvious.

The New Model .357 (bottom) has been reworked to look more like the old model flat-top (top) than its New Model brother positioned for comparison in middle.

Main differences between standard Colt SAA (top) and New Frontier version are the adjustable sights, flat-top frame and the bright Royal Blue finish on latter.

The twelve-inch Buntline .45 (top) is a scarce variation in the post-World War II Single Action Army series. The 4¾-inch version beneath was shortest standard length.

The Colt SAA has been widely copied by overseas makers. This Arminius, made in West Germany, is a virtually exact copy. While the author feels it is of excellent quality, it has very little potential for collectors.

to its big brother in appearance and operation, the main difference being smaller dimensions all around, an aluminum frame and a frame-mounted firing pin. A 4¾-inch barrel was standard. This series was expanded and changed to include 9½-inch-barreled Buntline models, .22 magnum models, dual-cylinder models, and nickel-plated versions. Eventually, around 1962, the aluminum frame was dropped for a zinc alloy frame which is known as the K series. Later, in 1970, a version with an investment cast steel frame color case-hardened just like the traditional Colt SAA was introduced called the Peacemaker and New Frontier .22s. This last series was discontinued in 1976.

In 1982 Colt announced a revival of the New Frontier

.22 version with a "cross-bolt safety." This whole .22 single-action line of Colts is a sleeper area for collectors as interest and prices are moderate, yet collecting potential is high.

In 1961 Colt introduced a flat-top target model of the Colt SAA called the New Frontier. It differed from the standard Colt SAA by having a flat-top frame mounting an Accro adjustable rear sight, a ramp front sight and Colt's finest Royal Blue finish with the traditional color case-hardened frame. This model was made in 4¾-, 5½-, 7½-

Buntline Scout (top), from the aluminum-framed series, is compared to New Frontier Buntline .22 convertible with case-hardened frame. Latter was discontinued in 1972, but a newer version was reintroduced in 1982.

and 12-inch barrel lengths, the first and last mentioned being quite rare. Chamberings include .38 Special (rare), .357, .44 Special (scarce), and .45 Colt. This was the finest production single-action ever produced by Colt. This high quality combined with the low numbers produced (less than 8000 total) make this series one of the premier groups for collectors. No barrel and caliber combination was produced in large numbers and most combinations are scarce to rare.

Colt stopped production of both the SAA and New Frontier series in 1975. Both models were brought back in 1976 with some changes. The barrel threads, the cylinder bushing, the ratchet and hand were all different in the New Model Colt SAA as well as a few subtle changes in the frame. This new series saw the reintroduction of the .44 Special and the .44-40 cartridge into the line. In 1981 Colt announced production of the Colt SAA and New Frontier would be discontinued as parts were used up. Production of these models was expected to cease in 1982.

When the dust settles and production of the Colt SAA and New Frontier finally ends, this last group of Colt single-actions very likely will supply some of the rarest and most valuable specimens for collectors. As with pre-WWII Colt SAAs, care must be taken that rare calibers, barrel lengths, finishes or combinations thereof are factory original. If there is any doubt, a factory letter should be sought.

There have been a great number of foreign imports that are copies to one extent or another of the traditional Colt and Ruger type single-actions. Most of these came from Italy and Germany with a few from Switzerland. In Karwan's opinion none of these imports has any particular collecting potential except one. That is the Virginian, made by Hammerli of Switzerland and imported by Interarms from 1973 to 1976.

Other than not having a bushed firing pin hole the Virginian is an extremely high quality piece rivaling Colt in quality of fit, finish and materials. The Hammerli name has always been associated with high quality, so that is no surprise. Made in .357 and .45 Colt and with 4¾-, 5½-, and 7½-inch barrels, this is the only imported single-action worth a second glance by collectors, in Karwan's opinion.

In the past few years several custom gunsmithing companies have announced the production of limited editions. The approach seems to be to take a group of standard-production single-actions, such as Ruger's Super Blackhawk, give them some custom features such as a shortened barrel, high-polish blue, plated parts, ad infinitum. These are given a fancy name and sold as a "Limited Edition."

As long as one buys only such guns as those put out by quality operations such as Mag-na-port and at or near the original price offering you are getting a good dollar value.

"It has been my experience, however, that the collecting

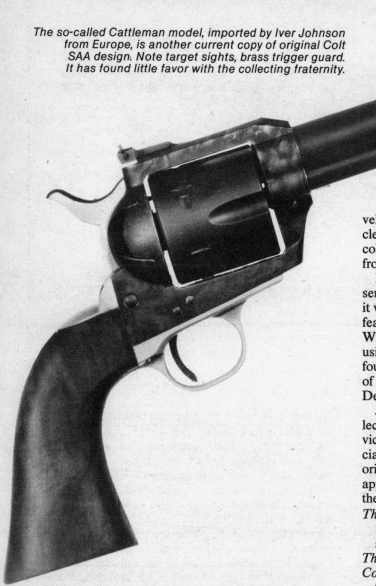

The so-called Cattleman model, imported by Iver Johnson from Europe, is another current copy of original Colt SAA design. Note target sights, brass trigger guard. It has found little favor with the collecting fraternity.

velop some expertise on the subject. At the end of this article, we have listed several books of particular value in collecting single-actions. More collectors get in trouble from lack of knowledge than any other single reason.

Haunt the gun shows and museums so that you can observe firsthand as many variations as possible. In that way it will become obvious to you what an original finish and features should look like and the values of various models. When dealing through the mail or by phone, rather than using the good/very good/excellent grading system, we've found the best approach is to actually describe the amount of original finish, the bore condition and any detractors. Demand the same from your correspondents.

Join the Ruger Collector's Association if you are collecting Rugers and take advantage of the factory letter service offered by both Colt and Ruger. The latter is especially important for the odd variations to help confirm their originality. Single-action revolvers are as American as apple pie and will be a favored area for collecting as long as there is an American.

The Book of Colt Firearms by R.L. Wilson and R.Q. Sutherland. Published by Robert Q. Sutherland, Kansas City, Missouri (out of print).

The Colt Heritage by R.L. Wilson, Simon & Schuster.

Colt's SAA Post War Models by George Garton, Beinfield Publishing, No. Hollywood, California.

Flayderman's Guide to American Firearms and their values, 2nd edition, by Norm Flayderman, DBI Books, Inc., Northfield, Illinois.

Gun Digest Book of Modern Gun Values, 3rd Edition, by Jack Lewis, DBI Books, Northfield, Illinois.

Gun Traders Guide, 9th Edition by Paul Wahl, Stoeger Publishing Co., Hackensack, New Jersey.

Know Your Ruger Single Action Revolvers 1953-63 by John C. Dougan, Blacksmith Corporation, Southport, Connecticut.

The Peace-Maker and its Rivals by John E. Parsons, William Morrow & Company, New York (out of print).

The Post-War Colt Single-Action Revolvers by Don Wilkerson, The Single Action Shop, Apple Valley, Minnesota.

The 36 Calibers of the Colt Single Action Army by David Brown, published by author, Albuquerque, New Mexico.

potential and huge increases in value hyped for these type guns is just not there in most cases. Most Ruger collectors walk right by such guns because they are not 'factory.' There has been a flurry of interest in the past in these guns, but that appears to have died down to a great extent. If you are interested in collecting some company's series by all means do so, just don't expect overnight value increases of 300-400% as some would have you believe is normal. Such prices are, in my experience, the exception rather than the rule," Karwan says.

We've purposely avoided commemoratives in this discussion mostly because it is a field that deserves separate treatment and is out of the scope of this treatise. Needless to say, the commemorative field includes many single-actions including both Colts and Rugers and there is a substantial collector interest in these areas.

In collecting single-actions, be they old or modern, always try to get the specimen in the best condition possible. Read the books available on your area of interest to de-

The Hammerli Virginian, imported by Interarms a few years back, is the only imported single-action with significant collector potential. (Below) Though a good value at the original price, limited editions such as the Mag-na-port Classic are not the collection sensations that some would have us believe, according to investigations by Karwan.

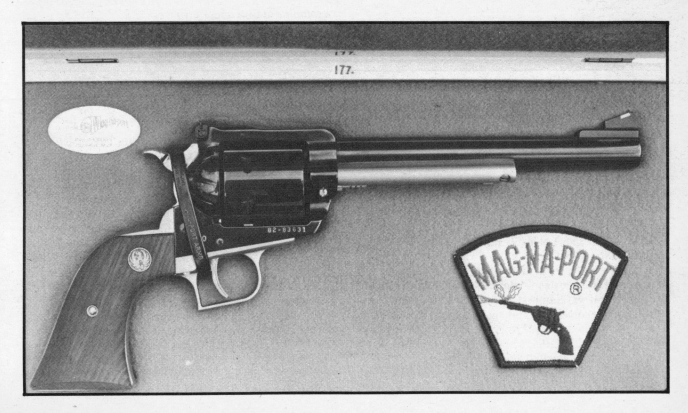

Chapter 11

PRESENTATIONS & COMMEMORATIVES

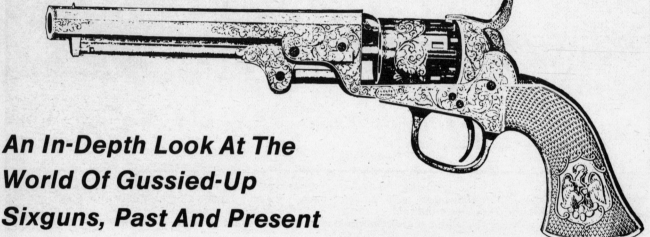

An In-Depth Look At The World Of Gussied-Up Sixguns, Past And Present

Examples of Colt decorative work is illustrated in old print from early catalog. This Navy Model .36 boasted engraving, checkered and carved ivory grips, with some metal gold plated.

ENGRAVING is an art virtually as old as mankind. The caveman who scratched crude pictures on the walls of his sandstone cave with a bit of flint was setting the tone for things to come. From that crude beginning, through the artistry of the Chinese, the Egyptians, the Greeks and Romans, we have reached the level of today's embellishment of firearms that has led to the presentation pieces and the more recent commemorative series of several manufacturers.

While the presence of highly ornate firearms evident in museums throughout the world indicates that they have been engraved and inlaid with silver, gold and even precious gems for centuries — almost since the invention of the firearm — it was Samuel Colt who created the idea of a presentation revolver. The early guns made in this country were manufactured or made by hand, then passed on to an artisan to decorate. Later, some gun manufacturers who wanted presentation guns tended to turn them over to specific artisans under contract. This practice still continues, although there have been in-house engravers and

gold and silver smiths in several of the gunmaking companies since the last century.

In the present and recent past there have been some great names in the field of engraving. Any single-action that boasts authentic Kornbrath engraving is high on the collector list. From about 1850 until 1900 L.D. Nimsche was considered the outstanding gun engraver in this country — although, as with all things artistic, his fame has increased more since his death than during his working years.

Nimsche was prolific. There is no way of knowing how many guns he actually engraved in his half-century of work, but it has been estimated at more than 5000. He engraved other items as well, including pocket watches, bracelets, watch fobs and other personal mementoes. While many engravers tend to specialize in specific patterns, Nimsche had the reputation, verified by examples of his work still in existence, that he could inscribe in metal virtually any design, be it a scroll, lettering, figure of an animal or even a portrait. He did not settle on a few basic

Alvin A. White was one of those Colt craftsmen who brought a high degree of artistry to the art of engraving and gold inlay work that has placed his work in high demand by the collectors of today. Factory-trained craftsmen often left such employment to open engraving and custom work shops of their own, catering to factories and even individuals.

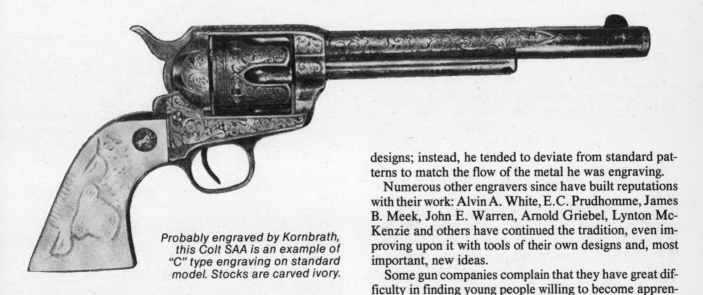

Probably engraved by Kornbrath, this Colt SAA is an example of "C" type engraving on standard model. Stocks are carved ivory.

designs; instead, he tended to deviate from standard patterns to match the flow of the metal he was engraving.

Numerous other engravers since have built reputations with their work: Alvin A. White, E.C. Prudhomme, James B. Meek, John E. Warren, Arnold Griebel, Lynton McKenzie and others have continued the tradition, even improving upon it with tools of their own designs and, most important, new ideas.

Some gun companies complain that they have great difficulty in finding young people willing to become apprentices and thus learn the techniques for such gun ornamentation. However, if one looks at some of the work coming out

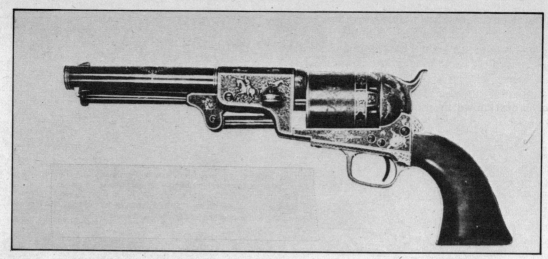

This fine example of early Colt engraving with gold inlays now is on display at the Connecticut State Library. Such artistry is seldom duplicated in the modern day.

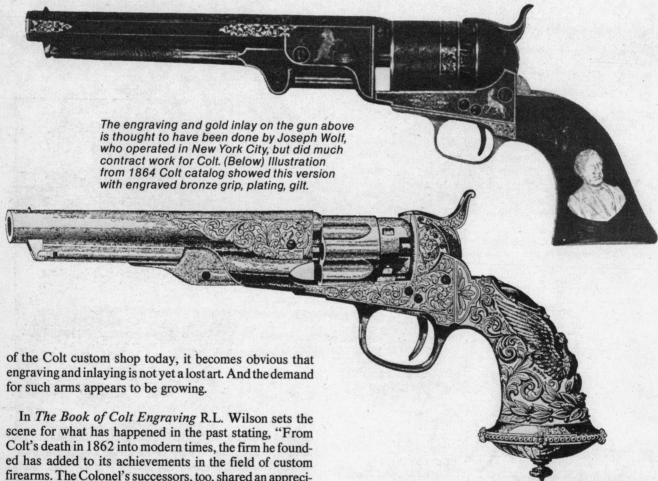

The engraving and gold inlay on the gun above is thought to have been done by Joseph Wolf, who operated in New York City, but did much contract work for Colt. (Below) Illustration from 1864 Colt catalog showed this version with engraved bronze grip, plating, gilt.

of the Colt custom shop today, it becomes obvious that engraving and inlaying is not yet a lost art. And the demand for such arms appears to be growing.

In *The Book of Colt Engraving* R.L. Wilson sets the scene for what has happened in the past stating, "From Colt's death in 1862 into modern times, the firm he founded has added to its achievements in the field of custom firearms. The Colonel's successors, too, shared an appreciation of quality, history and the uniqueness inherent with the products marked with the name Colt. A few of the best known clients who took pride in their custom Colts included Buffalo Bill Cody, Bat Masterson, George Armstrong Custer, U.S. Grant, John J. Pershing and Douglas Mac-Arthur, the artists Frederic Remington and George Catlin, Western stars Tom Mix, Chuck Connors and John Wayne and several Presidents of the United States..."

One such piece, a fully custom Paterson, was presented to Theodore Roosevelt and now is museum-preserved. The ivory-handled Colt Single Action Army revolvers that General George Patton wore throughout the European campaign also came out of the Colt custom shop. As a matter of interest, someone once mistakenly identified the grips of the Patton pair as being of mother-of-pearl. Patton's typical rejoinder was that "only a New Orleans pimp would have pearl handles on a gun!" The late Tom Mix, who preferred pearl grips, would have taken great exception. So, too, would a lot of New Orleans pimps!

While the custom shop in Hartford does a lot of other things besides fancy up firearms, this is the facet for which it probably is best known; these are the guns that get talked and written about and which catch the eye of the public.

Over the years a host of experts have worked in that shop. Some have passed on, some have opened their own shops, while others have remained at their Hartford benches. The expertise of such individuals as the earlier mentioned Alvin A. White, Earl Giggey, Bob Burt, Leonard Francolini, Dan Goodwin, Bryson J. Gwinnel and Steven Kamyk adds up to a lot of talent. With the shop continuing to grow and the staff training new talent, Colt should have the largest shop in the world by 1985.

For the past few years Colt has come up with one special gun annually that is auctioned off usually at a major sporting goods show. In 1976 a Bicentennial Dragoon with gold

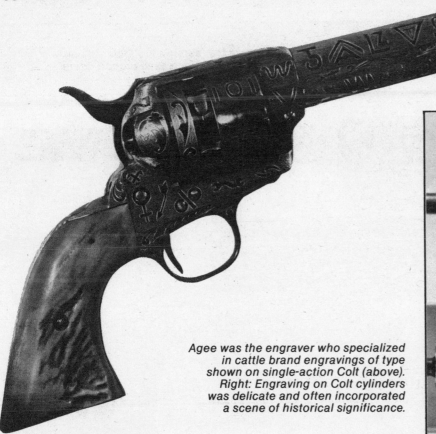

Agee was the engraver who specialized in cattle brand engravings of type shown on single-action Colt (above). Right: Engraving on Colt cylinders was delicate and often incorporated a scene of historical significance.

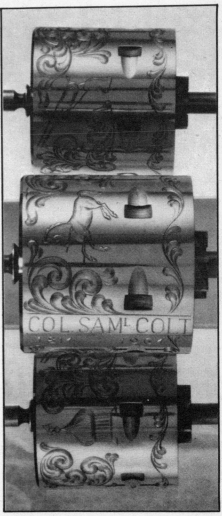

inlays and heavy engraving was auctioned off for $55,000. The following year a Colt Tiffany-gripped SAA was sold by sealed bid for a high of $49,500. Funds from these sales are donated to the U.S. Olympic Fund to aid competitive shooters.

There was a time when a presentation-quality gun was available only to the wealthy — or perhaps as a gift from Colonel Colt to some individual who might be able to do the firm some good. Any number of presentation guns went

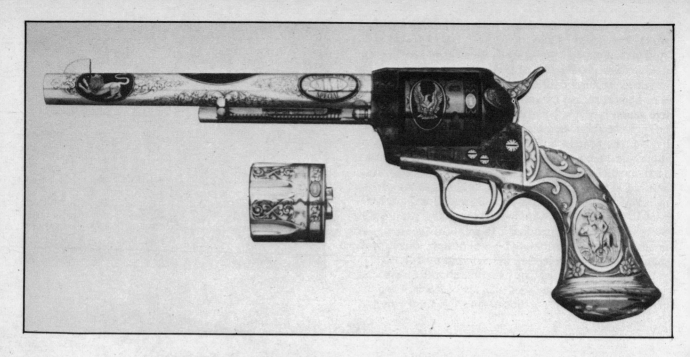

Tiffany-engraved revolvers such as this Colt example still are available from the factory's craftsmen, if one is willing to foot the bill. With the increases in prices of gold in last decade, cost has increased proportionately.

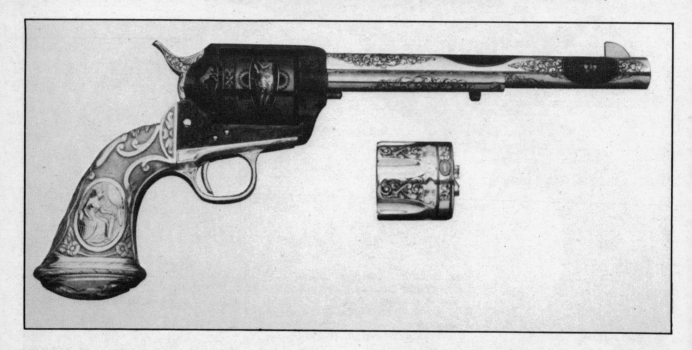

into the safes and strong boxes of politicians and military leaders of more than a century ago with the idea that they might influence sale to the government. Similar guns were presented also to foreign dignitaries with a bread-cast-upon-the-waters thought in mind. Such favor-oriented gifts are frowned upon today and it has been many years since U.S. gun manufacturers have followed such a policy of gentle bribery. It should be noted, however, that back in the days when Fidel Castro was calling himself a patriot rather than a communist, one U.S. firm did send him a highly engraved, gold-inlaid presentation pistol. The officers of the firm have wished many times since that they could get the gun back and melt it down!

Today engraving is available in A class, which covers about one-quarter of the gun's surface, progressing through the alphabet to class D, which covers virtually all of the exterior. Class A engraving for a single-action SAA these days starts at $545 from Colt, while the price of Class D engraving on the same gun would begin at $1043.

Some consider the commemorative issue the poor man's custom gun, if one wants to look at it in that light.

This Colt commemorative usually is a stock gun that has been given some special treatment to pretty it up. The number manufactured depends largely upon the potential sale, of course, while the original retail price has been kept at a reasonable level for the potential collector. The exception, perhaps, would be the John Wayne Commemorative, which was issued in 1982 as the last of the Colt Single Action Army models — at least, as we have known them for a century-plus. Of this particular model only 3100 guns have been made and the price is close to $3000 per gun. It is estimated by some experts that the value will double in five years.

The big swing to commemoratives began in 1961 rather by accident, when Bob Cherry, a gun dealer in Genesco, Illinois, ordered 104 Colt Derringers to recognize the 125th anniversary of the founding of his town. These Derringers were gold plated overall and sold in a box lined in velvet and satin. The price at the time was $27.50. Today, these guns, fully authenticated, go for some $500 each on the collector market. The fact that there were so few makes them valuable.

In 1961 Colt issued six commemorative models ranging

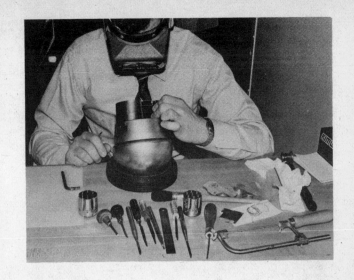

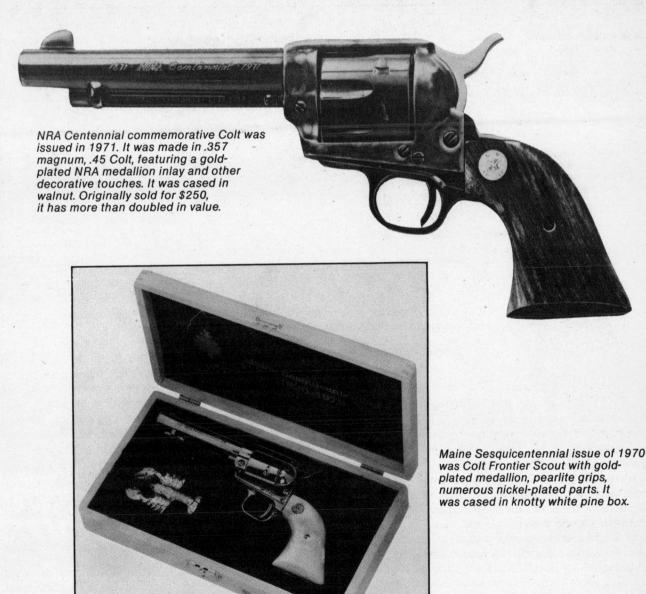

NRA Centennial commemorative Colt was issued in 1971. It was made in .357 magnum, .45 Colt, featuring a gold-plated NRA medallion inlay and other decorative touches. It was cased in walnut. Originally sold for $250, it has more than doubled in value.

Maine Sesquicentennial issue of 1970 was Colt Frontier Scout with gold-plated medallion, pearlite grips, numerous nickel-plated parts. It was cased in knotty white pine box.

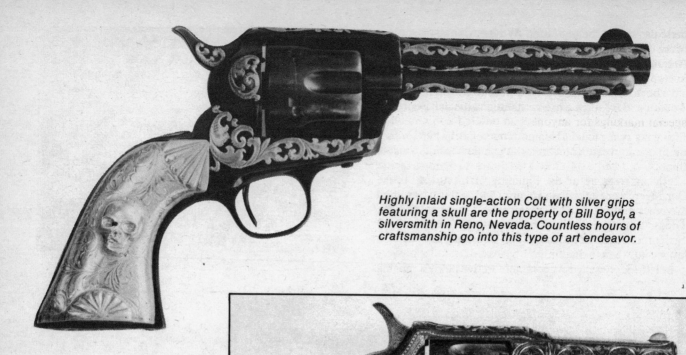

Highly inlaid single-action Colt with silver grips featuring a skull are the property of Bill Boyd, a silversmith in Reno, Nevada. Countless hours of craftsmanship go into this type of art endeavor.

Remington also did excellent job of prettying-up standard models during the period in which firm made handguns.

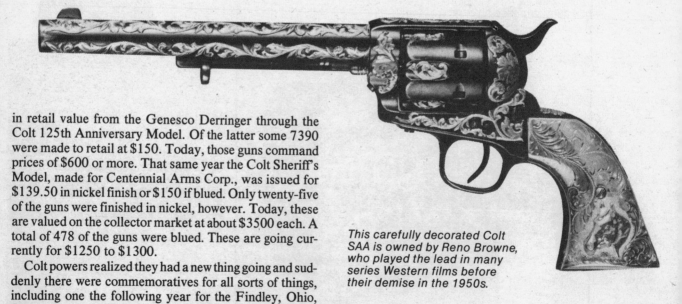

in retail value from the Genesco Derringer through the Colt 125th Anniversary Model. Of the latter some 7390 were made to retail at $150. Today, those guns command prices of $600 or more. That same year the Colt Sheriff's Model, made for Centennial Arms Corp., was issued for $139.50 in nickel finish or $150 if blued. Only twenty-five of the guns were finished in nickel, however. Today, these are valued on the collector market at about $3500 each. A total of 478 of the guns were blued. These are going currently for $1250 to $1300.

Colt powers realized they had a new thing going and suddenly there were commemoratives for all sorts of things, including one the following year for the Findley, Ohio, Sesquicentennial. Don't laugh. Originally 110 .22 LR guns were made to commemorate this event. They sold for $89.50 retail. Today those guns sell for $650 up. There also were twenty sets of cased .22 magnums made valued

This carefully decorated Colt SAA is owned by Reno Browne, who played the lead in many series Western films before their demise in the 1950s.

these days at $3250 to $3350! At the other extreme, some of the commemorative runs numbered in the thousands. In twenty years or so they have doubled their value, but have not gained the monumental worth of the limited editions.

"During that era," according to Bob Cherry, "Colt would produce a special barrel length, special finish and special markings for anyone who ordered a minimum of fifty guns of a model. This continued until 1966, with a number of private commemorative issues being brought forth."

Colt officials began to realize they had created something of a monster. Thus, in 1965 they established their Commemorative Committee initially composed of Herb Glass, Charles Kidwell, Bob Cherry and Wally Beinfield. Since then the committee has had a rotating membership whose duty it is to determine what events or individuals in

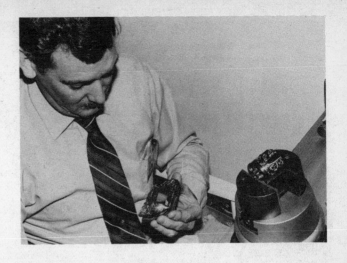

Remington Model 1890 Army single-action revolver is tastefully engraved and outfitted with mother-of-pearl grips. (Below) This highly decorated Colt with Tiffany grip was displayed at the 1978 trade show, later auctioned off.

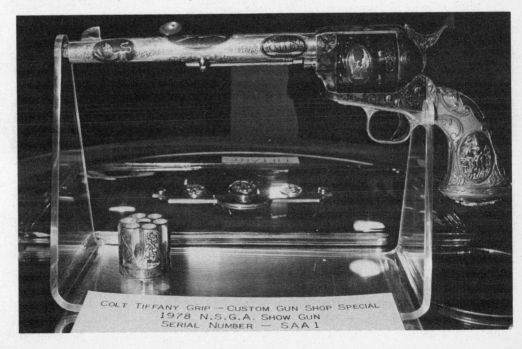

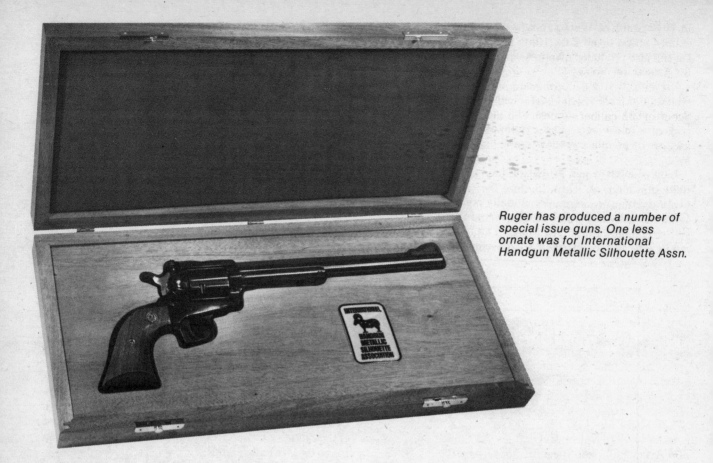

Ruger has produced a number of special issue guns. One less ornate was for International Handgun Metallic Silhouette Assn.

history truly deserve commemorating.

Since the Bicentennial of 1976 commemorative action has slowed for Colt. The 1982 introduction of the John Wayne commemorative marked the recent high point, coupled with the demise of the original design of the Colt SAA.

On the longarms scene Remington produced numerous models to commemorate the firm's 150th anniversary in 1965, with Winchester climbing on the bandwagon the following year. In the years since there have been numerous rifle and shotgun makers who have turned out commemorative issues, but Colt has had the handgun market virtually to itself, with the exception of Ruger, who has done some cautious production that will be discussed later.

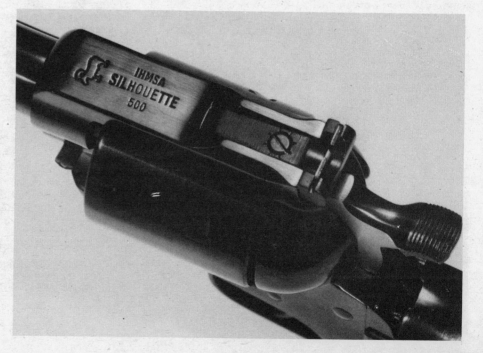

The IHMSA guns are designed to be fired in competition, so are marked simply and without any expensive inlays to fall out.

In 1977 Smith & Wesson produced an ornate Model 25 double-action to mark the 125th anniversary of its founding and also produced a limited run on behalf of the Texas Rangers at one point.

In the case of the Colt commemoratives, most have been pretty much standard models — with concentration on the Scout in .22 caliber — cosmetic changes incorporating grips of exotic woods, gold or silver plating on some parts and, of course, the commemorative message inscribed on the barrel.

In Chapter 10 some mention was made of the special-issue guns made by Ruger for the Mag-na-port series. As explained, this manufacturer entered the special issue and commemorative business with a bit more thought than perhaps had been shown by others. The special guns were produced on contracts with a specified number of guns pre-sold, thus taking the risk element out of the production.

In 1979 a hundred Super Blackhawk .44 magnums were issued with the logo of the International Handgun Metallic Silhouette Association etched on the right side of the frame and "Limited Edition" under the cylinder on the same side of the frame. These guns all had 7½-inch barrels, with the initials IHMSA etched on the top strap.

A similar edition — this time of five hundred — was issued in 1980, these with 10½-inch barrels. Each of these came in a mahogany presentation case with the IHMSA logo enclosed. The top strap was engraved with "IHMSA SILHOUETTE 500."

In early 1979 Sturm, Ruger offered a limited edition of 304 Arizona Ranger Specials. These were the .45 Blackhawk with a special series of serial numbers on the grip frame. All were made with a stainless steel grip frame, hammer and trigger, although all other parts are blued. Barrel length on these commemoratives was 4⅝ inches and each was equipped with smooth walnut grips. The logo of the Arizona Rangers — a horseman with mountains in the background, the scene enclosed in an outline of the state — was stamped on the top strap with the words "ARIZONA RANGERS" on the top of the barrel. Three hundred of these were shipped to Arizona, while Bill Ruger retained numbers 301 through 304 for his own collection. Number 1 went to the state's governor, while the next 249

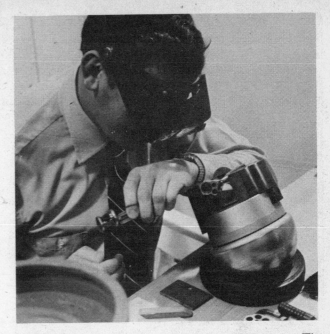

guns were sold to members of the Arizona Rangers. The final fifty were sold to the public in the state.

Mag-na-port got back into the cooperative act with a series of Blackhawk War commemoratives. Badger Shooting Supply ordered 150 of these .45 Blackhawks to honor the Sac chieftain, Blackhawk, who led his people and those of the Fox tribe in the upper Midwest in 1832 in an attempt to regain lost Indian lands.

These guns were equipped with 7½-inch barrels, each of them Mag-na-ported and sealed at the factory against firing. These guns are fitted with custom sights, while the trigger and hammer are jeweled, the ejector rod house and grip frame finished with nickel satin. The rest of the gun was blued. All of these guns were cased in walnut lined with scarlet velvet, a commemorative medallion set in the lid.

Ruger also turned out a thousand .357 magnum single-actions for the Bass Anglers Sportsman Society in late 1981. These guns were less ornate than some the firm had produced on similar special order, since there were few changes from the production model. The front sight held a red insert, while the rear sight was outlined in white; the BASS emblem was etched into the left side of the frame and the words "BASS Limited Edition 1981" are etched in the back strap with a special identifying serial number for the series. Each of the guns came in a cherry wood box with appropriate BASS markings.

In 1982 a special issue of five hundred .44 Super Blackhawks was made for the Michigan Association of Chiefs of Police. This single-action carries the badges of the Michigan police chiefs, sheriffs and state police engraved in triple relief on the cylinder. A gold and blue logo of the

Each of the IHMSA issue has been marked with a special serial number, with the steel ram insignia of the organization prominently stamped into metal of butt.

Ruger introduced roll-engraved cylinders early in his firm's production, marking the Bearcat with name, decoration. (Below) Special run of Texas Ranger commemorative .45 Colts were highly engraved with silver plate, ivory grips.

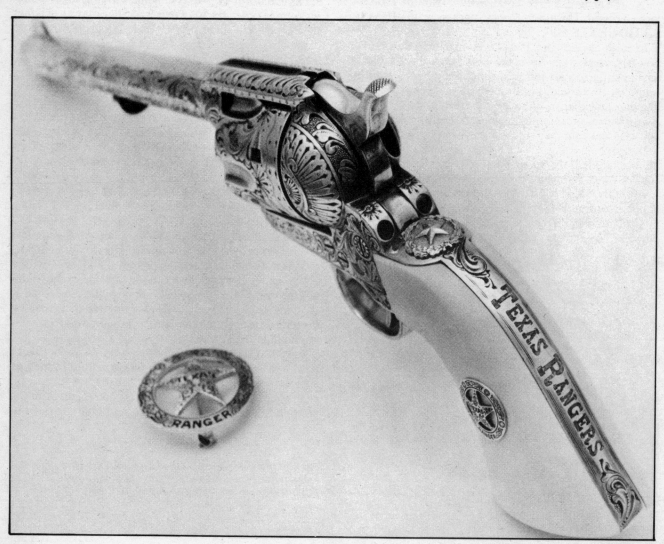

organization is inset in the grip, and the side plates, hammer and barrel are gold plated.

The .44 Old Army percussion also has come in for a share of this specialized business. The National Muzzle Loading Rifle Association ordered a hundred blued Old Army models in 1974, then added their own emblem to the grip panel. These were sold to members of the organization on a drawing basis.

The Ruger Collector's Association also has had an influence on special issues and in 1975 ordered a hundred stainless steel Old Army revolvers. Serial numbers on these guns range from 1500 to 1599 with a star preceeding the number. The initials RCA were engraved on the top strap and each gun was furnished with an authenticating letter from the maker. One of these guns was engraved and later sold to an RCA member through auction.

In 1976 the same organization purchased the last two

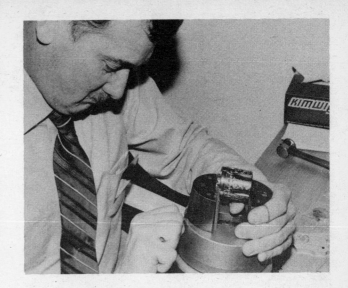

hundred stainless steel Ruger percussions marked with the Bicentennial logo. These also were offered to members of the association with an authenticating letter. Six of these guns were retained by the organization for engraving. They are being auctioned off to RCA members on a periodic basis, each of the guns encased in a presentation box.

This chapter would not be complete without mention of Charles Schreiner III, ramrod of the historic YO Ranch down in Mountain Home, Texas. With his sons, Charles

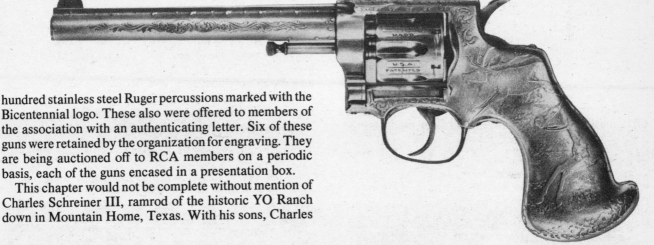

Above: Smith & Wesson craftsmen, or those under contract, produced their own versions of custom handguns for those customers who could afford the product. (Below) The less expensive Texas Ranger commemorative featured a badge inlayed in the walnut grip, a Texas Star on back strap, while the commemorative legend was inlaid in the barrel.

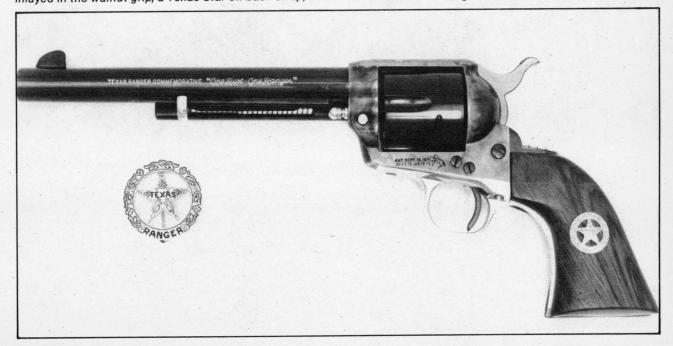

Western film actress Reno Browne had her name inlaid in gold in the ejector rod housing of her Colt SAA.

IV and Walter, he has done his own bit for the commemorative scene.

Back in 1968 Schreiner III decided it was time someone did something to note the efforts of the Texas Rangers. Thus, he financed the purchase of one thousand Colt SAAs. Two types of commemorative resulted. Selling for that time at $650 was an unengraved gun with the legend,

"Texas Ranger Commemorative — One Riot... One Ranger," engraved and inlaid on the barrel. Inset in the left walnut grip was a miniature Texas Ranger badge, while a full-size engraved silver Texas Ranger badge accompanied the sixgun. The barrel was blued, while the frame was case-hardened steel and the trigger guard and grip frame of brass. There were eight hundred of these guns.

That was the beginning only. The other two hundred guns were offered in three grades of engraving, prices starting at $1000 and graduating to $10,000, depending upon how much ornamentation was desired. Most of the guns were silver-plated, bearing the same gold-inlaid legend on the barrel with the words Texas Rangers deeply engraved on the back strap. Again, a badge was inlaid into the grip,

Texas' YO Ranch, which sponsored Texas Ranger commemoratives, decided to mark its own centennial by issuing a special run of Colt SAA revolvers. They were engraved and ornamented by San Antonio engraver Frank Hendricks.

The last Colt Single Action Army to be made is John Wayne commemorative. It features a likeness of late actor on the cylinder, ivory grips, quality engraving. Some of profit from sale is given to John Wayne Cancer Clinic.

but this time the grips were of ivory. These guns had been purchased undecorated from Colt and turned over to Frank Hendricks of San Antonio for engraving and other ornamentation. Today the guns are worth roughly three times their original sale, according to Walter Schreiner.

More recently the Schreiners have come up with a limited issue of two hundred YO Ranch commemoratives. Fifty of these are in what they term Premier grade with eighty percent engraving coverage. Each is silver-plated and fitted with ivory grips by the same Frank Hendricks who did the work on the Texas Ranger series. Each revolver has a gold YO Ranch medallion overlay on the left side of the grip and another gold overlay on the back strap, while a gold eagle is inlaid on each side of the hammer. Gold bands also are inlaid on the cylinder and on the barrel, one at the muzzle, the other near the cylinder. Inlaid in the trigger guard is a Star of Texas in gold. The inscription on the left side of the barrel reads: "1880 YO Ranch Centennial 1980." On the right side is inscribed: "A Century Of Ranching In Texas."

According to Walter Schreiner, the Premier grade six-guns are finished in antique silver-plating with the surfaces next to the gold bands and the eagle blued to make the yellow of the gold more prominent.

Each Premier is furnished with an original bronze of an old-time cowboy, fully outfitted, holding a YO branding iron in his hand. This bronze, created by H. Clay Dahlberg of Hunt, Texas, is numbered to match the serial number of the Premier.

The remaining 150 YO Ranch Commemoratives are what the Schreiners describe as Deluxe grade, with sixty percent engraving coverage by Hendricks. They are silver-plated with ivory grips and the YO medallion in silver on the left grip and another silver medallion on the back strap. The barrels are engraved with the same legends as the Premier grade. Each of the Deluxe grade guns comes in a specially designed wooden case with a glass top, accompanied by a history of the YO Ranch.

The Premier grades are priced at $8000 each, while the Deluxe is $2500.

This highly decorated Buntline with shoulder stock and screwdriver was the only one of its kind turned out by Colt craftsmen in the modern era. It was auctioned off at sporting goods dealers show to benefit Olympic Fund.

THE WHITE HAT MOB

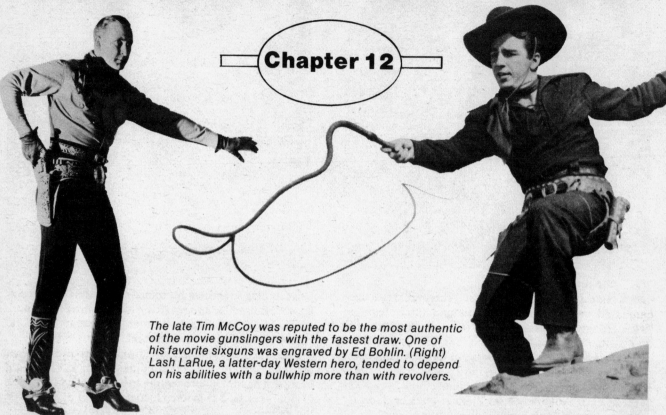

Chapter 12

The late Tim McCoy was reputed to be the most authentic of the movie gunslingers with the fastest draw. One of his favorite sixguns was engraved by Ed Bohlin. (Right) Lash LaRue, a latter-day Western hero, tended to depend on his abilities with a bullwhip more than with revolvers.

THERE WAS little real similarity between Rock Hudson and John Wesley Hardin just as there was little room for comparison in looks, demeanor — or profession — between the late Tyrone Power and the equally late Jesse James. Yet it is the writers, directors and the interpretations of actors who have popularized the American West, not only in this country but around the world.

All of this popularity goes back to Thomas Edison and the fact that the first film to tell a story was a Western. It was titled *The Great Train Robbery* and starred a little-known actor, G.M. Anderson, who was to become known as Bronco Billy Anderson, the first cowboy film star. Born in 1882, the veteran died in Los Angeles in 1971 at the age of 89, having seen the series Western go full cycle from birth to box-office death in a period of only fifty years.

The second great Western star was William S. Hart, who had lived in the West and had a flair for authenticity. Bronco Billy didn't know one gun from another in those days and even less about horses, so he used whatever gun the property man had been able to buy the cheapest at the nearest hockshop. Since the original train robbery film was made in New Jersey, not far from New York City, there were more pawn shops than experts.

Nonetheless, Anderson had retired by 1916 after making four hundred films and a fortune. In 1957, at age 72 and

more than thirty years of oblivion, he was given a special Academy Award by the Academy of Motion Picture Arts and Sciences.

Bill Hart, trained as a Shakespearean actor, made his first Western in 1914 and was at or near the top of the cowboy heap for ten years when he made his last film and retired.

But it was Tom Mix who set the trend for cowboy stars to come. He was a flamboyant character who had spent time with Wild West shows and knew what the public wanted. The public demanded action and color, not Shakespearean acting. Mix, upon reaching popularity, set about creating a mystique that wore what amounted to a tailored uniform topped by a white hat, handmade boots and a silver-decorated, hand-carved gunbelt. His horse was almost as decorative with silver-mounted saddle, bridle and martingale.

While Anderson had been satisfied with any handgun that would fire blanks and Bill Hart sought authenticity, Mix was interested in guns that would fire rapidly and thus pick up the pace of his gunfight scenes. He often combined a double-action in one hand, a single-action in the other. Later, he seemed to concentrate on Colt double-action police and military models. His shirts were hand embroidered, his hats had the widest brim and highest crown Stetson could make and his chaps were decorated with silver.

Early John Wayne tended to use whatever sixgun he was issued by the studio property master. In later years he went for authentic guns, holsters to match his role.

Bill Boyd, in portraying Hopalong Cassidy over twenty years, maintained a clean but aristocratic image that included ivory-handled, highly engraved matched guns.

Similarity Between The B-Picture Movie Cowboys And The Frontiersmen Of History Lies In The Fact That There Is An American West

But it was Tom Mix who caught the image of the public and lasted longer than any other Western star. He made his first film in 1910, handling stock and acting as a stuntman. By 1917 he was a top star and at the peak of his career was making $17,000 a week; that in the era when there was no income tax! His last screen appearance was in 1935 in a fifteen-chapter serial, *The Miracle Rider.* In spite of the fact that he was nearing 60, he still was able to command $40,000 for four weeks of his time. In that final film, Mix seemed to be attempting to return to credibility. His outfits were less florid and instead of the nickel-plated twin six-guns with their pearl grips, he carried a standard blued Colt SAA with standard hard rubber factory grips. He died in 1940 in an auto accident in Arizona and was buried in Los Angeles' Forest Lawn Memorial Park in a silver casket.

But the Tim Mix syndrome continued until the end of the series Western film and at one point it appeared that cowboy stars were attempting to see which could get the most brocade on his shirt, the most silver on his sixgun and the most carving on his saddle and gunbelt.

There were some exceptions. Tim McCoy, a Westerner before he brought an Indian tribe to Hollywood to make *The Covered Wagon,* took a dim view of the flamboyance. He tended toward black hats and clothing in keeping with the military uniform he once had worn as a cavalry officer. Buck Jones, who had been hired by Fox Films as a threat to Tom Mix, made an effort to steer away from the Mix

image, looking clean but plain, except for boots, spurs, gunbelt and the white horse he rode.

But from the Mix approach, virtually every cowboy star who ever made it to the screen favored the hand-tooled, silver-decorated gunbelt and distinctive handguns that either were engraved, furnished with exotic grips or otherwise individualized. One of the few who settled for plain walnut grips was Lash LaRue, who lasted for a decade through the Forties and Fifties. He had a different gimmick, a blacksnake whip.

The early John Wayne was on a par with McCoy and Jones in the plain bent of his dress; in fact, he played supporting roles to both of the stars in his youth. When he became a series star in his own right, he too went for the fancy gun rig and the chrome-plated, ivory-handled six-guns. It wasn't until years later that he began to settle for the authenticity that helped to make him an American legend.

Oddly, however, these same Western stars had their own effect upon the handgun market and particularly in the role of the single-action revolver. Gunmakers began to feature the "look" of some of the handguns used by the stars, making cosmetic changes to take advantage of the publicity offered by Hollywood.

In the following pages we'll look at several of the stars who bridge the era from the early silent Western films to the demise of the Saturday afternoon matinee cowboy.

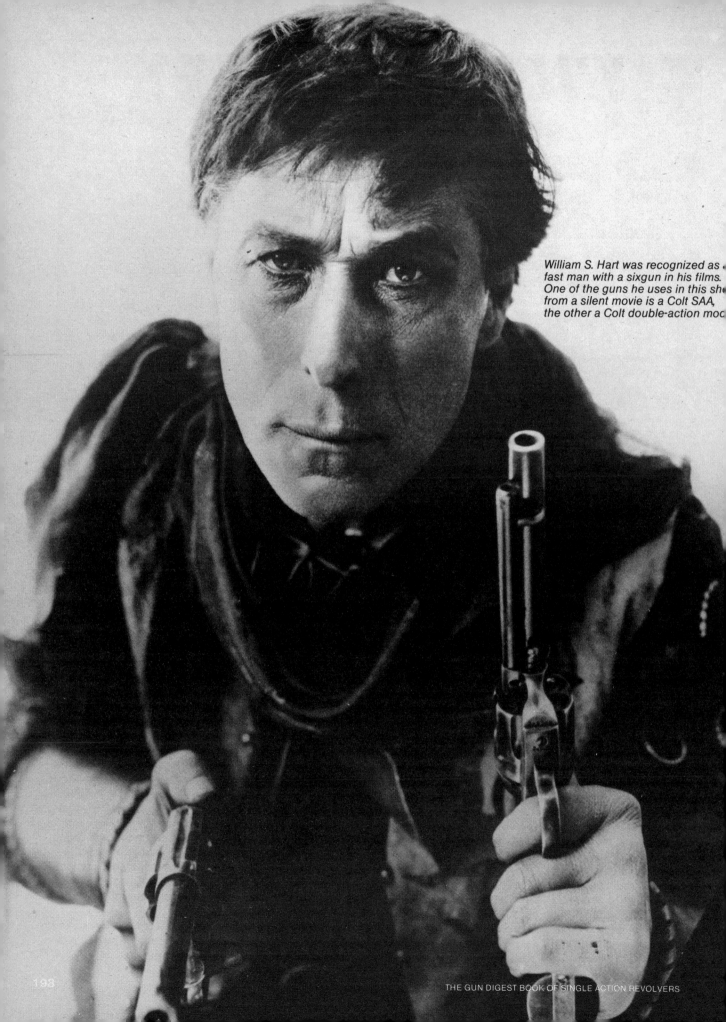

William S. Hart was recognized as a fast man with a sixgun in his films. One of the guns he uses in this shot from a silent movie is a Colt SAA, the other a Colt double-action mod

WILLIAM S. HART

The old hat that Hart wore in most of his movies still is owned by his son, as is a pair
of customized Colt Single Action Army revolvers which were presented to William S. Hart, Jr.,
on his second birthday. It required a lengthy search by the author to track down the guns.

ON A HIGH HILL near Newhall, California, lies Horseshoe Ranch, long the home of the late William S. Hart, the first Western film star to gain international fame. The ranch and Hart's home during his lifetime, *La Loma de Los Vientos*, now are a part of the 243-acre William S. Hart Park. At the time of his death in 1946 the film cowboy bequeathed the ranch to the people of Los Angeles County, designating in his will that it should be made into a public park for all to enjoy.

Between 1914 and 1925 Bill Hart was considered the epitome of the Western hero. Throughout his movie career — during which he wrote and produced many of the stories in which he starred — he was the fast-drawing, steely-eyed gunman, often a badman who was reformed by a good

woman in the course of the story. Although his first love seemed to be horses — especially his pinto, Fritz — he took great pride in his abilities and handling of a sixgun.

Hart was born in Newburgh, New York, on December 6, 1870, but his family settled near the Sioux Rosebud Reservation in South Dakota after living in Iowa, Kansas, Minnesota and Wisconsin. As a youngster Hart came to know the Sioux well, becoming familiar with their language and customs. It was during this period that he developed his love of the West and an almost overwhelming demand for authenticity that was to serve him later in films.

When Hart was 19 his father became nearly blind and his mother fell ill. As a result the family returned to New York. After working at numerous odd jobs Young Bill Hart

This highly ornamented Colt SAA presented to his son by the film star in former's infancy has weathered years well. Other guns are in museum at the old Hart Ranch.

The initials of the film star were inlaid in silver in the ivory grips that were inlaid in silver mountings. Note that the ivory since has cracked over the years.

made his stage debut in *Romeo and Juliet,* a far cry from ceremonial dancing with the Sioux.

For the next fifteen years he pursued a stage career and in 1914 met Thomas Ince, who offered him the chance to portray villians in a pair of two-reel films. Shortly after, he starred in his first Western, *On the Night Stage.* Almost overnight he replaced the ranking Western film star, Bronco Billy Anderson.

Hart made a series of films for Ince and eventually was able to take over his own production unit. He made dozens of Westerns for Artcraft until 1922, when the firm insisted he update his continuing plot of the good badman who redeems himself. By this time Tom Mix and Buck Jones were besting him at the box offices of the nation.

Hart, still maintaining his way was best, left Artcraft and signed to make a picture for United Artists, the com-

pany that had been formed by Douglas Fairbanks, Mary Pickford and Charles Chaplin. His one and only film for the firm — and also his last — was *Tumbleweeds.* Disappointed with the marketing, he sued United Artists for an accounting. He allegedly was blacklisted by the all-powerful studios and never worked again in a feature. However, in the late Thirties he did a sound prologue for *Tumbleweeds,* added music, and it was reissued, being belatedly proclaimed a minor classic.

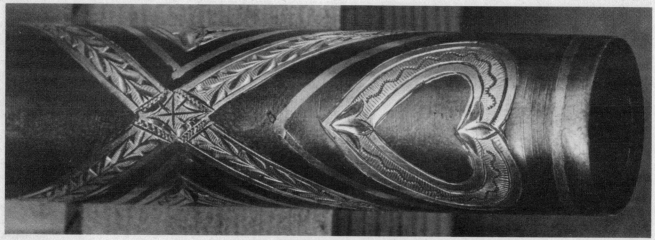

The series of silver hearts that have been inlaid into the barrel of the matched sixguns leave little doubt as to the thinking of Bill Hart in selecting this motif. William S. Hart, Jr., says the guns never were fired.

It is not known whether film star Hart was responsible for selecting the type of engraving for the sixguns, but in view of the Indian influences, it is a possibility.

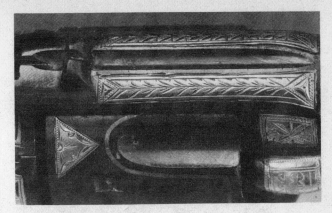

The engraving and inlay work in the sixgun was done at the Colt factory, according to a letter written to Colt, but it is possible that several craftsmen worked on it.

Some of Hart's early pictures were filmed in Oklahoma on the famed 101 Ranch operated by the Miller Brothers. Ironically the two men who were to edge him off the throne as the nation's Number One Cowboy both received much of their early training there. Tom Mix and Buck Jones each spent several seasons with the ranch and its Wild West show that toured the hinterlands. Other Silent Era movie cowboys such as Hoot Gibson and Art Acord also paid their dues by working at the 101.

Hart, of course, had little use for Mix and Jones both of whom tended to ignore authenticity in favor of showmanship. It was Mix who introduced the "cowboy uniform," which featured fitted pants, hand-made silver-inlaid boots and white ten-gallon hats. Jones and others through the final chapters of the feature Western, manned by Roy Rogers, Gene Autry and Rex Allen, adopted much the same type of showy attire; the same clothing tastes that have influenced the Urban Cowboy trend in more recent years.

The flutes in the revolver are inlaid with gold wire, while most of the decorative work is in silver. From the looks of the cylinder, a degree of rust is present.

The only cowboy actor appearing in B pictures ever to adopt Hart's seeming approach for realism was William Elliott — billed early in his career as Wild Bill Elliott. In his final years he adopted much the same type of realistic costuming as Bill Hart and many of the pictures in his final series, before the death of the B Western in the Fifties, cast him as an outlaw turned good, as had been the case with Hart three decades earlier.

Nonetheless, Hart's claim that "the truth of the West means more to me than a job and always will," was his ultimate undoing. Other than doing the sound prologue for *Tumbleweeds* in 1939, Hart never made another film, although he did coach both Johnny Mack Brown and later Robert Taylor in gun handling for their respective roles as Billy the Kid. In fact, both of the actors used a Colt Single Action Army that is alleged to have belonged to Billy the Kid during his heyday. Most reports state that Billy — William Bonney — preferred the Colt Lightning model — but Hart had gone to great pains to authenticate the revolver, bearing serial number 70361. In .44-40 caliber, featuring a 4¾-inch barrel, the gun had the name Billy crudely engraved on the backstrap.

Among the other guns owned by Hart in his movie heyday was one presented to him by Al Jennings, who was proclaimed from time to time — usually by himself or press agents — as the Last of the Train Robbers. True, Jennings had been involved in a series of train robberies, but most of them had been pretty unprofitable. Ultimately he was caught and sent to prison.

Upon his release he ended up in Hollywood, where he starred in several silent motion pictures — all of them bad — and eventually became an extra and occasional bit player. Oddly enough, a highly fictionalized version of his life was filmed in the Fifties, starring the late Dan Duryea. It was titled *Al Jennings of Oklahoma* and was fabricated from the finest fiction.

Ultimately Jennings and Hart became acquainted and the would-be outlaw presented the actor with one of his handguns, alleged to have been the veteran of numerous forays into lawlessness. The sixgun is a Colt Single Action Army model in .45 caliber, carrying the initials AJ carved into the right grip. As to just how authentic the sixgun is

it was the era prior to the introduction of the cartridge revolver, he often used a Colt Model of 1849 percussion in .36 caliber. But since most of his films covered the later era, he appeared to favor a Colt Single Action Army. This one, equipped with stag grips, has a 5½-inch barrel and is in .45 caliber, bearing serial number 249742. He also carried a Colt New Service double-action .45 in some of his films. Also equipped with stag grips, plus a lanyard ring at the butt, this one is factory numbered as 307955.

All of the guns described above are in the collection on display at the Horseshoe Ranch home near Newhall, as is another Colt SAA .45 bearing the serial number 25894. This particular sixgun was presented to Hart in 1917, at the height of his fame, by citizens of Dodge City, Kansas. The initials NRT are carved into the wood of the right grip. The gun had been the property of Sheriff Chak Beeson, who it is said had taken it from the body of the last badman to be killed on Dodge City's infamous Front Street.

In December 1921 Hart was married to Winifred Westover, an actress of note, who had appeared in an early

Hart's favorite handguns, all now on display at the museum at the Hart Ranch, include (from top): .36 percussion Colt Model of 1849 pocket pistol, Colt SAA with stag grips, double-action Colt .45, and a .44 single-action alleged to have belonged to Billy The Kid.

when it comes to its history of lawlessness may be open to question. Jennings was no more successful as an actor than he had been as a train robber. No one ever did imprison him for his acting as they had for train robbery, but there were those critics who seemed to think such a parallel action would have been a blessing to stage and screen.

Because of his limited acting success, Jennings often found himself in what has been termed dire straits. Taking a leaf from the notebook of Bat Masterson, it is alleged he would round up several old single-action revolvers that he could buy for a few dollars apiece. After carving his initials into the stocks, he would sell each of them as his own personal weapon that he had carried during his life of crime! That the single-action in the Hart collection did belong to Jennings is a fact. As for its previous origins, there is question.

In keeping with Hart's continuing demand for authenticity, he tended to favor two revolvers, depending upon what period in the history of the West he was portraying. If

William S. Hart, Jr., a college professor in Southern California, retains fond memories of his famed father. He has had the matched Colts for half a century-plus.

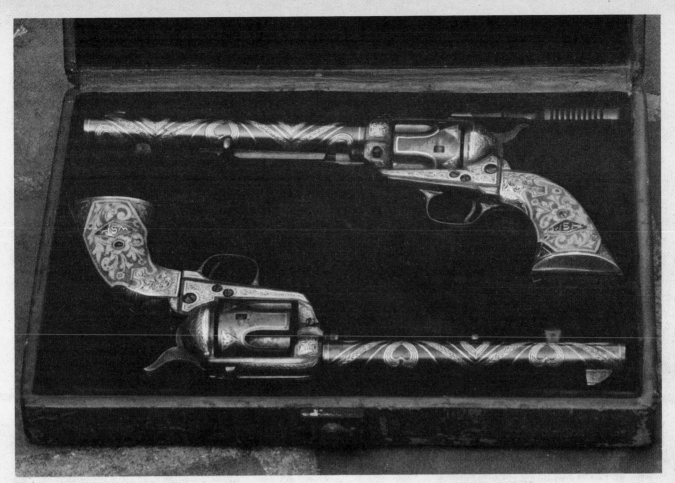

The ornate Colt Single Action Army revolvers with 7½-inch barrels still are maintained in the original box in which they were delivered to the silent screen star from the Colt factory at the peak of his cowboy fame.

screen classic, D.W. Griffith's *Intolerance*. The twosome separated some months later, but were not divorced until 1927.

At the time his son, William S. Hart, Jr., was born in 1922, the actor began casting about for a one-of-a-kind gift for the infant. When the younger Hart was only two years old, his father presented him with a beautiful hand-carved, silver-mounted saddle and a pair of highly engraved Colt Single Action Army revolvers.

The matched handguns were completely engraved with a design of hearts along their barrels. These hearts then were inlaid with intricate designs in gold and silver. The silver grips carry the initials WSH. The serial numbers on the guns were 246014 and 342963. Both were .45 caliber and boasted 7½-inch barrels.

In a letter to the Colt Company dated January 1925, following the delivery of the guns and their presentation during the previous Christmas festivities, Hart wrote:
Gentlemen:

I am enclosing photos of two guns of your make that I had inlaid and presented to my son, William S. Hart, Jr., age two years and four months. When the little fellow has grown to manhood and his Dad has crossed the Big Divide, he will be a two-gun Bill — just as his Dad was.

When I was a boy on the Frontier, I saw many guns that had been inlaid by some of those who liked fancy shootin' irons, but I never saw anything as handsome as the guns now owned by my son.

When the case is first opened their brilliancy is such one would think them studded with diamonds.

It gives me pleasure to send these photos to you. The old single-action Colt .45 is my favorite.

Very Sincerely Yours,
William S. Hart

These two guns, however, are not included in the collection at William S. Hart Park. Thus their whereabouts became something of a challenge and I set about attempting to locate them.

First, with the help of an old friend, Bill Murphy, I researched the files of the Los Angeles Times to learn that William S. Hart, Jr., had been one of nineteen students elected to Phi Beta Kappa, the national scholastic honorary fraternity, at the University of California, Los Angeles, in early 1943. I also learned that he had been a member of the city planning commission in Santa Monica, California, as late as 1974 and that his mother, Winifred Westover Hart, had died at the age of 78, in March 1978.

Bill Hart, wearing the hat that became his trademark, was the top gunslinger of the silver screen in early Twenties. Although he appears to be portraying a gentleman in this scene, you can bet his twin sixguns are beneath the coat!

A bit more investigation revealed that William S. Hart, Jr., still resides in Southern California. In making contact, I was not certain just how to pursue the question of what had happened to the pair of ornate matched sixguns. I had learned through my researches that, when the cowboy star had died in 1946 in New York City, he had left all of his wealth to charity. The ranch near Newhall had been a part of that bequest.

I located William S. Hart, Jr., in Santa Monica and learned that he is a professor, teaching business administration at the University of Southern California.

Initially he was reluctant to discuss the guns or his father, explaining that "I've never been a part of the Hollywood scene and I've attempted to maintain a low image over the years. I'm quite happy as a professor."

But subsequent discussion revealed fond memories of the late cowboy star. "I would be a bit careful in declaring the authenticity of some of the guns in my father's collection," he advised. "For example, he had what were said to be the guns of Wild Bill Hickok, but in my own researches into Western history, I've found it is pretty well established that Hickok's guns were buried with him." The son of the star also tended to express some degree of doubt as to the authenticity of the gun that allegedly had belonged to Billy the Kid.

"There was a gun that was presented to my father by Bat Masterson, however. After giving up law enforcement, Masterson went to New York and became a newspaperman. There was a presentation ceremony in the newspaper office, when Bat presented my father with a gun. But where that gun came from is anyone's guess. I doubt that it is the one with which he is supposed to have cleaned up Dodge City."

In his adolescence the younger Hart became acquainted with several frontier figures and badmen through his relationship with his father.

"One was an old man I knew as Uncle Billy Judson," he recalls. "I didn't know until much later that he was the last surviving member of the James gang. He also presented my father with a gun that he said he had carried while riding with Jesse and Frank James."

As for Al Jennings, William S. Hart, Jr., had known him for many years. "He died in 1962 not long after his wife died. In fact, he virtually starved himself to death. He said he had no reason to live any longer. He had to be nearly a hundred at that time. I went out to see him several times and he had just lost the will to live."

The younger Hart recalls his youth at the ranch in Newhall, when his father, the star, would send him out to work on nearby cattle spreads. "That's probably why I'm a college professor," he offers somewhat wryly.

"But I also recall being amazed with my father's dexterity with his sixguns. I saw him shoot the head off a rattlesnake once and with a sixgun in each hand, cocking and firing single action, he would fire so rapidly that the twelve shots sounded like a machine gun. There may be those who are faster today, but as a youngster, I was impressed.

"Also, he had broken his hand during a dam break in 1926. I'm sure he must have been even faster in handling a gun before that."

As for the highly ornate matched sixguns presented to him by his father in his infancy, William S. Hart, Jr., indicated that they now are in the hands of a private collector who chooses to remain unnamed. However, he did act as liaison in arranging for us to take photos of them.

The words of William S. Hart in writing to Colt in 1925 were not in error. The guns do sparkle like diamonds and, in gazing upon them, one has to admire the workmanship of a bygone era that went into them.

William S. Hart may be only a shadowy figure on a few remaining reels of film, but his memory will continue to be maintained in the park and museum in the Southern California hills that bear his name.

Riding his pinto, Hart invariably portrayed a badman with a heart of gold. Note authenticity of holster, gun belt.

TOM MIX

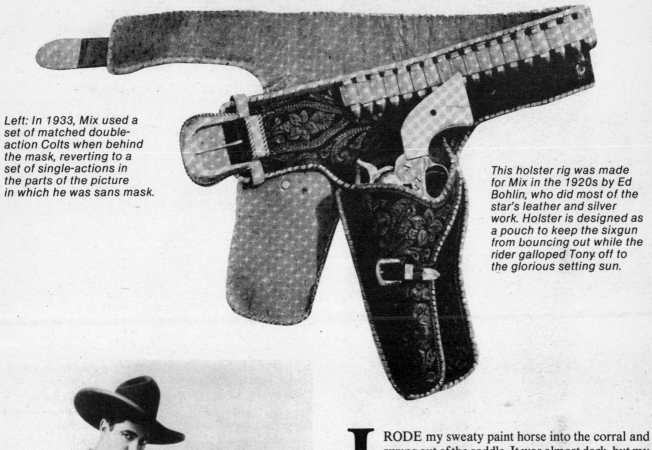

Left: In 1933, Mix used a set of matched double-action Colts when behind the mask, reverting to a set of single-actions in the parts of the picture in which he was sans mask.

This holster rig was made for Mix in the 1920s by Ed Bohlin, who did most of the star's leather and silver work. Holster is designed as a pouch to keep the sixgun from bouncing out while the rider galloped Tony off to the glorious setting sun.

From his earliest days as a star, Tom Mix tended to use a handgun smaller than the Colt SAA, because of small size of his hands. The Colt New Service was one of his favorites, often substituting for SAA in many a scene.

I RODE my sweaty paint horse into the corral and swung out of the saddle. It was almost dark, but my father was standing at the barn door.

"You're late," he said. His tone wasn't quite so accusatory as it sometimes was, although his expression said he wasn't happy about the sweat on the horse's sides.

He knew why I was late. I'd been practicing trick riding again, on the way home from school. He was aware of my youthful ambitions to be a movie cowboy, but he'd never knocked the desire. I've always suspected my old man, a cowboy in his day, felt he'd have made a better hero than some who were riding cross the screens of the Thirties.

"Tom Mix is dead."

That was all he said, but my childhood memories crowded in on me with a sense of loss. It was 1940 and I was 15 years old. Until then, I'd never considered the fact that Tom Mix could die. He was one of the immortals.

Tom Mix had been my hero in those days before World War II. I'd met him only once, in 1932, at the age of 8 or so, when he had made a personal appearance at a neighborhood theater. He had done a stage show with his wife, Mabel Ward, and a team of backup talent. Dressed in white, Mix had ridden onto the stage on Tony, the horse's silver saddle and bridle glinting in the spotlight.

There were hundreds of kids like myself in the audience, most of us properly brainwashed by the Ralston-Purina Company, which then sponsored the Tom Mix Ralston

Mix's abilities as a horseman may have been superior to his actions with a handgun. In the Twenties, he jumped his horse across this Cahuenga Wagon Cut. It's now part of the Hollywood Freeway and is covered by concrete.

But that day, as I watched Mix on the theater stage, I was enraptured. He was in his mid-fifties by then, but when he fired his sixguns and rifle, he never missed. In fact, he announced at one point that with a single shot he would hit two poker chips mounted on a whirling disc. He fired and two chips were shattered. It wasn't until years later that I realized it was a trick and had been done with bird shot. Even then, I didn't care. The series of tricks performed by Tony made him seem smarter than a lot of adults we knew.

That personal appearance was accompanied by an old silent film wherein Mix battled Arabs in the Near East, saving the heroine from a fate worse than increased oil prices It had been filmed in the era when Tom Mix made $17,500 a week — four times the salary of the President of the United States!

It was announced from the stage that any youngster wishing to meet Tom Mix and Tony should show up behind the theater. It took me a lot of years to realize that was the only way they could clear the theater of youngsters so another contingent of paying customers could get seats. Otherwise, we'd have sat in the same seats through the day's four shows!

Tom Mix had his own travel trailer and a custom horse trailer for Tony parked behind the theater. He came out of the trailer, still wearing his white outfit and his sixgun on each hip, to smile and shake hands with all of us. As I recall, he looked tired and the smile may have been a bit forced. And he finally said that was all, that he had to rest. He went back into the trailer and slowly the other youngsters began to disband, moving toward the street.

I was alone there in the alley, still staring at the door of the trailer, hoping Mix would come out again. Finally, I turned and started away. But I stumbled and fell, skinning my knee. I started to cry, I recall. A moment later, the door of the trailer opened and the man in the white suit peered out. He watched me for a moment as I struggled up, trying to appear manly, trying to stifle the tears.

"Are you all right?" he asked, advancing to the steps of the trailer.

"I hurt my knee," I told him tearfully. Then he came down the steps, gathered me up in his arms and sat down on the trailer steps, trying to comfort me. I don't remember what Tom Mix said to me after that. All I know was that I was happy, sitting there on his lap, unconcerned that my

Mix seemed to have a hang-up about having his signature on his possessions, including a neon sign on top of his home. This signature was inlaid in gold on a shotgun he was presented by Marlin at the height of his career.

Straight Shooters. It was all part of a sales campaign to sell a cereal most of us didn't like much. By sending in boxtops, you could become a member and, for more boxtops, they'd send you all sorts of premiums having to do with Mix and his past. Every kid in my gang had become a collector and my greatest joy in the mid-Thirties was a genuine, full-scale wooden model of Tom Mix's Colt .45. Made of pine, it was broken a lot and was continually being repaired with model-airplane glue.

When engaged in such derring-do as crashing his horse through a window, Mix didn't subject his high-priced ornate guns to damage. Here he wears a standard rubber-gripped single-action. In later years, he found that if you fell on the gun, it could hurt. He substituted rubber guns.

mother would be looking for me in front of the theater. With Tom Mix was where she finally found me.

Tom Mix was a legend, much of his background created by Hollywood press agents. Biographies of the era stated that he was born in a log cabin near El Paso, Texas; that he had been a sheriff in Colorado, a soldier in the Philippines and the Boxer Rebellion; that he had fought on both sides in the Boer War.

In recent years, most of this legend has been refuted. Actually, he was born near DuBois, Pennsylvania, served in the U.S. Army for a time but never left the East Coast, and later drifted into a job as a deputy marshal in Dewey, Oklahoma, where the Tom Mix Museum now is located.

But he was a cowboy and a showman. He worked on several ranches in Oklahoma and ultimately the famed Miller 101 Ranch, which combined raising cattle and horses with show business, since the Miller Brothers sent a rodeo troupe on the road each year.

It was while working in Oklahoma that Mix became involved with motion pictures. Selig Studios from Chicago came to the area to film a semi-documentary, *Life in the Great Southwest*. Mix served as a horse wrangler and later as a stuntman on the film. He was signed by Colonel William Selig to appear in a series of short Westerns and even comedies. He made more than three hundred silent films before the advent of sound, when he retired tem-

When not riding across the silver screen, Mix usually went armed. He favored this Smith & Wesson .357 magnum as one he could carry in a shoulder holster. Ivory behind his name has been colored red, making the letters stand out.

porarily to travel the country with a circus.

Studio press agents always insisted that Mix did all of his own death-defying stunts and throughout much of his career this was true. However, if you look at the films he did in the Thirties, it's obvious that stuntmen took over some of the tougher assignments in his later years.

Be that as it may, there is no doubt that Tom Mix made the whole world horse conscious. His first movie horse, bought from the Miller Ranch string, was called Old Blue. He trained the horse in numerous tricks, teaching it to rear on signal, fall and to play dead. When the horse died, Mix had it buried and erected a monument reading: "In memory of Old Blue, the Best Horse I Ever Rode. We Grew Old Together."

Meantime, Mix had realized there would come a day when Old Blue no longer would be able to run as hard as films required. According to legend, he spotted a colt running behind the wagon of an Italian fruit vendor in Los Angeles. Mix bought the colt for an alleged sum of $17.50. He named the young gelding Tony.

Tom Mix was the first film cowboy to insist his horse be given billing and it was not long before the theatre one-sheets and three-sheets advertising coming attractions billed the team as Tom Mix and Tony.

Thinking back to the episode in the theatre, where Mix

did his two-for-one shot, my recollections are a bit vague after nearly half a century, but I have the feeling the guns he used were not Single Action Colts. I do remember that they were blued and had mother-of-pearl grips. In reviewing the guns now on display at the Tom Mix Museum in Dewey, Oklahoma, I suspect that he was using a pair of .38 Official Police Colts that he carried in many of his films.

Mix, as has been indicated, was perhaps more of a showman than he was a genuine cowboy. He tended not to allow authenticity to get in the way of a thrill or a good scene in his films. As a result, he often carried a Colt Single Action in the holster that would be most visible to the camera. But in the other holster — he usually was a two-gun man — he carried a double-action so he could fire more rapidly!

At the time of his death, Bud Abbott of the team of Abbott and Costello, had a pair of single-action Colts in his collection, with a carefully tooled double holster rig that had belonged to Tom Mix. One of the guns was an old black powder model, while the other was newer and built to handle smokeless powder. Inasmuch as the shooting done during filming was with black powder blanks, the difference wasn't particularly important. This matched set and the rig were sold to a private collector, incidentally, who prefers not to be identified.

Mix, it would appear, was a gun collector of some note

before such collecting really became a national hobby. After serving with the Army, Mix turned up at the Miller Brothers 101 Ranch at Marland, Oklahoma, where he was employed from 1906 to about 1909. He later was a bartender in Dewey, then the town marshal. Despite all of the publicity claims, this may well have been his only actual exposure to the law enforcement business. The Dewey museum does hold documents stating he was a Texas Ranger and a deputy U.S. marshal, but it would appear that these were honorary commissions that he received after reaching star status in Western films.

Mix also bought a small ranch and when the Selig Moving Picture Company came out from Chicago to do a film called *Life in the Great Southwest,* the erstwhile cowboy was signed on as livestock wrangler. He also is credited with handling some of the stuntwork.

Colonel Selig must have liked Mix, for he signed him to a series of short films. During this early part of the silent era, Mix acted, wrote and even directed some of the movies. From this early beginning, he developed the type of character that was to make him famous. His hero didn't drink, smoke or swear, although Mix did all three in private life. It was Mix who designed the "cowboy uniform" that a host of followers on the silver screens of the nation would attempt to emulate or even outdo. He had hand-tailored silk shirts, silver-studded chaps, boots inlaid with silver, guns that were either stocked in ivory or mother-of-pearl. His spurs often were diamond studded as was his belt buckle. The fact that the average cowboy of the era he was portraying made about $30 per month and could afford none of these fancy items went ignored by Mix and those who followed. Mix once described his character as "a cow-

This pair of Colt Single Action Peacemakers are displayed currently at the Tom Mix Museum in Dewey, Oklahoma. The top sixgun, with mother-of-pearl grips, is chambered in .45 caliber, while the other is chambered for the .38.

This Smith & Wesson Model 3 American also is on display at the Tom Mix Museum. A collector item, it apparently was given to Mix during his heyday to add to his collection. As far as we can determine, it was not used in his films.

boy who rides into town with nothing but his horse, his clothes and his guns, and happens into a situation." The fact that the saddle, clothes and guns Mix used in his films cost thousands of dollars didn't lend a great deal of credibility to the simplicity of the plots, but the audiences loved it!

The method of shooting used by Mix in his screen characterizations would drive an avid target shooter to tears. He seemed to take no sort of aim. Instead, he used an upward and downward motion that looked more like a karate chop than a shooting stance. Thus, he would fire the two guns alternately. As mentioned earlier, his guns usually were a combination of the Colt SAA, which was cocked and fired closer to the cameras with his more dexterous right hand, while a near look-alike Colt double-action was fired with the left. The double-action feature didn't make it necessary to seek the hammer with his left thumb and made it possible to keep up his sixgun rhythm.

Mix made a series of so-called talking pictures in the early Thirties, but at that time he was well over 50 years

In his last film, "The Miracle Rider," made in 1935, the cowboy star carried this standard Colt .45 SAA, giving up the engraved, pearl-handled sixguns he favored for a return to authenticity in his role of a Texas Ranger.

This set of double-action Colt Official Police revolvers was carried by Mix in most of his pictures. They were nickel-plated with mother-of-pearl grips. These are the guns he is reputed to have used for personal appearances.

This matched pair of Colt double-actions in .38 caliber was used by Mix in making pictures. Note the scratches on the nickel plating, worn edges on the pearl grips.

old. After one particular fall, he decided he'd had it and went back to the circus, where he had passed several years while sound was finding its way and technicians finally discovered they could record voices in an outside environment. In 1935 he formed his own circus, but it fell on hard times. He returned to the screen in 1936 to make his only serial, *The Miracle Rider.* He received $40,000 for four weeks work, but the circus folded a few months later in spite of this infusion of money.

Mix had been talking to Twentieth-Century-Fox about a super Western that would gather in all the old Western stars. He was headed for Hollywood, crossing the Arizona desert, when his high-speed Cord convertible missed a detour. In the crash a heavy metal box was thrown against his neck. He was dead when a road crew reached him. The date was October 12, 1940.

Today, near Florence, Arizona, the site of the accident, there is a moument of native rock that is topped by a metal statue of a riderless horse. A plaque is inscribed:

In Memory of Tom Mix, Whose Spirit Left
His Body On This Spot and Whose Characterizations
and Portrayals in Life Served Better to Fix
Memories of the Old West in the Minds of
*   Living Man.*

A number of the guns that Tom Mix owned during his lifetime had been given to individuals. Some of these are in private collections today. However, the bulk of his collection — which included fourteen handguns, nine rifles and five shotguns — is located in the **Tom Mix Museum** in Oklahoma.

At the time of his death, Mix's will left all of his personal items to a California attorney, Ivon D. Parker. There was an instant clamor for these items from fans and collectors. Parker, however, felt that the collection should preserved. He built a special room at his house to protect the collection and it was virtually hidden from the public until the time of his own death. At that time the Tom Mix collection was awarded by probate to his sons and nephews, who soon discovered the reason the elder Parker had virtually hidden the items. The demand for souvenirs had become even greater in the years since Mix's death.

The problem was solved when the people of Dewey and nearby Bartlesville, Oklahoma, decided there should be a museum devoted to the film cowboy. They raised $40,000 in less than two weeks with which to buy the collection and house it.

Today, the Tom Mix Museum draws thousands of visitors to the small Oklahoma community where Mix was the town marshal. In addition to the guns is an entire range of paraphernalia having to do with the cowboy's long career. One can spend hours browsing through the photos, documents and assorted items of show business days long gone.

The revolvers owned by Mix cover a broad range, many of them having been given to him. Several are inscribed with his name, while others are rather standard, unadorned models that perhaps held some sentimental value for the cowboy star. But there is little doubt that each of these six-guns has its own story.

Author feels this set of Colt Officers Model .38s was used by Mix for on-stage shooting demonstration viewed in the former's childhood. Note the target-type sights. Grips are of ivory carefully scrimshawed, marked with TM brand.

WILD BILL ELLIOTT

He Went For Authenticity In The William S. Hart Tradition, But Still Liked Dressed-Up Sixguns!

WILLIAM ELLIOTT went through a number of names and a lot of guns before he won success as a Western star.

He was born as Gordon Elliott in Pattonsburg, Missouri, in 1903, but was raised in Kansas City, where his father was associated with the stockyards. It was there that young Elliott came to know cowboys and learned to handle a horse in helping to cut and separate cattle in the shipping yards. By the time he was 16 he had won a number of trophy buckles in rodeos, but a few years later he was studying dramatic arts at the famed Pasadena Playhouse in California.

Still billed as Gordon Elliott, he entered motion pictures in 1928, appearing in minor roles in a number of equally minor feature films. He played villians in romances, detective stories and a few Westerns before he was featured in a Warner Brothers musical, *Wonder Bar*.

Four years later, in 1938, Elliott finally hit his stride. He was chosen to play the lead in a serial, *The Adventures of Wild Bill Hickok*. The studio changed his name from Gordon to William. The serial was a box-office success and he was rushed into another serial, *Overland with Kit Carson*. However, the name, "Wild Bill" Elliott that had been used for billing purposes stuck and he was carried on studio advertising under that name through a series of Western features he made for Columbia Pictures.

In 1943 Elliott moved on to Republic Studios, where he took over the role of Red Ryder from Don Barry. His co-star portraying Little Beaver was a youngster named Bobby Blake. The little Indian, of course, since has grown to adulthood to star in such features as *Tell Them Willie Boy*

Bill Elliott went through several phases in his movie career. He started by portraying villians, progressing to hero roles in series and ultimately to feature films.

216

Is Here and television's *Beretta.* During this era the Wild Bill tag was dropped and he was billed usually as Bill Elliott.

During this developing period Bill Elliott sought an image that would make him a bit different from the singing cowboys of the day with their $200 spangled shirts. Oddly enough, Elliott bore a resemblance to the late William S. Hart. He took advantage of this and went for the same type of realism in his dress that Hart had used in his silent film portrayals. In his effort to develop a character of his own, Elliott also wore his guns with the butts forward as though

for a cross-draw. However, he drew by simply turning his hands outward, drawing the gun on his right hip with his right hand, the left gun in the same way. To many of us, this appeared awkward and unwieldy, but Bill Elliott made it work. In fact, the old cowboys who made up the stuntman brigade and the hard-riding posse for most of Hollywood's Westerns proclaimed him the best and fastest gun-handler since Colonel Tim McCoy.

During the late Forties Elliott was elevated out of the Red Ryder series, being replaced by Allen Lane. The new Elliott films for Republic Studios allowed him to go even

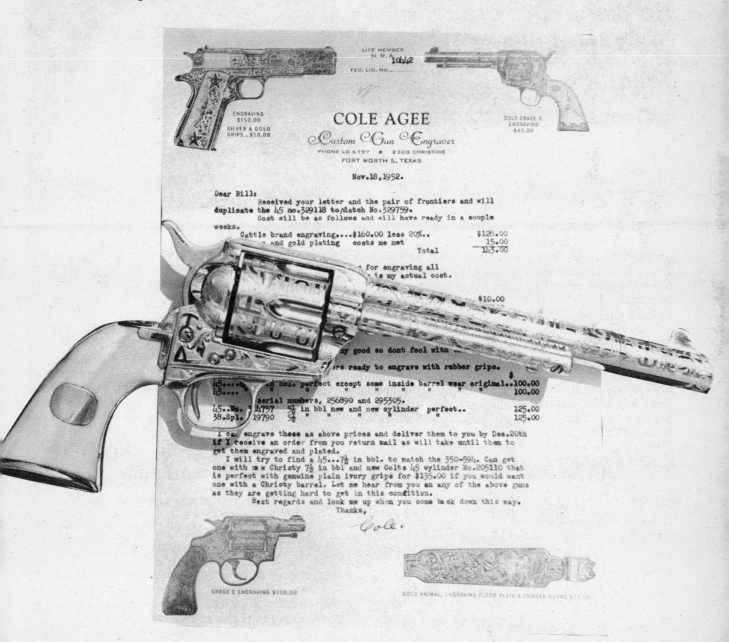

This Colt SAA with 7½-inch barrel was engraved on special order by C. Agee for Bill Elliott. It is backgrounded by correspondence between the pair.

This matched pair of single-action .45s also belonged to Elliott during his heyday as a Western film star. Wood grips were made by Elliott. Elongated diamond bears his initials. Replacement grips of ivory were made by T.L. Bish.

farther in adopting the type of character originated by William S. Hart: the "good badman," with the fast guns and the grim outlook on life that usually had him starting out as a misunderstood gunman who redeems himself in the end. But even in this bigger-budget series, often made in color, Elliott continued to do his good deeds with his guns slung butt forward. For him, it had become a comfortable style.

Toward the end of his career, Elliott moved on to Allied Artists, where he continued his good badman portrayals, utilizing adult plots that usually ended with blazing gunfire. But by 1954 the day of the B-Western had come to a close, the new Western television series and re-edited

Hopalong Cassidy pictures on the home screen cutting into theater attendance.

During the next three years Elliott appeared in several non-Western roles, but still in an adventure theme, completing his contract. He retired from the screen in 1957. For a time he toured the rodeo circuit and hosted a television show that featured his own films, while continuing to raise horses and cattle at his ranch in Calabasas, California. Ultimately he moved to a ranch outside of Las Vegas, Nevada, where he died of cancer in 1965.

In the early days of his heroics, Elliott apparently used whatever sixguns the studio prop department issued him, but he ultimately developed his own likes and dislikes, settling on a pair of standard Colt Single Action Army revolvers with 5½-inch barrels. In keeping with his feeling for authenticity, these were unadorned, except for bone grips.

However, Bill Elliott did have an appreciation for fine hardware. In 1963 Tommy L. Bish, a gun writer of the period and a well known arms collector, purchased from another collector three highly engraved Colt SAA models, which were purported to have belonged to Elliott. Bish recognized the cattle brand engraving on all three of the sixguns as that of the late Cole Agee, who had operated out of Fort Worth, Texas, prior to his death.

Bish had become intrigued with the background of the guns and contacted Elliott, who not only stated the guns had belonged to him, but that he still had letters from Agee discussing the price for engraving the guns, and the express receipt for their return to him. Elliott, as it turned out, had sold the set of matched .45s with 5½-inch barrels for $2500, then had sold the 7½-inch barreled Peacemaker to the same collector for an additional $500. According to the letter from Agee to Elliott, cost of the engraving, with some chrome and gold plating, was only $143 per gun in that era of 1952, when the engraver worked on them. Serial number of the Peacemaker is 350594. The matched .45s are numbered 329118 and 329759.

The three Colts all are pre-World War II models. The matching pair are identically engraved and chrome-plated, except for the cylinders, hammers, triggers, screws and ejector rods, which Agee plated in gold. The 7½-inch Peacemaker was fully chromed and outfitted with custom-made grips of elephant ivory mounted with silver.

At the time Bish obtained them, the matched pair with 5½-inch barrels had grips of walnut. He later learned that Elliott had made the grips himself. Each set was inlaid with an oblong silver diamond carrying the Western star's initials, BE, as well as a large raised silver star where the Colt emblem normally is inset.

Bish fashioned elephant ivory stocks for each of these sixguns, but retained the original grips made by Elliott, aware of their collector interest.

The three guns no longer are in his possession. Bish sold the Elliott Colts several years ago to an oil company executive in Tulsa, Oklahoma.

"At the time I thought I was getting a hellish big price," he acknowledges. "But today, they would be worth many times that amount."

There is a touch of regret in Bish's tone as he says this, as though he wishes he had retained ownership as much for the nostalgia value as the monetary.

Tommy L. Bish and Wild Bill Elliott display the trio of engraved Colts which Bish purchased at a gun show. Elliott later authenticated the fact that he had owned them.

REX ALLEN

The Last Of The B-Western Cowboys Is Down To His Last Sixgun

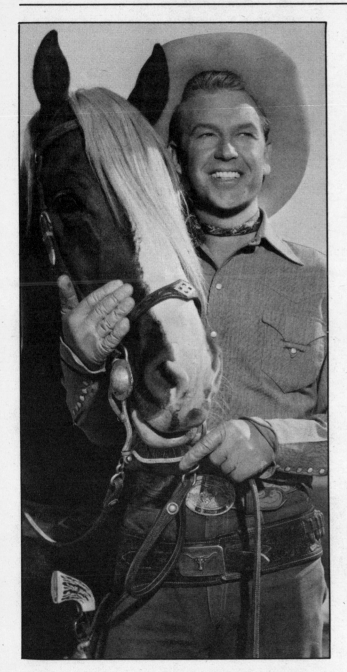

In his first film, Arizona Cowboy, *Rex Allen was rather conservative in dress, wearing a tightly tooled gunbelt and carrying a Colt SAA with stag grips. (Left) Silver-mounted saddle and engraved sixguns were stolen from museum. Saddle was later recovered, but the guns weren't.*

A SKINNY teenage boy came down from the Winchester Mountains north of Willcox, Arizona, in the late Thirties to win a state music contest with his $5 Sears, Roebuck guitar and thus launch a career that would make him the last of the singing cowboys of the B-Western era that ended with the birth of the television frontier types.

The engraved sixguns that Rex Allen carried through some of his thirty-five Western films were installed in the museum in his hometown of Willcox a dozen years ago, then disappeared one night, along with the silver-mounted saddle, bridle and martingale that the cowboy had used on his horse, Koko, through most of his screen adventures.

"There were two burglars who took the gear," Allen recalls today. "One of them was caught in Texas and we got the saddle and other horse tack back, but the guns and the holster rig disappeared with the other man who's never been caught."

Allen was all-fired proud of those matched sixguns and the holster rig, too. The silver grips had his name engraved in them and the guns had been inlaid with gold by Sunset Trails, a Los Angeles outfit. The grips, Allen feels, were discarded a long time ago as they would have made the gun too easy to identify. But back when he was first starting to make the film series that made him the successor to Roy Rogers, he paid $2500 for that pair of guns and the silver- and gold-mounted belt and twin holsters that went with them. That was in the Forties, when $2500 was a lot of money. "In fact," Allen drawls today, "you have no idea of how many weeks I had to work at Republic Pictures to pay for those guns. They were not exactly noted for the money they paid any of us."

At the time he left Chicago for Hollywood, Allen had another set of Colt Single Action Army revolvers customized by an Illinois craftsman. "Those guns had my name engrved on them, along with the Diamond X brand. One of them is in the Country Music Hall of Fame in Nashville. The other one was stolen a long time ago.

"I'm down to one sixgun today. I keep it around for sentimental reasons, although I use it on occasion when I do a guest shot on television or a personal appearance. It's a pretty much ordinary .455 Colt revolver with chrome plating and hard rubber grips. It's a pre-World War II model and some of the plating is starting to flake off. However, I bought that gun from Audie Murphy more than twenty-five years ago. It's been with me a long time."

The late Audie Murphy, a Western star in his own right, was a collector of Colt Single Action Army revolvers who tended to sort out that collection periodically, selling off some of the duplications. That is how Allen came to pay $100 for the sixgun.

The gunbelt stolen from the Arizona museum was custom made to Allen's specification by Cliff Ketchum, who operated the San Fernando Valley Saddlery in those days.

"It was a real work of art," Allen recalls, "but with the price of gold and silver, compared to the days when I had it made, I suspect the precious metal has been stripped off a long time ago and sold as scrap."

The single-holster rig that he still has and which he used in a number of pictures was made by Leddy Brothers, a saddlery in San Angelo, Texas. It also is silver mounted, with his name set in silver letters across the back of the belt. The holster has been skeletonized so that the barrel and cylinder are visible through openings in the leather. It rides on Allen's left hip with the gun butt forward for a cross draw.

In spite of the fact that he learned to play the guitar and sing back there in the Arizona mountains where his family had a ranch that "raised a lot of rocks and a few cattle," Rex Allen came by his knowledge of guns and shooting in realistic, practical fashion.

Allen continued to remain conservative in his earliest films, although traces of silver were showing in his cowboy hardware such as the gunbelt. The engraved SAA Colts were maintained primarily for public appearances.

This gunbelt, custom-made for Allen by Leddy Brothers in Texas, is still in the actor's possession. It was made at the height of his fame as the last singing cowboy of the B-Western era, which came to an end in mid-1950s.

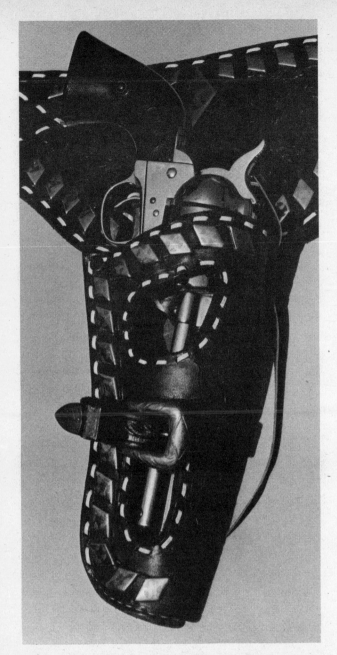

Rex Allen designed the cut-out holster which revealed the barrel, part of the cylinder. There was no great practical reason, but it made him different from the other cowboys of the screen who rode the same ranges.

dues-paying member of the Professional Rodeo Cowboys Association.

Giving up the rodeo trail, Allen landed a job on an Arizona radio station and a year later was with a station in New Jersey, singing country and Western songs, some of which he had written himself. By 1946 he had followed in the footsteps of Gene Autry, joining the National Barn Dance, which was broadcast nationally from Chicago. He also had signed a recording contract.

"My first rifle was given to me when I was about 10," Allen recalls. "It wasn't so much a gift as it was a survival tool. In those days we had to learn to shoot well if we were going to eat well." Even today, as other hunters at such events as the Grand National Quail Hunt in Oklahoma can testify, Rex Allen is a deadly shot with a quail gun.

Shortly after graduation from high school in 1938, Allen hit the road with his guitar with the intention of becoming a rodeo star. He rode a lot of wild bulls and bucking horses. As he puts it, "I had a few of them try to ride me," before he decided music offered a better future. However, he still is a

A few pounds heavier and 30 years older, Rex Allen is still able to wear the sixgun rig that he favored in his days as a movie cowboy. He still records country-Western music and narrates Disney films, commercials.

The last sixgun that Rex Allen retains belonged to the late Audie Murphy, another top cowboy of the screen. The Colt SAA has no front sight, since Murphy found it easier to draw, fire blanks.

The sixgun purchased from Audie Murphy a number of years before the actor's death in a plane crash has all matching serial numbers, adding to collector value. (Below) Some areas of the checkered hard rubber grips are virtually worn smooth, indicating a lot of use.

The Colt Single-Action Army model carries serial number 260920, indicating that it was manufactured well prior to World War II, probably in 1904, say factory records.

Meantime, Allen's baritone had found a new outlet in narrating films for Disney and in commercials. In spite of these successes in varied fields, Rex Allen still is called Mister Cowboy throughout the West and makes numerous rodeo appearances each year.

As though to complete the circle, his oldest son, Rex Allen, Jr., has been making a name in country music and is slated to do a film, *The Singing Cowboys,* at this writing. Rex Allen's silver-mounted saddle will be taken from its place of honor in Willcox's Museum of the Southwest so the younger Allen can ride off into the sunset in the same sparkling style as did his father.

"I'm planning on lending him my gunbelt, too," the senior Allen explains. "And I'm looking for some fancy grips for that old sixgun I got from Audie Murphy. It sort of seems to me that Audie might like the idea of the tradition being carried on by another generation. I know I do."

Raised as an Arizona cowboy, Rex Allen always has been an excellent horseman, but he had to learn to handle a sixgun when he got into films. His previous shooting had been primarily with a rifle and shotgun for game.

When Gene Autry had a feud with the studio, Republic Pictures quickly replaced him with Roy Rogers. Later, with Rogers thinking of going on his own, the studio didn't want to be caught flat-footed. Thus, Rex Allen was brought in as a threat and to keep brother Roy under control. This may seem a bit cold-hearted, but it is a system as old as Hollywood. Buck Jones was brought in as a possible replacement for Tom Mix, then twenty years later a singing cowboy named Bob Baker was brought to Universal Studios as a replacement for Jones. In spite of the situation, today Rex Allen and Roy Rogers are close friends.

In 1949 Republic Pictures offered Allen a chance to star in *Arizona Cowboy.* That was the first of a long series of films for the studio and by 1951 he was among the top five Western stars, remaining on that roster for the next four years, when all of the studios dropped their series Westerns to concentrate on the television short form. At that time Allen was cast in television's *Frontier Doctor* series, which lasted for several years.

Even today, Rex Allen still is known as Mister Cowboy in large segments of the nation. His son, Rex Allen, Jr., is slated to follow in his footsteps with a new film being planned to also star young Roy Rogers, Jr.

Chapter 13

Modern quick-draw rig from George Lawrence carries holster low, tied down just above knee. Basketweave holster is metal lined, permitting cylinder rotation.

LEATHER HOLSTERS for single-action revolvers are only slightly more than a hundred years old in development. For the most part, those citizens who carried handguns in the Nineteenth Century, did so with the barrels stuck in their belts or concealed in pockets. Earlier, those who were able to afford firearms generally could afford only one and that one was a long arm, providing the dual role of protection and a harvester of protein.

Those who rode horses were likely to carry two handguns in holsters which were slung over the saddle. These holsters were generally made of one piece of leather, cut to fit the two guns. In the East carrying guns in the open was frowned upon and handguns were almost always carried concealed in pockets until shortly after World War I.

Prior to the War Between the States, the mounted cavalryman who was issued a single-action revolver also was issued a leather holster. The gun was carried on the right side, but the soldier was supposed to crossdraw it with the left hand and the holster was designed to carry the gun butt-forward. This was so that the right hand could wield the cavalry saber.

Later, when the cavalry adopted the Colt Army Model 1860 black powder revolver, the holster was designed the

Modern Revolver Holsters Are Directly Descended From Their Frontier Ancestors

SINGLE-ACTION LEATHER

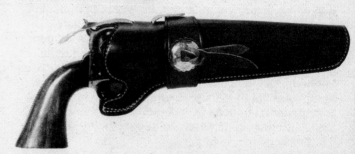

Bianchi's replica mid-1800s Slim Jim holster is designed for black powder revolvers, belt-slotted for high ride.

Gunfighter figures displayed at the Frontier Museum Historical Center, Temecula, California, have been thoroughly researched for authenticity in clothing and equipment worn. Note the high riding holsters and no tie-downs. Gunmen of the Old West, on both sides of the law, were convinced that an accurate first shot was most important.

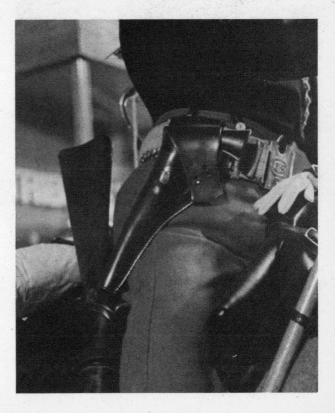

Pre-Civil War saddle holster set stands in the background, designed to hang across the saddle and carry two black powder revolvers. Later, American cavalrymen were issued full-flap holsters for crossdraw from butt forward carry. Holster position, right, was comfortable when mounted.

Civilian black powder holster of Slim Jim type dated from 1850s and 1860s. The half-flap design closed down over gun handle with short leather strap slipped through loop sewn on holster body. Gun fit well into narrow holster.

This early holster shows some excellent hand tooling, still in good condition. Design shows no top flap or safety strap, leather is cut away from trigger area.

same way, and included the full flap, still common with military holsters. Then, the rider was supposed to hold the reins in the left hand while he drew and fired his sidearm with the right hand, twisting his wrist to grab the forward-facing gun butt. John Bianchi, in his definitive book, *Blue Steel & Gunleather,* says that this design persisted for military holsters until 1905, when the army changed to a right-handed holster with the butt to the rear.

The Model 1885 holster, adopted by the cavalry, was a half-flap design, developed from the earlier full-flap style. The holster was made from a single piece of leather, formed roughly to the shape of the gun it carried. After cutting, the single sheet of leather was folded or rolled in half and stitched in the back and included a plug in the bottom or muzzle end to help keep out dirt. The holster was designed to ride high on the hip as the wearer mounted and rode. The half-flap was cut to cover the top of the gun and fold down to snap closed. Some versions were cut to carry the Colt Single-Action Army, others for the Smith & Wesson Schofield which was cavalry issue during the decade of the 1880s.

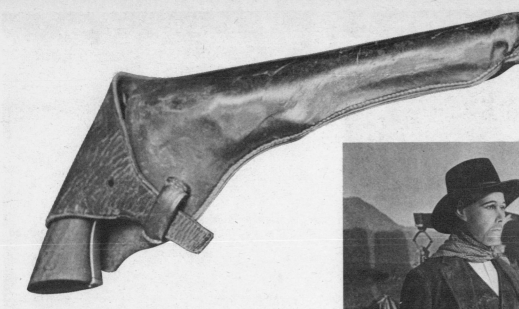

Another early black powder Slim Jim holster with flap closed, above, displayed in Bianchi's Frontier museum.

After the war the nation's economy was in rags; the migration West was under way. Many veterans from both the North and the South had become used to carrying a handgun for protection, rather than the long rifle of their fathers. Those cavalrymen who were armed with the full-flap, butt-forward holstered gun knew its disadvantages. Many were taken into the local saddlemaker shop to be converted for a normal right-hand draw. Many other holsters were made up to suit the customer about to head West to seek a new life after the war.

A direct descendant of the cavalry full-flap model was the Slim Jim holster, which found favor with many handgun packers. The Slim Jim had no flap at all. Open at the

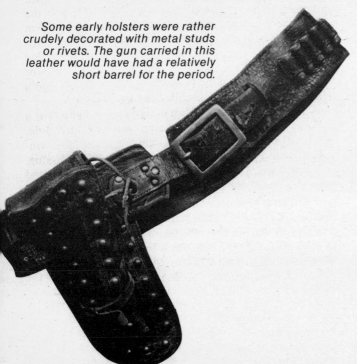

Some early holsters were rather crudely decorated with metal studs or rivets. The gun carried in this leather would have had a relatively short barrel for the period.

Those who carried two guns a hundred years ago, did so for the additional five or six shots, not to blaze away with both guns from two hands, as in later movies.

top, it was carried on the right hip, high up on the belt, gun butt to the rear. The name describes the shape; the gun was deep in the holster, the lower portion of the holster not much bigger around than the gun barrel, with the leather cut away to expose the rear of the trigger guard and trigger. A stitched strip of leather extended up over the bottom of the trigger guard on most Slim Jims.

As the new cartridge revolvers were developed by Remington, Colt and Smith & Wesson, they became popular in the West. Holsters took on the one-piece Kansas Loop look. The general design, or at least the look, is still popular today on holsters built for single-action revolvers. The belt loop is formed by doubling over the back leather, leaving it attached to the holster body and forming a leather skirt between holster body and the wearer's hip. The holster muzzle area was pushed through a slit-formed band in the skirt. The belt loop was and is wide enough for most any cartridge belt width the Westerner wore, somtimes three or

Two-gun holster set is intended for a pair of Colt .44 Richards conversion revolvers. Slim Jim holsters are still in excellent condition, construction and fit.

U.S. Cavalry holster Model 1884, .45 Colt 7½-inch barrel, with canvas cartridge belt, carried before this century.

Cartridge revolvers built by Smith & Wesson, Colt and Remington were popular in the West and some holsters took on the Kansas and Texas Loop look, still in favor.

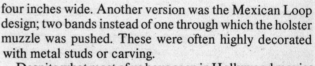

Functional loop design carried revolver deep inside holster. When mounted, rider might slide holster around to rear or to front of hip position for security on trail.

four inches wide. Another version was the Mexican Loop design; two bands instead of one through which the holster muzzle was pushed. These were often highly decorated with metal studs or carving.

Despite what most of us have seen in Hollywood movies over the years, the Western frontiersman neither wore his gun low on his thigh, nor tied down the holster with thong. As near as can be determined, the universal location was high on the hip, close to the body. When mounted, the holster might be slipped around the right hip to about the pocket location, or completely around to the left side for cross-draw. The left side carry would provide better gun protection as the rider rode so many hours in the saddle.

Upon dismounting, the gun would be readjusted to a location just about at the right trouser pocket, by the right hip but still carried high and snug. The draw-down gunfight at high noon is mostly a figment of latter-day writers' imaginations and a fast draw was uncommon. The holster was mainly a place to keep the gun safe while mounting and riding a horse without a safety strap or tie-down.

In the latter part of the Nineteenth Century, some gunfighters developed what is called the Texas Low-Cut holster. This was a standard loop design holster cut away to allow more of the gun handle to show and be easy to grab, but it still was carried high and tight.

For more firepower two guns and two cartridge belts might be worn. This arrangement gave ten or twelve shots from one hand, not five or six from each. Typically, the Colt Single Action Army often was loaded with five rounds, the hammer down on an empty chamber as a safety measure. If the traveler needed more firepower in hostile country, he probably carried a lever-action rifle chambered the same as his revolver, commonly in .44-40.

As Western movies became popular early in this century, the image of the gunfighter — good guy or bad guy — included a low riding holster, sometimes almost to the knee. These were more often than not highly decorated with silver and tooled leather, tied down with thong at the muzzle end of the holster, and designed with a hammer loop. The adversaries stroll out to the middle of the street and

Typical loop-type holsters worn by Texas cowboys, plain and tooled, dating from the 1880 period. Plain leather model shows open muzzle while the tooled holster appears to be closed. Both would be worn high on owner's hip.

face each other. The townsfolk scurry for cover and a place to watch. The camera gives us a close-up of one or both shifting their gun belts lower and slipping off the hammer safety strap. They slap leather and the bad guy drops to the ground.

Mostly, it never happened that way. Good aim was more important than a fast draw. Most shootings were from behind a tree, around the corner of a building, through the saloon doorway or into the sleeping cowboy at night. If a gunfight was unavoidable, the first man to get off an accurate shot was usually the winner. Unless there was something wrong with the other guy, you didn't get a chance for a second shot. You drew your gun with moderate speed, took aim and shot deliberately. Low-hung, tied-down holsters were unheard of and unnecessary.

Gunfighters began to cut away some of the holster leather to expose more of the gun handle for an easier grab, known as the Texas Low-Cut, with no tie-down.

Texas Loop holster is shown above with .45 caliber Colt Model 1878 double-action revolver, muzzle protruding below leather. Holster could accommodate similar size single-action and may have done so during its life.

Matched pairs of holsters are rare, dating from early days, and here is an ornate duo carved and decorated for an equally matched pair of Merwin Hulbert revolvers. The set, with knife, was obviously owned by a person of means.

Moving into the time after the turn of the century, holsters took on a more familiar, modern look, as shown by this pair from the Twenties or Thirties.

ing inside the leather holster provided almost frictionless fast draw while holding only portions of the gun frame in the holster. As the draw commenced, there was no leather touching the gun to slow it down; the metal-to-metal contact was immediately broken. Quick-draw competition grew rapidly, spreading across the country, even to cities like Chicago, St. Louis, Kansas City, as well as the more obvious Western cities such as Tombstone, Los Angeles, Las Vegas, Phoenix, and others where one would expect it.

This interest, which peaked in the early Sixties, led to additional design development of leather goods for fast-draw holsters and belts. Ojala developed what is believed

The double loop holster wsa popular with outlaws as well as lawmen in the period before 1900. This stud-decorated model seems to have belonged to the Marshal of Laredo, Texas, if the attached badge is authentic.

The winning of the West was not the end of holster development for the single-action revolver, of course. Development continues today. A big surge in the popularity of the single-action handgun took place in the 1950s with the advent of fast-draw competition. Live ammunition and blanks were used by the specialists, shots timed with sophisticated electronic timers to split seconds. Holsters for the competitors became known as Hollywood holsters and achieved a high level of engineering and development before the sport declined from its peak of popularity.

Arvo Ojala was a movie stuntman, a fast-draw artist and coach of many Western actors. He developed the fast-draw holster to a high state of the art. He produced his first sheet metal lined holster in the early Fifties. The metal lin-

Fast-draw competition evolved into the walk-and-draw timed shoots. The holster was canted with muzzle forward, a minimum of leather touching the gun. The draw was a twisting motion, left hand thumbing hammer.

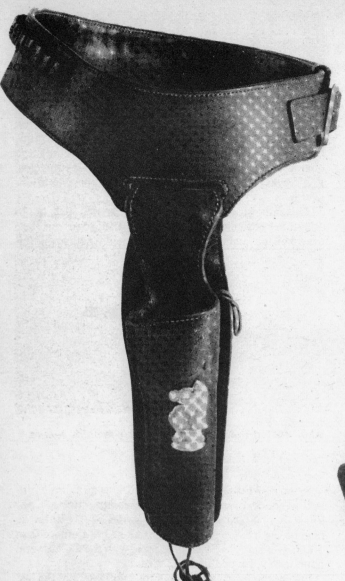

The forward muzzle rake holster design came about for two reasons: One, it was fast to draw and, two, it prevented over-eager quick-draw competitors from shooting themselves. The fast-draw cowboys were beginning to let a blank round go before the gun had cleared leather, putting powder burns in feet and legs. So the holster was built with a forward rake of thirty or forty degrees from vertical. The too-fast shot went harmlessly into the ground. Ojala's patented design had a number of other features, as well. The internal metal construction of the holster permitted not only a fast, safe draw, but allowed the cylinder to turn while still within the holster. The single-action revolver could be cocked and cylinder rotation started as it was being drawn, reducing the clocked time to complete the action.

While most of the latter day fast-draw artists carry their holstered single-actions low, the gun butt only slightly above the level of the naturally falling hand, one of the early pioneers of fast-draw maintained his holster at high carry. More than anyone outside Hollywood, four-time national fast draw champion Dee Woolem may be credited with starting the movement as an organized sport.

The holster above was built by Arvo Ojala and worn by actor Richard Boone in his Paladin *television series.*

to be the first muzzle-forward design for competition, something not seen on the frontier a hundred years ago. The rigs were constructed in Ojala's shop under the direction of Andy Anderson, who later went on to his own leather business, under the Gunfighter name brand.

Before moving into a discussion of the modern quick-draw and other single-action holsters, one final mention of the full-flap military holster: The design is still in production, for the issue Model 1911A1 Colt .45 automatic pistol, virtually unchanged for more than six decades until John Bianchi redesigned the holster for more modern needs. The military full-flap is still there, but the new design is more versatile, offering left or right-hand carry, high or low on the belt, easier draw, exposed or concealed, while still providing maximum security for the gun. It is designated the Model 66 by Bianchi.

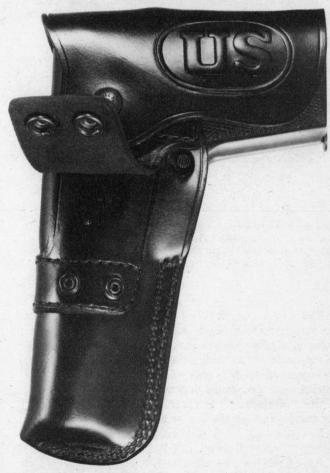

A modern descendant of the military full-flap holster is Bianchi's Model 66 for the familiar .45 M1911 Colt ACP. New model offers belt mount on right or left side or crossdraw carry. Flap snaps on or off for faster draw; completely removed for concealment carrying.

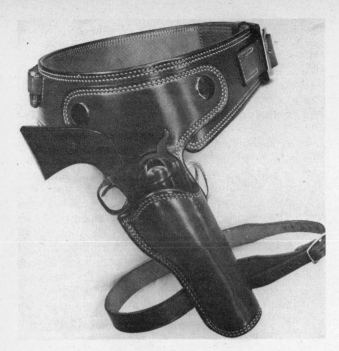

Competition fast-draw rig shows lower gun position, forward rake muzzle angle, a minimum of leather around the gun and a hefty buckled strap for thigh tie-down.

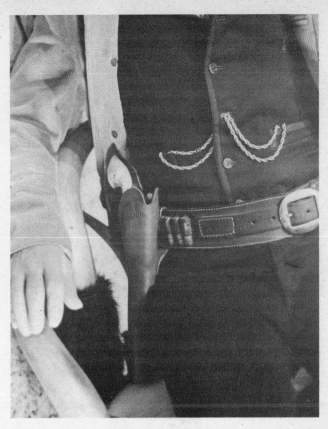

When seated, the waist-high gun carry remains secure.

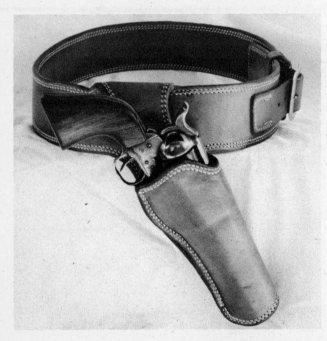

Forward rake angle is more extreme on this fast-draw model. Such a rig would be impractical for a gunman on horseback but will clear leather with speed.

In the mid-Fifties Woolem was working as a "train robber" at the Knott's Berry Farm tourist attraction at California. Armed with a Colt SAA loaded with blanks, he held up the train each hour, guessing he did so more than 100,000 times. He began practicing with the Colt several hours a day, for additional realism.

One of the legendary tests of the gunfighters of the last century was the silver dollar trick. The shooter held a silver dollar on the back of his gun hand, waist high, dropped the dollar, and fired a shot before the dollar hit the ground. With one week of practice, Dee Woolem found he was able to beat the fall with ease. He was making his own holsters and found that with improvement he was able to fire off two shots before the dollar landed. After several more months of practice and a few more holster improvements, Woolem was able to fire three shots before the dollar hit the dirt. This was faster than even a double-action revolver or an automatic pistol. He experimented some with a low holster, but moved the placement up to waist level at this time, with the gun butt hitting his forearm about midway between waist and elbow.

Woolem maintains the higher holster position is not only faster, but safer than the low position. With the low carry, the gun is cocked while still in the holster, lifted out of the leather, and the muzzle swings up and across some part of the leg or foot. With the high carry, the gun is snapped out the back of the holster and the muzzle swings clear down-range, not passing across any part of the body. Woolem still believes the high carry to be the best, as did the early real-life gunfighters.

Bianchi Model 1873 double-loop single-action holster is a modern version with maximum security and safety. Note how double-stitched leather protects trigger guard.

For more than a century, the favorite basic ingredient of holsters and gunbelts has been leather. Prices rise and fall, based on diverse economic factors, but the best hides are always in demand by holster makers.

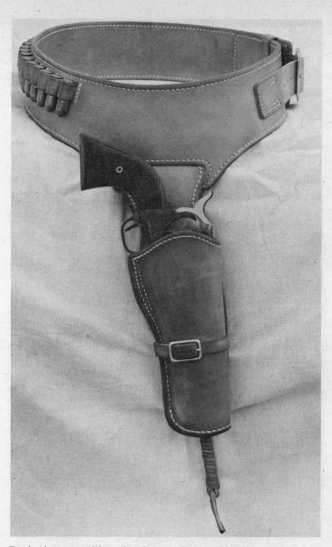

Typical competition rig shows plenty of leather on the cartridge belt, semi-contoured to fit the wearer's body. Muzzle hangs straight, with moderate drop.

Woolem's tours of the country demonstrating fast-draw helped the sport to gain popularity and support. He first toured for Great Western Arms using their Great Western single-action, then for Crosman, using their Hahn CO_2-powered BB gun, and finally was with Daisy for the same purpose.

Woolem has this to say about his high carry: "You shoot from hip level, you sure can't hit much if you shoot from down around your knee. So, from a low holster you must lift the gun and swing it up through an arc, to hip level. I carry my gun as near as possible to where I'll shoot it. The gun has less distance to travel. If my hand is anywhere near as fast as his, I'll beat the low gun wearer every time."

After development of the Arvo Ojala steel-lined holster, perhaps the next most important was that of the forward tilt muzzle holster design attributed to Andy Anderson. A WWII combat wound left Anderson with a stiff right wrist, affecting his gun handling from the holster. As a commercial art student, he gained knowledge of the human bone structure and began to analyze his problem. He found that when the hand holding a gun is simply held down naturally at holster level the muzzle points slightly forward, not

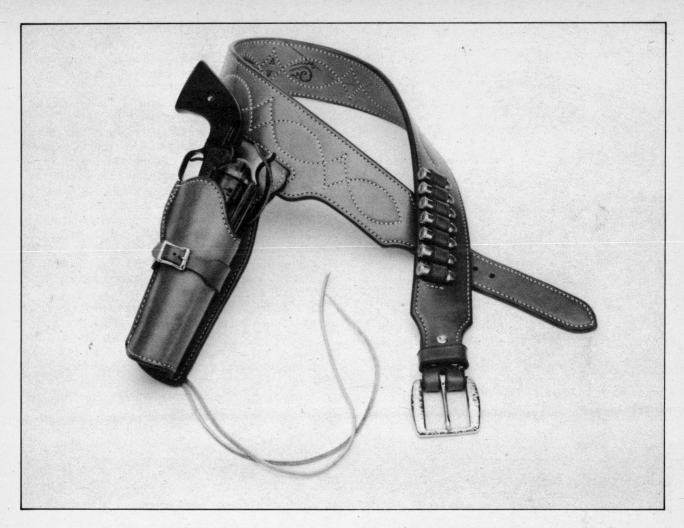

The Cobra Gunskin outfit in New York has obtained the rights to the name and designs of famed fast-draw holster maker Andy Anderson. The Gunfighter rigs which Anderson developed are available from Cobra in several variations.

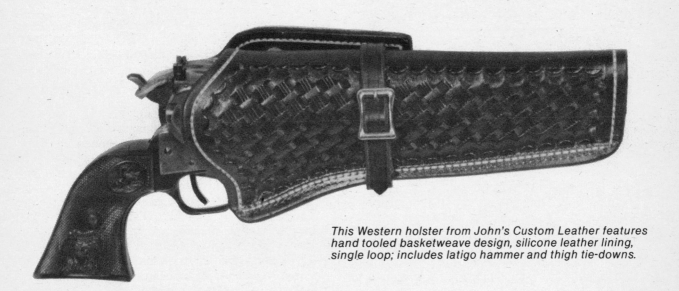

This Western holster from John's Custom Leather features hand tooled basketweave design, silicone leather lining, single loop; includes latigo hammer and thigh tie-downs.

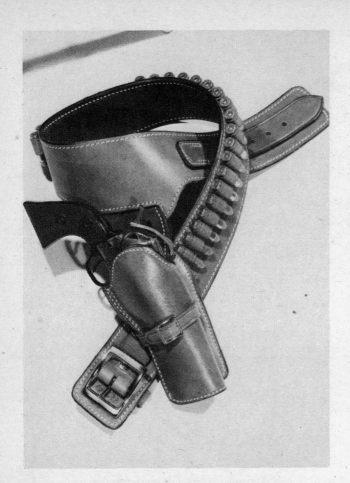

straight down or to the rear. The higher toward the hip the hand is held, the more the muzzle wants to point forward. Anderson reasoned that a holster mounted at the same natural angle would permit a faster, safer, more accurate draw. He was right.

Anderson moved to Los Angeles in 1958 and opened his Gunfighter shop, producing special fast-draw rigs. As the popularity of fast-draw and his own rigs grew, Anderson presented single-action fast-draw live ammunition classes twice a year for nearly a decade. Many of the top fast-draw gunners use his rigs today. In addition to the muzzle rake design, Anderson is credited with producing the first contoured gunbelts, fitting snugly around the flair of the hips smoothly and comfortably. He was the first to offer rigs designed for the walk-and-draw competition, a variant of the original fast-draw sport. His Gunfighter stitch, now so popular on rifle slings and boots, was first offered on Anderson's Gunfighter Walk & Draw Standard Fast Draw rig.

Andy Anderson is now retired, due to medical problems, but his name and design rights are assigned to Cobra Gunskins in New York state, which offers several of his original and updated single-action holster rigs. Cobra continues to consult with Anderson on their new design developments.

The modern single-action revolver holsters owe much to the early frontiersmen and saddle makers of a century ago. Aside from Cobra with its Andy Anderson designs, most

Safariland's modern version of the gunfighter rig is their Model 40 Virginian. The holster has a fifteen degree forward rake, cylinder area is steel lined, held free of contact with gun. Gunbelt contains standard thirty cartridge loops, contoured body fit.

This highly carved and tooled Buscadero belt and holster rig is from George Lawrence leather, in the early Mexican tradition. Thirty cartridge loops are sewn to the belt which measures three inches through the body and 5½ inches wide at the holster drops for comfort.

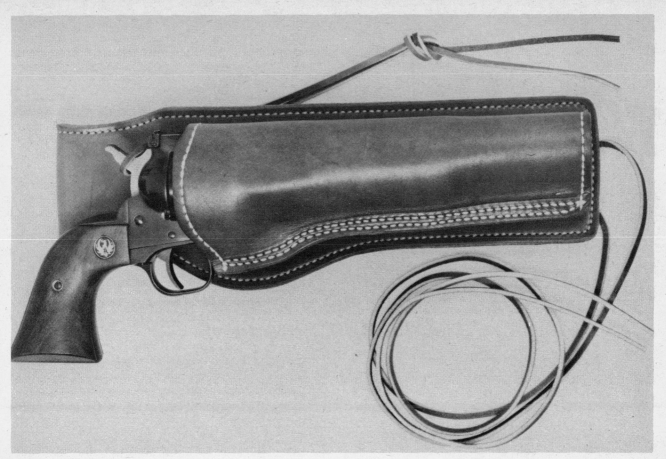

Model 48 Blazer Western holster is from Smith & Wesson leather, of traditional design. Low cut leather exposes trigger guard and gun handle, two sets of leather thong tie-downs and thong loop for single-action hammer spur.

Roy's Custom Leather, best known for Pancake holster, also offers the design to fit most single-action revolvers.

of the big holster makers also produce several single-action holsters and rigs. Among those turning out replicas and modern designs are Bianchi Gunleather, John's Custom Leather, George Lawrence, Roy's Custom Leather Goods, Safariland, and Smith & Wesson Leather. Each is carefully constructed of the best leather available, fitted to the specific single-action revolver for which it is designed, and finished to last for years.

Leather has been the traditional protector and carrier of single-actions for more than a hundred years. It would appear that leather will continue in that role for the next century of single-action use.

Chapter 14

THE LONG, THE SHORT & THE SMALL

Over The Decades, Some Have Wanted Behemoth Revolvers, Others Have Wanted Midgets; The Trend Continues!

I LEARNED a long time back that it requires no rehearsal to be miserable. In my relatively wild youth I had both elbows broken, so I don't care much for recoil or barrel whip in a handgun. For example, a few rounds out of a .44 magnum leaves me with swollen elbows for a week.

But there are those who insist *macho* is based upon how much recoil you can take without verging on tears. Elmer Keith, who conducted the early experiments with the .44 magnum, is one who subscribes to that school of thinking and he's welcome to his belief. Everyone to his own thinking.

There is another school of thought having to do with the mini-calibers such as .22 rimfire. There have been a host of

revolvers made in this diminutive over the years and some police officers even today carry a .22 rimfire Derringer as a hideout gun. It's true that in at least one instance an elephant was killed with a cartridge of that size. When it comes to handling a felon, the feeling of a lot of folks, including myself, is that the .22 RF is sure-fire only if one has the opportunity to stick the muzzle in said felon's ear and pull the trigger.

Meantime, experimentation — even production — go on at both extremes: larger and smaller.

Going back some two decades to 1961, a gent named Clarence Bates of Compton, California, decided to go the .44 magnum one better. The Smith & Wesson Model 29 had been introduced only five years earlier, but Bates was

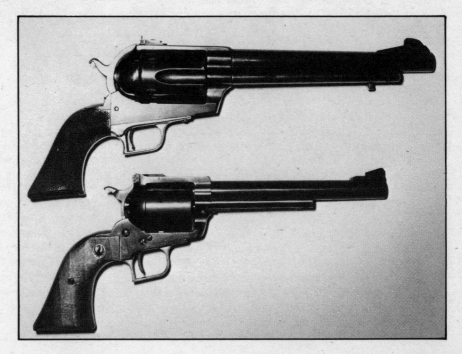

For the sake of comparison, a Ruger magnum Super Blackhawk is shown with the giant Bates made in .45-70.

Because of the design of the grip, Clarence Bates found he had little trouble in controlling the recoil of his .45-70 revolver. Shoulder strap helped hold up holster.

Below: The .45-70 cartridge which Bates loaded in his big sixgun is compared to the .44 magnum (center) and a .357 magnum cartridge. Tests showed power of round.

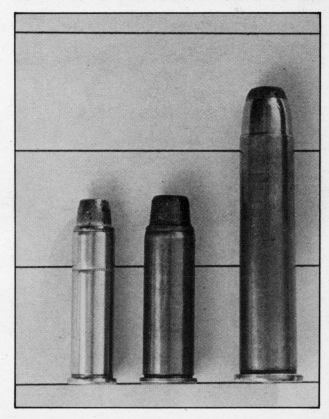

curious as to just where the search for more power and longer range in a single-action handgun reached the limits of practicality.

Bates, who had made a number of replicas of the Walker Colt in his own shop, decided to copy the Colt Single Action Army model in .45-70 caliber, retaining some Walker ideas.

The cartridge, of course, goes back a lot beyond Bates or his ideas. Originally designed to load a 500-grain bullet ahead of 70 grains of black powder, it was introduced in 1873 for the old trap-door Springfield military rifle and remained a standby of our army until 1892. In more recent years the cartridge has been loaded with smokeless powder for rifles of modern manufacture for big-game hunting.

Bates ended up with a handgun featuring a nine-inch barrel, and an overall length of sixteen inches. The revolver weighed five pounds four ounces; more than the Walker Colt. When loaded, its weight was upped to five ounces short of six pounds. A handful by any standard, this created some practical limitations.

Bates soon found that if he tried to carry this handgun in a regular belt holster he was constantly in danger of losing his pants, so he devised a holster that rode on his hip in cross-draw fashion, but it was afforded added support by a shoulder strap. In attempting to hold the gun on a target, even with a two-hand hold, there tended to be a bit of waver.

Penetration potential of the .45-70 is illustrated in this photo. Holes marked with "1" were bored through a three-sixteenths steel plate with the big bore Bates. The indentation marked "2" is .44 magnum factory load.

So how did this big shooter perform? The .45-70 cartridge loaded today with smokeless powder will drive a 405-grain bullet out of the muzzle of a rifle at 1320 feet per second (fps) for 1570 foot-pounds of energy (fpe). That's a lot of shove.

The .45-70 cartridge case has nearly twice the powder capacity of the .44 magnum and has plenty of obvious destructive power, when one starts firing into five-gallon paint cans filled with water. When the gun was tested nearly two decades back, the can was split wide open, the water driven fifteen feet or so into the air. Smaller cans of water were literally flattened and when the .45-70 bullet was fired into a ripe watermelon it resembled the aftermath of a watermelon-eating contest. In this instance a 400-grain gas-check bullet was used.

A Ruger Super Blackhawk was used as control in the test of Bates' creation. In the tests on the water-filled cans the results seemed about equal; the same was true of the watermelon test, although the Bates handful did scatter the bits of rind across a slightly larger area.

Penetration tests were performed on lengths of four-inch-thick hardwood. Factory cartridges in the .44 magnum failed to penetrate the wood. Several reloads were tried in the .44 handgun also. Inspection revealed that the factory loads penetrated about three inches, while the reloads went through about half the thickness of the four-by-fours.

At the other extreme the .45-70 — handloaded in three different bullet weights — penetrated the four inches of hardwood with seeming ease, tearing out large splinters on the back side. Bullet weights used were a 210-grain gas-check, a 250-grain gas-check, a 300-grain soft-point and a

The Bates .45-70 appears to have monstrous proportions compared to S&W Model 29 .44 magnum and the still smaller .357 S&W magnum.

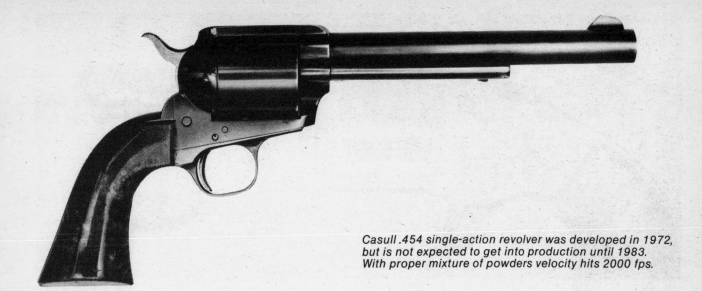

Casull .454 single-action revolver was developed in 1972, but is not expected to get into production until 1983. With proper mixture of powders velocity hits 2000 fps.

400-grain gas-check. The first two of these loads were backed with 19.5 grains of Unique powder; the second pair were loaded with 18.5 grains of the same powder. Bates had done some calculating with his slide rule prior to testing, to satisfy himself that the handgun he had built would withstand the pressures.

In trying the Bates .45-70 on three-sixteenths-inch steel plate, the 210-grain bullet penetrated easily, while the heavier bullets only dented the plate to a depth of half an inch. Factory loads in the .44 magnum dented the plate only a quarter-inch.

One reason for the military .45-70 rifle being discontinued was the parabolic trajectory that caused accuracy to suffer at extended ranges. The long-range shooting test on the .45-70 was hardly scientific, but it did show what the handgun could do in Bates' practiced hand. The target was a large white rock in Southern California's San Gabriel Mountains. Said rock was 275 yards away. Bates scored three hits out of five, the two misses disturbing the dust at the foot of the rock. The shooter with the .44 magnum — also familiar with the capabilities of his gun — scored five for five in the initial competition.

On the next five-round try, however, the magnum shooter scored three hits, while Bates had four hits on the rock

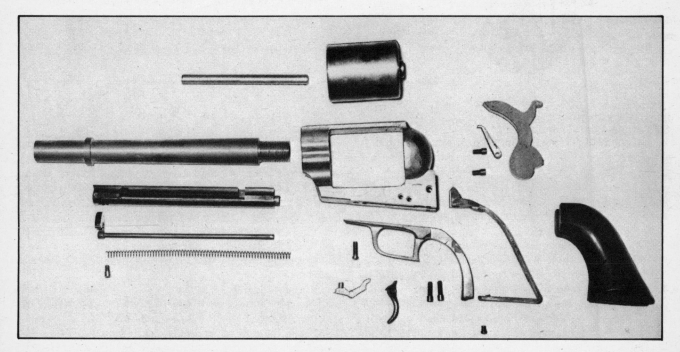

Dismantled Bates .45-70 shows the components that go into building the gun. The cylinder on this one has yet to be fluted in order to reduce the weight by a few more ounces. Ring on barrel will be milled to make ejector tube lug.

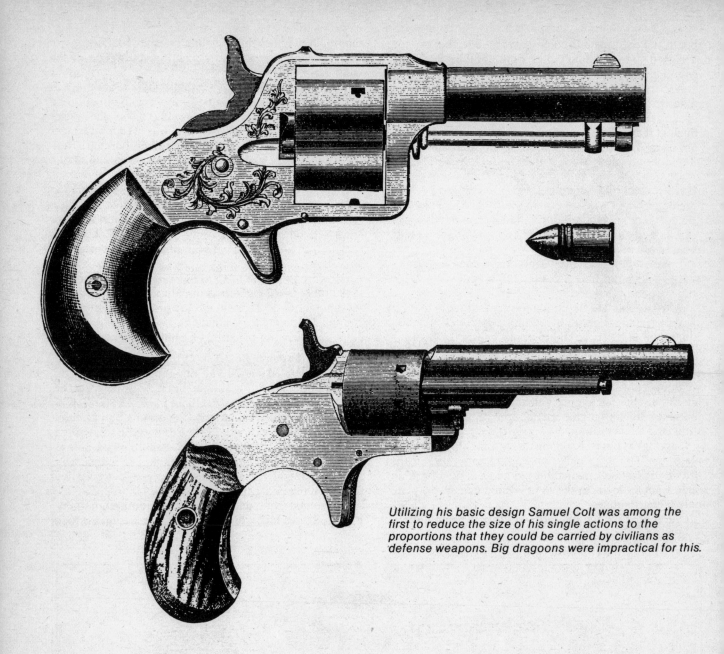

Utilizing his basic design Samuel Colt was among the first to reduce the size of his single actions to the proportions that they could be carried by civilians as defense weapons. Big dragoons were impractical for this.

with his monster. Later, when the rock was measured, it was found to be forty inches at the widest point and five feet high.

In working out reloads for the .45-70, Clarence Bates and Stuart Brainerd, a fellow shooter and personal friend, hoped to come up with a round that would drive a 250-grain bullet at 2000 fps.

It was not until Bates had an opportunity to chonrograph his loads — again matched against the Ruger Super Blackhawk — that he realized how far he had missed his goal. The best round he came up with recorded velocity on the chronograph screens at 1347 fps. This particular .45-70 cartridge was loaded with 19 grains of Unique powder behind a 250-grain gas-check bullet. On the other hand, the Ruger .44 magnum scored a high of 1540 fps using 22.3 grains of Hodgdon's H240 powder and a 243-grain gas-check bullet. When Bates tried an extra grain of powder in his .45-70, the velocity showed a decrease.

One shooter who was involved in the tests had some definite ideas: "The 400-grain slug, at better than 1000 feet per second, is a devastating load that, I think, could still be improved velocity-wise. Hercules 2400 powder proved less than satisfactory. Even 30 grains rattles around in the huge .45-70 case like beans in a castinette.

"This powder burns poorly unless densely loaded. Short of filling the balance of the case with corn meal, I can't think of any way to make 2400 burn properly in that particular case."

At that time Bates was using rifle primers in his reloads for proper ignition even with the Unique powder. The primers showed signs of excess pressure during the tests, although there were no problems of extraction. No pressure tests were made on these loads, but the various handbooks show that top loads offer pressures of no more than 25,000 pounds per square inch (psi).

After the experiment Bates went back to his drawing

board and equipment to come up with a five-shot cylinder designed so that the bolt slots were not located directly over the chambers.

As for construction of the Bates .45-70, the cylinder was fluted to reduce the weight, with the maker insisting that "it doesn't weaken the gun, because the metal is sufficiently thick at that point."

The cylinder and frame of the .45-70 was fashioned of 4130 chrome-moly steel, which was heat treated prior to machining; this was a precaution to prevent warpage. The barrel was of 1144 steel cut with eight grooves of .457 diameter. Twist was one turn in twenty-two inches. It was Bates' theory that speed of rotation with this twist would stabilize the long 400-grain bullets, while lighter bullets could be speeded up to maintain accuracy.

Following the tests, the gun was dismantled and inspected. An indication of the heat and pressure generated by this big cartridge was reflected in the rear of the barrel, where it joined the cylinder. The circumference had been eroded by gases escaping between barrel and cylinder. The original .003 clearance between the two parts had increased thus to .005. However, Clarence Bates already had fired some five thousand rounds through the gun prior to this inspection.

The sound of the .45-70 in a short barrel, especially in the confines of an indoor shooting range, verges on the horrendous, although recoil didn't seem to be a major factor. It was somewhat neutralized by the weight of the gun.

Bates made several .45-70 guns besides the one that was tested, although he stuck to the same design. The one-piece SAA-type grips were of lignum vitae wood, the trigger guard of cast brass, while tool steel was used for the inner parts. For the sake of accuracy, Bates incorporated a Redfield Sourdough, which he dovetailed into the ramp. At the rear was an adjustable Micro sight.

For those who may consider all of this experimentation somewhat dangerous, it should be remembered that Clarence Bates had spent his early days as a machinist and later became a mechanical engineer. He was aware of the potential problems and took great pains to see that his design was safe.

However, the Bates design has been swallowed by the past, while Smith & Wesson and Ruger still are selling all of the .44 magnums their plants can produce. There should be proof of something in that fact.

Which brings us to the .454 Casull, another entry in the bigger-than-big sweepstakes. This particular single-action was prototyped a decade back, but at this writing it still is not in actual production. Freedom Arms, Incorporated, of Freedom, Wyoming, however, says the gun should be in production in 1983.

One of the early efforts to come up with a compat defense handgun was the Chicago Protector. Thousands of these were sold as tourist items during the Chicago Exposition in 1890 for protection against the city's undesirables.

There seem to be few who discount the claim that the .454 Casull magnum is the most powerful handgun in the world. It has been proved that it will shove a 235-grain bullet down its 7½-inch barrel at velocities in excess of 2000 fps. That, incidentally, results in more than a ton of muzzle energy, or twice that of the .44 magnum factory-loaded cartridge. But this also creates chamber pressures of some 50,000 psi!

Dick Casull, the designer, has thus far not been able to interest ammunition companies in providing a factory round for his oversized baby, thus loads are created by hand. A standard .45 Colt case is used, but the primer pocket must be reamed out to handle a large rifle primer. The case, according to Casull's recipe, then is loaded with 2 grains of Unique powder, 25 grains of 2400, then is topped off by 4 grains of Bullseye before the 235-grain bullet is seated.

It is understood that several ammo companies have taken a look at this combination and, if they should ultimately load cartridges on a mass scale, probably would tone down the components to deliver perhaps 1850 fps with the 235-grain bullet.

Dean Grennell, a top reloading authority, feels that the mixture of the three powders could be dangerous, if one does not pay strict attention to loading procedures. He contends it is not a load he would recommend. It certainly would be unsafe in any other gun of current manufacture due to high pressures!

The handgun itself at first glance resembles the Colt SAA, but the cylinder is larger in diameter, is not fluted and is bored to load only five rounds. The early versions were heat-treated to Rockwell hardness of 43C. In addition to the thick cylinder walls, Casull also has cut the cylinder locking recesses so that they are between the chambers rather than over them. The frames are larger than those of the standard Colt or Ruger single-action, too, and the first were made of 4140 steel that had been invest-ment cast. Those being shown these days are of stain-less steel.

Those who have fired the Casull .454 contend that it has no more recoil than the .44 magnum, since the designer has fashioned the grip in the old plow-handle design to absorb some of that recoil.

Whether the Casull .454 will make its mark in history as have the Colt, Smith & Wesson and Ruger .44 magnums will only be known in the future.

At the other extreme there seems to be an effort to see how small a single-action revolver can be made and still be

Freedom Arms is producing the smallest single-action revolver made today. It is available in several barrel lengths; this model measures only 4¾ inches overall.

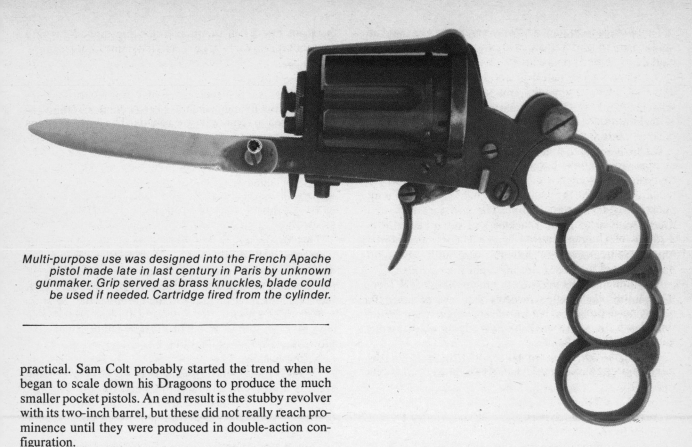

Multi-purpose use was designed into the French Apache pistol made late in last century in Paris by unknown gunmaker. Grip served as brass knuckles, blade could be used if needed. Cartridge fired from the cylinder.

practical. Sam Colt probably started the trend when he began to scale down his Dragoons to produce the much smaller pocket pistols. An end result is the stubby revolver with its two-inch barrel, but these did not really reach prominence until they were produced in double-action configuration.

In an effort to make firearms smaller, James Reid of Catskill, New York, turned out what he called the .22

Freedom Arms Model FA-1 is built to fire either a .22 short or long rifle cartridge. This firing version is held to belt buckle by a stud, can be removed to use. This is shortest of current series with one-inch barrel.

Knuckle-Duster Revolvers from 1869 to 1884, making more than 10,000 of them. This was marked *My Friend* and had a metal oblong with thumb hole rather than actual grips. There was no barrel, as the bullet fired directly from the cylinder. The gripless frame served as a set of brass knuckles for fist fighting, if quarters got too close.

Reid made several variations of this creation over the years, increasing calibers to .32, then to .41 before adding a 1¾-inch barrel to a model introduced in 1875.

A seeming adaptation of Reid's design was the French Apache pistol, which was made in Paris in the 1890 era. This particular model also fired through the cylinder without the necessity for a barrel. The grip actually was a traditional set of brass knuckles and slung beneath the cylinder was a double-edged dagger. There is no record of the manufacturer of this particular gun, but it was manufactured in .32 caliber featuring a pin-fire cartridge.

Mention has been made earlier of the Smith & Wesson Ladysmith single-action revolver that was designed for self-defense by ladies, but was discontinued when Daniel Wesson discovered it was being carried primarily by ladies of the oldest profession.

An odd-looking firearm called the Chicago Protector was mass-produced by the Chicago Firearms Company in the 1890s and it appeared more like a lady's vanity case than it did a defensive firearm. Thousands of these guns were sold to visitors to the Chicago Exposition of 1893 as protection against the holdup artists who preyed on tourists. The chromed firearm had no external trigger. Instead, the gun fit into the palm of the hand, the shaped butt against the heel of the hand, the fingers gripping the forward edge of the oddly shaped cylinder. The barrel extended between the fingers.

To fire this creation one simply clenched the fist. The butt mechanism served as the trigger. The force plunged a firing pin into the round held in the flat cylinder, at the same time turning another of the seven rounds into position to line up with the barrel. The Chicago Protector was made to fire a .32 round.

Whether by design or simple circumstance, Freedom Arms, the same outfit that is promoting the Casull .454, also has introduced today's smallest handgun, a .22 rimfire with a barrel only one inch in length. Overall length of the gun is three inches.

This single-action, however, is made in other barrel lengths as well. While the Casull .454 weighs 3⅛ pounds and measures fourteen inches overall, the most popular of the shorties, designated as Freedom Arms Model FA-1, has a 1.75-inch barrel that will handle either the .22 short or long rifle cartridge. It weighs only 4¼ ounces and measures 4.75 inches overall. The cylinder holds five rounds. However, a version to fire the .22 rimfire magnum holds only four rounds.

Dean Grennell, who ran some tests on one of these mini-sixguns states, "Presumably intended for use on large targets close in, the inherent accuracy is quite adequate on that basis. If you buy one for possible use in serious social shooting, you owe it to your own best interests and to those of your insurance underwriter to get in enough familiarization to handle it with competence and calm certainty."

The minute cylinder of the Freedom Arms FA-1 is bored to hold only five rounds of .22 rimfire ammo. The cylinder is fluted to bring the weight down to only 4¼ ounces.

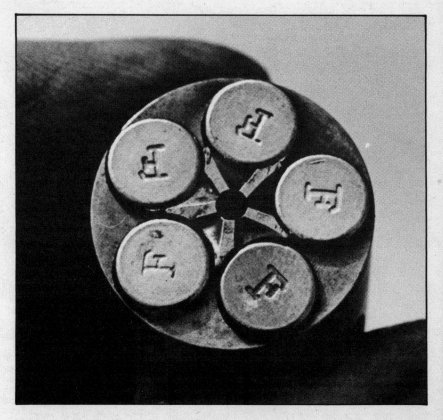

TODAY'S SINGLE-ACTIONS

HANDGUNS—SINGLE ACTION REVOLVERS

Abilene Single Action

ABILENE SINGLE ACTION REVOLVER
Caliber: 357 Mag., 44 Mag., 45 Colt, 6 shot.
Barrel: 4⅝", 6", 7½", 10" (44 Mag. only).
Weight: About 48 oz.
Stocks: Smooth walnut.
Sights: Serrated ramp front, click adj. rear for w. and e.
Features: Wide hammer spur. Blue or Magnaloy finish. From Mossberg.

Colt Single Action Army

COLT SINGLE ACTION ARMY REVOLVER
Caliber: 357 Magnum, 44 Spec., 44-40, or 45 Colt, 6 shot.
Barrel: 4¾", 5½", 7½" or 12".
Weight: 37 oz. (5½" bbl.). **Length:** 10⅞" (5½" bbl.)
Stocks: Black composite rubber with eagle and shield crest.
Sights: Fixed. Grooved top strap, blade front.
Features: See Colt catalog for variations and prices.

Colt New Frontier

Colt Single Action Army—New Frontier
Same specifications as standard Single Action Army except: flat-top frame; high polished finish, blue and case colored; ramp front sight and target rear adj. for windage and elevation; smooth walnut stocks with silver medallion, or composition grips.

COLT NEW FRONTIER 22
Caliber: 22 LR, 6-shot.
Barrel: 4¾", 6", 7½".
Weight: 29½ oz. (4¾" bbl.). **Length:** 9⅝" over-all.
Stocks: Black composite rubber.
Sights: Ramp-style front, fully adjustable rear.
Features: Cross-bolt safety. Color case-hardened frame. Available in blue or Coltguard finishes. Re-introduced 1982.

F.I.E."HOMBRE" SINGLE ACTION REVOLVER
Caliber: 357 Mag., 44 Mag., 45 LC.
Barrel: 5½" or 7½".
Weight: 45 oz. (5½" bbl.).
Stocks: Smooth walnut with medallion.
Sights: Blade front, grooved topstrap (fixed) rear.
Features: Color case hardened frame. Bright blue finish. Super-smooth action. Introduced 1979. Imported from West Germany by F.I.E. Corp.

F.I.E. "LEGEND" SINGLE ACTION REVOLVER
Caliber: 22 LR/22 Mag.
Barrel: 4¾".
Weight: 32 oz.
Stocks: Smooth walnut or black checkered nylon. Walnut optional ($16.95).
Sights: Blade front, fixed rear.
Features: Positive hammer block system. Brass backstrap and trigger guard. Color case hardened steel frame, rest blued. Imported from Italy by F.I.E. Corp.

F.I.E. E15 BUFFALO SCOUT REVOLVER
Caliber: 22 LR/22 Mag., 6-shot.
Barrel: 4¾", 7", 9".
Weight: 32 oz. **Length:** 10" over-all.
Stocks: Black checkered nylon.
Sights: Blade front, fixed rear.
Features: Slide spring ejector. Blue, chrome or blue with brass backstrap and trigger guard models available.

Freedom Arms Mini Revolver

FREEDOM ARMS MINI REVOLVER
Caliber: 22 Short, Long, Long Rifle, 5-shot, 22 Mag., 4-shot.
Barrel: 1″, 1¾″.
Weight: 4 oz. **Length:** 4″ over-all.
Stocks: Black ebonite or simulated ivory.
Sights: Blade front, notch rear.
Features: Made of stainless steel, simple take down; half-cock safety; floating firing pin; cartridge rims recessed in cylinder. Comes in gun rug. Lifetime warranty.

Freedom Arms Boot Gun
Similar to the Mini Revolver except has 3″ barrel, weighs 5 oz. and is 5⅞″ over-all. Has over-size grips, floating firing pin. Made of stainless steel. Lifetime warranty. Comes in rectangular gun rug. Introduced 1982. From Freedom Arms.

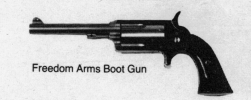
Freedom Arms Boot Gun

MITCHELL SINGLE ACTION REVOLVERS
Caliber: 22 LR/22 Mag., 357 Mag., 44 Mag., 44 Mag./44-40, 45 Colt.
Barrel: 4¾″, 5½″, 6″, 7½″, 10″, 12″, 18″.
Weight: About 36 oz.
Stocks: One-piece walnut.
Sights: Ramp front, rear adj. for w. & e.
Features: Color case-hardened frame, grip frame is polished brass. Hammer block safety. Introduced 1980. From Mitchell Arms Corp.

Mitchell Single Action

NAM MINI REVOLVER
Caliber: 22 LR, 22 Mag., 5-shot
Barrel: 1⅛″ (22 Short, LR), 1¼″ (22 Mag.), 1⅝″ (22 LR).
Weight: 4.5 oz. **Length:** 3.8″ over-all.
Stocks: Smooth plastic; walnut on magnum model.
Sights: Blade front only.
Features: Stainless steel, single action only. Spur trugger. From North American Mfg. Corp.

RUGER NEW MODEL CONVERTIBLE BLACKHAWK
Caliber: 45 Colt or 45 Colt/45 ACP (extra cylinder).
Barrel: 4⅝″ or 7½″ (6-groove, 16″ twist).
Weight: 40 oz. (7½″ bbl.). **Length:** 13⅛″ (7½ bbl.).
Stocks: Smooth American walnut.
Sights: ⅛″ ramp front, micro click rear adj. for w. and e.
Features: Similar to Super Blackhawk, Ruger interlocked mechanism. Convertible furnished with interchangeable cylinder for 45 ACP.

Ruger New Model Blackhawk

RUGER NEW MODEL BLACKHAWK REVOLVER
Caliber: 357 or 41 Mag., 6-shot.
Barrel: 4⅝″ or 6½″, either caliber.
Weight: 42 oz. (6½″ bbl.). **Length:** 12¼″ over-all (6½″ bbl.).
Stocks: American walnut.
Sights: ⅛″ ramp front, micro click rear adj. for w. and e.
Features: New Ruger interlocked mechanism, independent firing pin, hardened chrome-moly steel frame, music wire springs throughout.

Ruger New Model 30 Carbine Blackhawk
Specifications similar to 45 Blackhawk. Fluted cylinder, round-back trigger guard. Weight 44 oz., length 13⅛″ over-all, 7½″ barrel only.

Ruger New Model 357/9mm Blackhawk
Same as the 357 Magnum except furnished with interchangeable cylinders for 9mm Parabellum and 357 Magnum cartridges.

Ruger N.M. Super Blackhawk

RUGER NEW MODEL SUPER BLACKHAWK
Caliber: 44 Magnum, 6-shot. Also fires 44 Spec.
Barrel: 7½" (6-groove, 20" twist), 10½".
Weight: 48 oz. **Length:** 13⅜" over-all (7½" bbl.).
Stocks: Genuine American walnut.
Sights: ⅛" ramp front, micro click rear adj. for w. and e.
Features: New Ruger interlocked mechanism, non-fluted cylinder, steel grip and cylinder frame, square back trigger guard, wide serrated trigger and wide spur hammer. Deep Ruger blue.

Ruger Super Single-Six

RUGER NEW MODEL SUPER SINGLE-SIX CONVERTIBLE REVOLVER
Caliber: 22 S, L, LR, 6-shot. 22 Mag. in extra cylinder.
Barrel: 4⅝", 5½", 6½" or 9½" (6-groove).
Weight: 34½ oz. (6½" bbl.). **Length:** 11¹³⁄₁₆" over-all (6½" bbl.).
Stocks: Smooth American walnut.
Sights: Improved patridge front on ramp, fully adj. rear protected by integral frame ribs.
Features: New Ruger "interlocked" mechanism, transfer bar ignition, gate-controlled loading, hardened chrome-moly steel frame, wide trigger, music wire springs throughout, independent firing pin.

SEVILLE SINGLE ACTION REVOLVER
Caliber: 357 Mag., 9mm Win. Mag., 41 Mag., 44 Mag., 45 Colt, 45 Win. Mag.
Barrel: 4⅝", 5½", 6½", 7½".
Weight: 52 oz. (4⅝", loaded)
Stocks: Smooth walnut, thumbrest, or Pachmayr.
Sights: Ramp front with red insert, fully adj. rear.
Features: Available in blue or stainless steel. Six-shot cylinder. From United Sporting Arms of Arizona, Inc.

SEVILLE SHERIFF'S MODEL S.A. REVOLVER
Caliber: 44-40, 44 Mag., 45 ACP, 45 Colt.
Barrel: 3½".
Weight: 45 oz. (loaded).
Stocks: Smooth walnut. Square butt or birdshead style.
Sights: Sq. butt—ramp front, adj. rear; birdshead—blade front, fixed rear.
Features: Blue or stainless steel. Six-shot cylinder. Available with square or birdshead grip style. From United Sporting Arms of Arizona, Inc.

TANARMI S.A. REVOLVER MODEL TA22S LM
Caliber: 22 LR, 22 Mag., 6-shot.
Barrel: 4¾".
Weight: 32 oz. **Length:** 10" over-all.
Stocks: Walnut.
Sights: Blade front, rear adj. for w. & e.
Features: Manual hammer block safety; color hardened steel frame; brass backstrap and trigger guard. Imported from Italy by Excam.

TANARMI SINGLE ACTION MODEL TA76
Same as TA22 models except blue backstrap and trigger guard.

THE VIRGINIAN DRAGOON REVOLVER
Caliber: 357 Mag., 41 Mag., 44 Mag., 45 Colt.
Barrel: 44 Mag., 6", 7½", 8⅜"; 357 Mag. and 45 Colt, 5", 6", 7½".
Weight: 48 oz. (6" barrel). **Length:** 11⅞" over-all (6" barrel).
Stocks: Smooth walnut.
Sights: Ramp-type Patridge front blade, micro. adj. target rear.
Features: Color case-hardened frame, spring-loaded floating firing pin, coil main spring. Firing pin is lock-fitted with a steel bushing. Introduced 1977. Made in the U.S. by Interarms Industries, Inc.

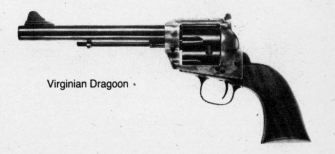

Virginian Dragoon

Colt 1847 Walker

COLT 1847 WALKER PERCUSSION REVOLVER
Caliber: 44.
Barrel: 9″, 7 groove, RH twist.
Weight: 73 oz.
Stocks: One-piece walnut.
Sights: German silver front sight, hammer notch rear.
Features: Made in U.S. by Colt. Faithful reproduction of the original gun, including markings. Color cased frame, hammer, loading lever and plunger. Blue steel backstrap, brass square-back trigger guard. Blue barrel, cylinder, trigger and wedge. Accessories available. Re-introduced 1979.

WALKER 1847 PERCUSSION REVOLVER
Caliber: 44, 6-shot.
Barrel: 9″.
Weight: 72 oz. **Length:** 15½″ over-all.
Stocks: Walnut.
Sights: Fixed.
Features: Case hardened frame, loading lever and hammer; iron backstrap; brass trigger guard; engraved cylinder. Imported by Sile, Navy Arms, Dixie, Armsport.

Walker 1847

Colt First Dragoon

COLT 1st MODEL DRAGOON
Caliber: 44.
Barrel: 7½″, part round, part octagon.
Weight: 66 oz.
Stocks: One piece walnut.
Sights: German silver blade front, hammer notch rear.
Features: First model has oval bolt cuts in cylinder, square-back flared trigger guard, V-type mainspring, short trigger. Ranger and Indian scene on cylinder. Color cased frame, loading lever, plunger and hammer; blue barrel, cylinder, trigger and wedge. Polished brass backstrap and trigger guard. Re-introduced in 1979. From Colt.

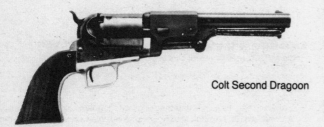

Colt Second Dragoon

Colt 2nd Model Dragoon Revolver
Similar to the 1st Model except this model is distinguished by its rectangular bolt cuts in the cylinder, straight square-back trigger guard, short trigger and flat mainspring with roller in hammer.

Colt 3rd Model Dragoon Revolver
Similar to the 1st Model except has oval trigger guard, long trigger, flat mainspring and rectangular bolt cuts.

Dixie Third Dragoon

DIXIE THIRD MODEL DRAGOON
Caliber: 44 ((.454″ round ball).
Barrel: 7⅜″.
Weight: 4 lbs., 2½ oz.
Stocks: One-piece walnut.
Sights: Brass pin front, hammer notch rear.
Features: Cylinder engraved with Indian fight scene; steel backstrap with polished brass backstrap; color case-hardened steel frame, blue-black barrel. Imported by Dixie Gun Works.

BABY DRAGOON 1848 PERCUSSION REVOLVER
Caliber: 31, 5-shot.
Barrel: 4", 5", 6".
Weight: 24 oz. (6" bbl.). **Length:** 10½" (6" bbl.).
Stocks: Walnut.
Sights: Fixed.
Features: Case hardened frame; safety notches on hammer and safety pin in cylinder; engraved cylinder scene; octagonal bbl. Imported by Sile, F.I.E., Dixie.

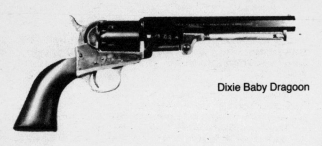

Dixie Baby Dragoon

NAVY MODEL 1851 PERCUSSION REVOLVER
Caliber: 36 or 44, 6-shot.
Barrel: 7½".
Weight: 44 oz. **Length:** 13" over-all.
Stocks: Walnut finish.
Sights: Post front, hammer notch rear.
Features: Brass backstrap and trigger guard; some have engraved cylinder with navy battle scene; case hardened frame, hammer, loading lever. Imported by Shore, (36 cal. only), The Armoury, Navy Arms, Valor, F.I.E., Dixie, (illus.) Richland, Euroarms of America, Sile, Armsport, Hopkins & Allen, CVA.
Price: Brass frame .... **$31.50 to $119.95**
Price: Steel frame .... **$40.95 to $140.95**
Price: Kit form .... **$30.95 to $87.95**
Price: Engraved model (Dixie) **$97.50**
Price: Also as "Hartford Pistol," Kit (Richard) ...... **$59.95** Complete **$79.95**
Price: Also as "Hartford Dragoon Buntline" (Hopkins & Allen) **$166.95**
Price: Navy-Civilian model (Navy Arms) **$118.00**
Price: Single cased set, steel frame (Navy Arms) **$180.00**
Price: As above, civilian model (Navy Arms) **$185.00**
Price: Shoulder stock (Navy Arms) **$45.00**

Dixie 1851 Navy

ARMY 1851 PERCUSSION REVOLVER
Caliber: 44, 6-shot.
Barrel: 7½".
Weight: 45 oz. **Length:** 13" over-all.
Stocks: Walnut finish.
Sights: Fixed.
Features: 44 caliber version of the 1851 Navy. Imported by Sile, Valor, The Armoury.

COLT BABY DRAGOON REVOLVER
Caliber: 31.
Barrel: 4", 7 groove, RH twist.
Weight: About 21 oz.
Stocks: Varnished walnut.
Sights: Brass pin front, hammer notch rear.
Features: Unfluted cylinder with Ranger and Indian scene; cupped cylinder pin; no grease grooves; one safety pin on cylinder and slot in hammer face; straight (flat) mainspring. Silver backstrap and trigger guard. Re-introduced in 1979. From Colt.

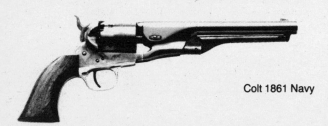

Colt 1861 Navy

Colt 1861 Navy Percussion Revolver
Similar to 1851 Navy except has round 7½" barrel, rounded trigger guard, German silver blade front sight, "creeping" loading lever.

1851 SHERIFF MODEL PERCUSSION REVOLVER
Caliber: 36, 44, 6-shot.
Barrel: 5".
Weight: 40 oz. **Length:** 10½" over-all.
Stocks: Walnut.
Sights: Fixed.
Features: Brass backstrap and trigger guard; engraved navy scene; case hardened frame, hammer, loading lever. Available with brass frame from some importers at slightly lower prices. Imported by Sile, The Armoury.

1851 NAVY-SHERIFF
Same as 1851 Sheriff model except: 4" barrel, fluted cylinder, belt ring in butt. Imported by Richland, Sile, Euroarms of America.

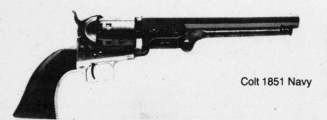

Colt 1851 Navy

COLT 1851 NAVY PERCUSSION REVOLVER
Caliber: 36.
Barrel: 7½", octagonal, 7 groove, LH twist.
Weight: 42 oz.
Stocks: One-piece varnished walnut.
Sights: Brass pin front, hammer notch rear.
Features: Made in U.S. by Colt. Faithful reproduction of the original gun. Color cased frame, loading lever, plunger, hammer and latch. Blue cylinder, trigger, barrel, screws, wedge. Silver plated brass backstrap and square-back trigger guard. Accessories available. Re-introduced in 1979.

Dixie New Model Army

Lyman 1851 Squareback Navy 36
Same as standard Colt model except 36 cal. only, has square-back trigger guard, nickel plated backstrap, color case hardened frame.

NEW MODEL 1858 ARMY PERCUSSION REVOLVER
Caliber: 36 or 44, 6-shot.
Barrel: 6½″ or 8″.
Weight: 40 oz. **Length:** 13½″ over-all.
Stocks: Walnut.
Sights: Blade front, groove-in-frame rear.
Features: Replica of Remington Model 1858. Also available from some importers as Army Model Belt Revolver in 36 cal., shortened and lightened version of the 44. Target Model (Iver Johnson, Navy) has fully adj. target rear sight, target front, 36 or 44 ($74.95-$152.45). Imported by CVA, Dixie, Navy Arms, F.I.E., Iver Johnson, The Armoury, Shore (44 cal., 8″ bbl. only), Richland, Euroarms of America (engraved and plain), Armsport, Sile.

Colt 1860 Army

LYMAN 44 NEW MODEL ARMY REVOLVER
Caliber: 44, 6-shot.
Barrel: 8″.
Weight: 40 oz. **Length:** 13½″ over-all.
Stocks: Walnut.
Sights: Fixed.
Features: Replica of 1858 Remington. Brass trigger guard and backstrap, case hardened hammer and trigger. Solid frame with top strap. Heavy duty nipples. From Lyman Products.

COLT 1860 ARMY PERCUSSION REVOLVER
Caliber: 44.
Barrel: 8″, 7 grooves, LH twist.
Weight: 42 oz.
Stocks: One-piece walnut.
Sights: German silver front sight, hammer notch rear.
Features: Made in U.S. by Colt. Steel backstrap cut for shoulder stock; brass trigger guard. Cylinder has Navy scene. Color case hardened frame, hammer, loading lever. Basically a continuation of production with all original markings, etc. Original-type accessories available. Re-introduced 1979.

Dixie 1860 Army

1860 ARMY PERCUSSION REVOLVER
Caliber: 44, 6-shot.
Barrel: 8″.
Weight: 40 oz. **Length:** 13⅝″ over-all.
Stocks: Walnut.
Sights: Fixed.
Features: Engraved navy scene on cylinder; brass trigger guard; case hardened frame, loading lever and hammer. Some importers supply pistol cut for detachable shoulder stock, have accessory stock available. Imported by Navy Arms, Shore, The Armoury, Dixie (half-fluted cylinder, not roll engraved), Lyman, Iver Johnson, Richland, Euroarms of America (engraved, burnished steel model), Armsport, Sile, Hopkins & Allen.

CVA 1861 ARMY REVOLVER
Caliber: 44, 6-shot.
Barrel: 8″ round.
Weight: 44 oz. **Length:** 13½″ over-all.
Stocks: One-piece walnut.
Sights: Blade front, hammer-notch rear.
Features: Engraved cylinder, creeping-style loading lever, solid brass trigger guard, blued barrel. Introduced 1982. From CVA.

1861 NAVY MODEL REVOLVER
Caliber: 36, 6-shot.
Barrel: 7½″.
Weight: 2½ lbs. **Length:** 13″ over-all.
Stocks: One piece smooth walnut.
Sights: Blade front, hammer notch rear.
Features: Shoots .380″ ball. Case hardened frame, loading lever and hammer. Cut for shoulder stock. Non-fluted cylinder. From CVA, Navy Arms, Armsport, Euroarms of America.

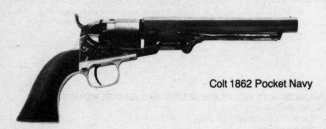
Colt 1862 Pocket Navy

COLT 1862 POCKET NAVY PERCUSSION REVOLVER
Caliber: 36.
Barrel: 5½″, octagonal, 7 groove, LH twist.
Weight: 27 oz.
Stocks: One piece varnished walnut.
Sights: Brass pin front, hammer notch rear.
Features: Made in U.S. by Colt. Rebated cylinder, hinged loading lever, silver plated backstrap and trigger guard, color cased frame, hammer, loading lever, plunger and latch, rest blued. Has original-type markings. Re-introduced 1979.

Colt 1862 Pocket Police Revolver
Similar to 1862 Pocket Navy except has 5½″ round barrel, fluted cylinder, different markings and loading lever. Faithful reproduction of the original gun.

NAVY ARMS 1862 LEECH & RIGDON REVOLVER

Caliber: 375".
Barrel: 7½".
Weight: 2 lbs., 10 oz. **Length:** 13½" over-all.
Stocks: Smooth walnut.
Sights: Fixed.
Features: Modern version of the famous Civil War revolver. Brass backstrap and trigger guard. Color case hardened frame. Copy of the Colt Navy but with round barrel. From Navy Arms.

1862 POLICE MODEL PERCUSSION REVOLVER

Caliber: 36, 5-shot.
Barrel: 4½", 5½", 6½".
Weight: 26 oz. **Length:** 12" (6½" bbl.).
Stocks: Walnut.
Sights: Fixed.
Features: Half-fluted and rebated cylinder; case hardened frame, loading lever and hammer; brass trigger guard and backstrap. Imported by Navy Arms (5½" only), Euroarms of America.

GRISWOLD & GUNNISON PERCUSSION REVOLVER

Caliber: 36, 44, 6-shot.
Barrel: 7½".
Weight: 44 oz. (36 cal.). **Length:** 13" over-all.
Stocks: Walnut.
Sights: Fixed.
Features: Replica of famous Confederate pistol. Brass frame, backstrap and trigger guard; case hardened loading lever; rebated cylinder (44 cal. only). Imported by Navy Arms, Sile.

ROGERS & SPENCER PERCUSSION REVOLVER

Caliber: 44.
Barrel: 7½".
Weight: 47 oz. **Length:** 13¾" over-all.
Stocks: Walnut.
Sights: Cone front, integral groove in frame for rear.
Features: Accurate reproduction of a Civil War design. Solid frame; extra large nipple cut-out on rear of cylinder; loading lever and cylinder easily removed for cleaning. Comes with six spare nipples and wrench/screwdriver. From Euroarms of America, Navy Arms, Dixie, Sile.

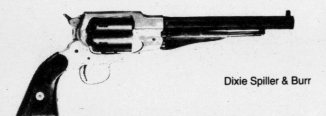

Dixie Spiller & Burr

SPILLER & BURR REVOLVER

Caliber: 36 (.375" round ball).
Barrel: 7", octagon.
Weight: 2½ lbs. **Length:** 12½" over-all.
Stocks: Two-piece walnut.
Sights: Fixed.
Features: Reproduction of the C.S.A. revolver. Brass frame and trigger guard. Also available as a kit. From Dixie, Navy Arms.

Dixie "Wyatt Earp"

DIXIE "WYATT EARP" REVOLVER

Caliber: 44.
Barrel: 12" octagon.
Weight: 46 oz. **Length:** 18" over-all.
Stocks: Two piece walnut.
Sights: Fixed.
Features: Highly polished brass frame, backstrap and trigger guard; blued barrel and cylinder; case hardened hammer, trigger and loading lever. Navy-size shoulder stock ($45.00) will fit with minor fitting. From Dixie Gun Works.

Ruger Old Army

RUGER 44 OLD ARMY PERCUSSION REVOLVER

Caliber: 44, 6-shot. Uses .457" dia. lead bullets.
Barrel: 7½" (6-groove, 16" twist).
Weight: 46 oz. **Length:** 13½" over-all.
Stocks: Smooth walnut.
Sights: Ramp front, rear adj. for w. and e.
Features: Stainless steel standard size nipples, chrome-moly steel cylinder and frame, same lockwork as in original Super Blackhawk. Also available in stainless steel in very limited quantities. Made in USA. From Sturm, Ruger & Co.

DIRECTORY OF MANUFACTURERS

AMMUNITION (Commercial)

Eclipse Cartridge, Inc., 26407 Golden Valley Rd., Saugus, CA 91350/805-251-6610
Federal Cartridge Co., 2700 Foshay Tower, Minneapolis, MN 55402
Frontier Cartridge Division-Hornady Mfg. Co., Box 1848, Grand Island, NE 68801/308-382-1390
Omark Industries, Box 856, Lewiston, ID 83501
Remington Arms Co., 939 Barnum Ave., P. O. Box #1939, Bridgeport, CT 06601
Service Armament, 689 Bergen Blvd., Ridgefield, NJ 07657
Super Vel, Hamilton Rd., Rt. 2, P. O. Box 1398, Fond du Lac, WI 54935
Winchester, Shamrock St.. East Alton. IL 62024

ANTIQUE ARMS DEALERS

Robert Abels, 2881 N.E. 33 Ct., Ft. Lauderdale, FL 33306/305-564-6985 (Catalog $1.00)
Wm. Boggs, 1243 Grandview Ave., Columbus, OH 43212
Ed's Gun House, Rte. 1, Minnesota City, MN 55959/507-689-2925
Ellwood Epps Northern Ltd., 210 Worthington St. W., North Bay, Ont. PIB 3B4 Canada
William Fagan, 126 Belleview, Mount Clemens, MI 48043/313-465-4637
N. Flayderman & Co., Squash Hollow, New Milford, CT 06776
Fulmer's Antique Firearms, Chet Fulmer, P.O. Box 792, Detroit Lakes, MN 56501/218-847-7712
Garcia National Gun Traders, Inc., 225 S.W. 22nd Ave., Miami, FL 33135
Herb Glass, Bullville, NY 10915/914-361-3021
James Goergen, Rte. 2, Box 182BB, Austin, MN 55912/507-433-9280
Goodman's for Guns, 1002 Olive St., St. Louis, MO 63101/314-421-5300
Griffin's Guns & Antiques, R.R. 4, Peterborough, Ont., Canada K9J 6X5/705-748-3220
The Gun Shop, 6497 Pearl Rd., Cleveland, OH 44130/216-884-7476
Hansen & Company, 244 Old Post Rd., Southport, CT 06490
Holbrook Antique Militaria, 4050 S.W. 98th Ave., Miami, FL 33165
Jackson Arms, 6209 Hillcrest Ave., Dallas, TX 75205
Lever Arms Serv. Ltd., 572 Howe St., Vancouver, B.C., Canada V6C 2E3/604-685-6913
Lone Pine Trading Post, Jct. Highways 61 and 248, Minnesota City, MN 55959/507-689-2922
Charles W. Moore, R.D. 2, Box 276, Schenevus, NY 12155/607-278-5721
Museum of Historical Arms, 1038 Alton Rd., Miami Beach, FL 33139/305-672-7480 (ctlg $5)
New Orleans Arms Co., 5001 Treasure St., New Orleans, LA 70186
O.K. Hardware, Westgate Shopping Center, Great Falls, MT 59404
Old West Gun Room, Old Western Scrounger, 3509 Carlson Blvd., El Cerrito, CA 94530/415-527-3872 (write for list)
Pioneer Guns, 5228 Montgomery, (Cincinnati) Norwood, OH 45212
Pony Express Sport Shop, Inc., 17460 Ventura Blvd., Encino, CA 91316
Martin B. Retting, Inc., 11029 Washington, Culver City, CA 90230
Ridge Guncraft, Inc., 125 E. Tyrone Rd., Oak Ridge, TN 37830/615-483-4024
San Francisco Gun Exch., 124 Second St., San Francisco, CA 94105
Santa Ana Gunroom, P.O. Box 1777, Santa Ana, CA 92701
Ward & Van Valkenburg, 114-32nd Ave. N., Fargo, ND 58102
M.C. Wiest, 125 E. Tyrone Rd., Oak Ridge, TN 37830/615-483-4024
J. David Yale, Ltd., 2618 Conowingo Rd., Bel Air, MD 21014/301-838-9479
Lewis Yearout, 308 Riverview Dr. E., Great Falls, MT 59404

SINGLE ACTIONS — (Foreign)

Armoury Inc., Rte. 202, New Preston, CT 06777
Armsport, Inc., 3590 N.W. 49th St., Miami, FL 33142/305-592-7850
Connecticut Valley Arms Co., Saybrook Rd., Haddam, CT 06438 (CVA)
Dixie Gun Works, Inc., Hwy 51, South, Union City, TN 38261/901-885-0561
Euroarms of American, Inc., P.O. Box 3277, 1501 Lenoir Dr., Winchester, VA 22601/703-661-1863
Excam Inc., 4480 E. 11 Ave., P.O. Box 3483, Hialeah, FL 33013
Firearms Imp. & Exp. Corp., (F.I.E.), P.O. Box 4866, Hialeah Lakes, Hialeah, FL 33014/305-685-5966
Interarms Ltd., 10 Prince St., Alexandria, VA 22313 (Mauser, Valmet M-62/S)
Mitchell Arms Corp., 116 East 16th St., Costa Mesa, CA 92627/714-548-7701
Navy Arms Co., 689 Bergen Blvd., Ridgefield, NJ 07657
Richland Arms Co., 321 W. Adrian St., Blissfield, MI 49228
Shore Galleries, Inc., 3318 W. Devon Ave., Chicago, IL 60645
Sile Distributors, 7 Centre Market Pl., New York, NY 10013/212-925-4111

SINGLE ACTIONS — (U.S.-made)

Colt Firearms, P.O. Box 1868, Hartford, CT 06102/203-236-6311
Freedom Arms Co., Freedom, WY 83120 (mini revolver, Casull rev.)
Hopkins & Allen Arms, 3 Ethel Ave., P.O. Box 217, Hawthorne, NJ 07507/201-427-1165
Iver Johnson Arms Inc., P.O. Box 251, Middlesex, NJ 08846
Mitchell Arms Corp., 116 East 16th St., Costa Mesa, CA 92627/714-548-7701
O.F. Mossberg & Sons, Inc., 7 Grasso St., No. Haven, CT 06473

Navy Arms Co., 689 Bergen Blvd., Ridgefield, NJ 07657
North American Arms, 310 West 700 S., Provo, UT 84601/801-375-8074
Ruger (See Sturm, Ruger & Co.)
Smith & Wesson, Inc., 2100 Roosevelt Ave., Springfield, MA 01101
Sturm, Ruger & Co., Southport, CT 06490
United Sporting Arms of Arizona, Inc, 2021 E. 14th St., Tucson, AZ 85719/602-632-4001 (handguns)

HANDGUN GRIPS

Ajax Custom Grips, Inc., 12229 Cox Lane, Dallas, TX 75234/214-241-6302
Art Jewel Enterprises, Box 819, Berkeley, IL 60163/312-941-1110
Bingham Ltd., 1775-C Wilwat Dr., Norcross, GA 30093
Fitz Pistol Grip Co., P.O. Box 55, Grizzly Gulch, Whiskeytown, CA 96055
Gateway Shooters' Supply, Inc., 10145-103rd St., Jacksonville, FL 32210 (Rogers grips)
The Gunshop, R.D. Wallace, 320 Overland Rd., Prescott, AZ 86301
Herrett's , Box 741, Twin Falls, ID 83301
Hogue Combat Grips, P.O. Box 2036, Atascadero, CA 93423/805-466-6266 (Monogrip)
Russ Maloni, 40 Sigman Lane, Elma, NY 14059/716-652-7131
Millett Industries, 16131 Gothard St., Huntington Beach, CA 92647
Monte Kristo Pistol Grip Co., P.O. Box 55 Grizzly Gulch, Whiskeytown, CA 96095/916-778-3136
Mustang Custom Pistol Grips, 27616 Tyler, Romoland, CA 92380
Pachmayr Gun Works, Inc., 1220 S. Grand Ave., Los Angeles, CA 90015
Robert H. Newell, 55 Coyote, Los Alamos, NM 87544/505-662-7135
Rogers Grips (See Gateway Shooters' Supply)
A. Jack Rosenberg & Sons, 12229 Cox Lane, Dallas, TX 75234/214-241-6302
Russwood Custom Pistol Grips, 40 Sigma Lane, Elma, NY 14059
Jean St. Henri, 6525 Dume Dr., Malibu, CA 90265 (custom)
Schiermeier Custom Handgun Stocks, 306 No. 1st St., Kent, WA 98031
Jay Scott, Inc., 81 Sherman Place, Garfield, NJ 07026/201-340-0550
Sile Dist., 7 Centre Market Pl., New York, NY 10013/212-925-4111
Southern Gun Exchange, 4311 Northeast Expressway, Atlanta (Doraville), GA 30340 (Outrider brand)
Sports Inc., P.O. Box 683, Park Ridge, IL 60068/312-825-8952 (Franzite)

SINGLE ACTION HOLSTERS

American Sales & Mfg. Co., P.O. Box 677, Laredo, TX 78040/512-723-6893
Belt Slide, Inc., 1301 Brushy Bend, Round Rock, TX 78664/512-255-1805
Bianchi Holster Co., 100 Calle Cortez, Temecula, CA 92390
Ted Blocker's Custom Holsters, Box 821, Rosemead, CA 91770/213-442-5772 (shop: 4945 Santa Anita Ave., Temple City, CA 91780)
Edward H. Bohlin, 931 N. Highland Ave., Hollywood, CA 90038/213-463-4888
Bo-Mar Tool & Mfg. Co., P.O. Box 168, Carthage, TX 75633/214-693-5220
Brauer Bros. Mfg. Co., 2012 Washington Ave., St. Louis, MO 63103
J.M. Bucheimer Co., P.O. Box 280, Airport Rd., Frederick, MD 21701
Chace Leather Prods., Longhorn Div., 507 Alden St., Fall River, MA 02722/617-678-7556
Cobra Ltd., 1865 New Highway, Farmingdale, NY 11735/516-752-8544
Colt, P.O. Box 1868, Hartford, CT. 06102/203-236-6311
Eugene DeMayo & Sons, Inc., 2795 Third Ave., Bronx, NY 10455
Ellwood Epps Northern Ltd., 210 Worthington St. W., North Bay, Ont. P1B 3B4, Canada (custom made)
The Eutaw Co., Box 608, U.S. Highway 176W, Holly Hill, SC 29059
Galco, 7383 N. Rogers Ave., Chicago, IL 60628
Hoyt Holster Co., P.O. Box 69, Coupeville, WA 98239/206-678-6640
Don Hume, Box 351, Miami, OK 74354/918-542-6604
The Hunter Corp., 3300 W. 71st Ave., Westminster, CO 80030/303-427-4626
John's Custom Leather, 525 S. Liberty St., Blairsville, PA 15717/412-459-6802
Kirkpatrick Leather, Box 3150, Laredo, TX 89041/512-723-6631
George Lawrence Co., 306 S. W. First Ave., Portland, OR 97204
Liberty Organization Inc., P.O. Box 306, Montrose, CA 91020/213-248-0618
Nordac Mfg. Corp., Rt 12, Box 124, Fredericksburg, VA 22401/703-752-2552
Kenneth L. Null-Custom Concealment Holsters, R.D. #5, Box 197, Hanover, PA 17331 (See Seventrees)
Arvo Ojala, 3960 S.E. 1st, Gresham, OR 97030
Old West Inc. Leather Prods., P.O. Box 2030, Chula Vista, CA 92012
Pioneer Products, 1033 W. Amity Rd., Boise, ID 83075/208-345-2003
Red River Frontier Outfitters, P.O. Box 241, Tujunga, CA 91042/213-352-0177
Rogers Holsters, 1736 St. Johns Bluff Rd., Jacksonville, FL 32216
Roy's Custom Leather Goods, Hwy, 1325 & Rawhide Rd., P.O. Box G, Magnolia, AR 71753/501-234-1566
Safariland Leather Products, 1941 So. Walker Ave., Monrovia, CA 91016/213-357-7902
Safety Speed Holster, Inc., 910 So. Vail, Montebello, CA 90640/213-723-4140
Buddy Schoellkopf Products, Inc., 4949 Joseph Hardin Dr., TX 75236
Seventrees Systems Ltd., R.D. 5, Box 197, Hanover, PA 17331/717-632-6873 (See Null)
Sile Distr., 7 Centre Market Pl., New York NY 10013/212-925-4111
Smith & Wesson, 2100 Roosevelt Ave., Springfield, MA 01101
Milt Sparks, Box 7, Idaho City, ID 83631
Robert A. Strong Co., 105 Maplewood Ave., Gloucester, MA 01930
Triple-K Mfg. Co., 568 Sixth Ave., San Diego, CA 92101
Universal Leathergoods, Inc., 6573 E. 21st Pl., Tulsa, OK 74124
Viking Leathercraft, P.O. Box 203, Chula Vista, CA 92012/714-423-8991
Whitco, Box 1712, Brownsville, TX 78520 (Hide-A-Way)